T0361135

INTERNATIONAL ECONOMICS
FIFTH EDITION

This study guide and workbook accompanies the text *International Economics*, fifth edition, Robert M. Dunn Jr. and John H. Mutti. Revised and updated to take account of the latest developments in international economics, it provides brief chapter summaries and practise problems to enhance the understanding of material presented in class.

For each chapter in *International Economics*, fifth edition, the study guide provides a summary, a list of objectives and different types of questions with worked short answers at the end of the book. The answers are in multiple choice, true or false, short answer and essay format.

Dana M. Stryk is Assistant Professor of Economics and Program Coordinator of Women and Power Leadership Programs at George Washington University.
Robert M. Dunn Jr. is Professor of Economics at George Washington University and **John H. Mutti** is the Sydney Meyer Professor of International Economics at Grinnell College, USA.

INTERNATIONAL ECONOMICS
FIFTH EDITION

STUDY GUIDE AND WORKBOOK

Dana M. Stryk

To accompany the textbook by

Robert M. Dunn Jr. and John H. Mutti

Routledge
Taylor & Francis Group

LONDON AND NEW YORK

First published 1996
by John Wiley & Sons, Inc.

Published 2013 by Routledge
2 Park Square, Milton Park, Abingdon, Oxon OX14 4RN

Simultaneously published in the USA and Canada
by Routledge
711 Third Avenue, New York, NY, 10017, USA

Routledge is an imprint of the Taylor & Francis Group, an informa business

© 1996, 2000 Dana M. Stryk

All rights reserved. No part of this book may be reprinted or reproduced or utilized in
any form or by any electronic, mechanical, or other means, now known or hereafter
invented, including photocopying and recording, or in any information storage or
retrieval system, without permission in writing from the publishers.

British Library Cataloguing in Publication Data
A catalogue record for this book is available from the British Library

Library of Congress Cataloging in Publication Data
A catalog record for this book has been applied for

ISBN 13: 978-0-415-22830-5 (pbk)

TABLE OF CONTENTS

LIST OF TABLES

LIST OF FIGURES

CHAPTER 2

PATTERNS OF TRADE AND THE GAINS FROM TRADE: INSIGHTS FROM CLASSICAL THEORY

IMPORTANT POINTS

1. The concept of absolute advantage originates from Adam Smith's labor theory of value. The real cost of a commodity is the labor time required to produce the good. For example, if a shoemaker makes a pair of shoes in five hours and a tailor sews a dress in ten hours, the real cost of these goods is five and ten hours respectively. Individuals trade these goods using the real exchange rate or barter terms of trade. In the previous example, the tailor requires two pairs of shoes for each dress she creates since dress production requires twice the number of labor hours as shoe manufacturing.

2. An example can illustrate how absolute cost differences lead to mutual gains from trade. In Table 2-1 the number of days required to produce cloth and wine are listed.

Table 2-1: Absolute Cost Example

Days of Labor Required to Produce	Country	
	England	France
Wine (1 barrel)	160	20
Cloth (1 bolt)	40	200

Since England takes fewer days to produce one bolt of cloth (40 days versus 200 days), it has an absolute advantage in the production of cloth. France has an absolute advantage in the production of wine since it only needs 20 days to produce a barrel, compared to 160 days in England. Without trade, one bolt of cloth exchanges for 1/4 barrel of wine in England, reflecting the fact that wine production requires four times as many days as cloth production. In France, one bolt of cloth exchanges for 10 barrels of wine.

Based on absolute cost differences, England should move its resources out of wine and into cloth production, while France should specialize in wine production. England will export cloth to France in exchange for wine only if it receives more than 1/4 barrel of wine for every bolt of cloth exported. France will purchase imported British cloth only if it pays less than 10 barrels of wine for every imported bolt of cloth.

Assuming the number of days used to produce cloth and wine in both countries remains unchanged, total production will increase as a result of specialization. Suppose that prior to trade, each country produces one barrel of wine and one bolt of cloth. This means that England uses 200 days for production while France uses 220 days. With specialization, England devotes all its resources to cloth production, producing 5 bolts of cloth. France produces 11 barrels of wine. Total cloth production increases by 3 bolts of cloth (2 bolts produced prior to trade, 5 bolts with specialization), while total wine production increases by 9 barrels of wine (2 barrels produced prior to trade, 11 barrels with specialization). Both countries gain from specializing since total world production and consumption increases.

3. The absolute advantage theory does not help to explain trade patterns when one country can produce both goods at a lower absolute cost. Instead, the concept of comparative advantage explains the basis for trade. David Ricardo showed that the requirements for mutually beneficial trade depend upon relative costs. More specifically, a country with an absolute disadvantage in the production of all goods has a relative advantage in the production of at least one commodity. In Table 2-2, England has an absolute advantage over France in the production of cloth and wine.

Table 2-2: Comparative Cost Example

Days of Labor	Country	
Required to Produce	England	France
Wine (1 barrel)	40	100
Cloth (1 bolt)	30	150

In the absence of trade, production constrains each country's consumption of the two goods. Labor hours used to produce wine mean that less cloth can be produced. Production in each country incurs an opportunity cost, measured by the amount of one good given up in order to produce the other commodity. In England, the opportunity cost of producing one bolt of cloth is measured in terms of lost wine production. If one bolt of cloth is produced, 30 production days are devoted to cloth production and cannot be used for wine production, which means that for every bolt of cloth produced, 3/4 barrel of wine cannot be produced. Thus, the opportunity cost of producing one bolt of cloth in England is 3/4 barrel of wine. (This rate is calculated by determining how many bolts of cloth or barrels of wine could be produced if 30 days exist for production: $3/4 \text{ barrel} = \dfrac{30 \text{ days for production}}{40 \text{ days per barrel of wine}}$) In France, the opportunity cost of producing an additional bolt of cloth is 3/2 barrels of wine. This country uses 150 production days to produce one bolt of cloth. In that same time, the country could have produced 3/2 barrels of wine. (This rate is calculated by determining how many bolts of cloth or barrels of wine could be produced if 150 days exist for production: $3/2 \text{ barrel} = \dfrac{150 \text{ days for production}}{100 \text{ days per barrel of wine}}$)

Based on these opportunity cost calculations, England has a comparative advantage in the production of cloth since the opportunity cost of cloth production in England (3/4 barrel of wine) is less than the opportunity cost of cloth production in France (3/2 barrels of wine). According to the Ricardian model of comparative advantage, England should specialize in the production of cloth while France specializes in the production of wine even though England has an absolute advantage in the production of both goods.

In order for both countries to have an incentive to engage in trade, the terms of trade must lie between the two opportunity cost ratios. If this value is 1 bolt of cloth for 1 barrel of wine, each country gains from trade. Previously, France had to give up 3/2 barrels of wine to get one bolt of cloth. With trade, France obtains one bolt of cloth for one barrel of wine, a savings of 1/2 barrel. England benefits from trade since it can obtain more wine for every bolt of cloth (3/4 compared to 1).

Total production increases as a result of specialization. Suppose that prior to trade, each country produced one bolt of cloth and one barrel of wine. (This implies that England has 70 production days and France has 250 production days. To find these numbers, add the amount of time needed to produce one unit of each good for each country.) With specialization, each country maintains the same number of production days, but specializes in its comparative advantage good. England moves all of its resources into cloth production and produces 7/3 bolts of cloth (70 production days/30 days per bolt=7/3 bolts of cloth). Without specialization, total world production equaled 2 bolts of cloth. With specialization, production of cloth increases by 1/3 bolt.

As England moves its resources into its cloth production, France moves its resources into wine production, producing 5/2 barrels of wine (250 production days/100 days per barrel=5/2 barrels of wine). Without specialization, total world production equaled 2 barrels of wine. With specialization, production of cloth increases by 1/2 barrel.

4.   The economic models developed in the text to analyze trade issues make several common assumptions. Perfect competition exists in goods and factor markets. This eliminates the possibilities of monopoly or oligopoly power and minimum wage restrictions. The amount of production inputs is assumed constant, meaning that a population boom or a change in the labor force participation rate does not occur. The level of technology is also constant and is determined outside the models. Trade

between countries occurs without any transportation costs or other barriers to trade (tariffs, quotas) which could influence the price of tradable goods. Tastes and preferences are fixed, and factors of production are domestically mobile but cannot cross international borders. Prices will change and goods will flow until the value of imports equals the value of exports in an open economy with free trade.

5. The comparative cost examples in Table 2-2 (study guide) utilized the concept of opportunity cost. Assuming scarce resources, the production of one good entails foregoing the production of another good. Since land, labor and capital have alternative uses, using specific amounts of these inputs to produce one bushel of wheat incurs a cost measured in terms of the foregone alternative. Producing 1 bolt of cloth in France means foregoing the production of 3/2 barrels of wine.

6. The Production Possibilities Curve (PPC) provides a graphical representation of different output combinations each country could produce with a given level of resources. Tables 2-3 and 2-4 illustrate the production possibilities for England and France respectively. The opportunity cost of one ton of steel in England is 1 bushel of wheat. In order to produce an extra ton of steel, England must forego the production of 1 bushel of wheat. The opportunity cost of steel in France is 4 bushels of wheat.

Table 2-3: England's Production Possibilities in Wheat and Steel

Wheat	180	160	140	120	100	80	60	40	20	0
Steel	0	20	40	60	80	100	120	140	160	180

Table 2-4: France's Production Possibilities in Wheat and Steel

Wheat	360	320	280	240	200	160	120	80	40	0
Steel	0	10	20	30	40	50	60	70	80	90

This information can be represented graphically. Figure 2-1 illustrates the PPC for England.

Figure 2-1: The Production Possibilities Curve for England.

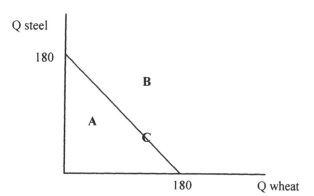

Points such as A indicate feasible and inefficient production. England could increase the production of wheat without decreasing the production of steel. Points such a B are not feasible with existing resources and technology. Points such as C, along the PPC, are considered feasible and efficient.

The slope of the PPC measures the rate at which one good can be transformed into the other good. This is also called the marginal rate of transformation, and is equal to the ratio of the marginal costs of production (MRT = MC_{wheat}/MC_{steel}). Firms will produce at the point on the PPC where the ratio of the price of the two goods (P_{wheat}/P_{steel}) equals the MRT. Since the PPC in Figure 2-1 is linear, the slope is constant, implying the opportunity cost of wheat production does not change.

10.   The PPC represents the production side of the economy. To capture consumer tastes and preferences, indifference curves are used. Indifference curves represent all possible combinations of goods that yield the same level of utility. The shape of an indifference curve depends upon the individual's preferences. If two goods are perfect substitutes (i.e. one apple is as good as one orange), the indifference curve is a straight line. Indifference curves used in this textbook are convex to the origin, reflecting the fact that the two goods are imperfect substitutes. The slope of the indifference curve, also known as the marginal rate of substitution (MRS), measures the rate at which consumers are willing to substitute the consumption of one good for the consumption of another. The MRS is equal to the ratio of the marginal utilities (MU_{wheat}/MU_{steel}). Since, by assumption, consumers seek to maximize utility subject to a budget constraint, consumption occurs where the ratio of the prices of the goods (P_{wheat}/P_{steel}) equals the MRS.

Trade models use community indifference curves to represent the tastes and preferences of all consumers within a country. Aggregating tastes and preferences leads to some problems. Income distribution affects the way in which tastes and preferences appear in the indifference curves. If trade makes some consumer wealthier and others poorer, the value consumers place on changes in income affect welfare conclusions. To avoid these problems, tastes and preferences are assumed to be identical across all individuals.

11.   Combining the PPC and the indifference curves illustrates equilibrium for a closed economy. Without trade, a country must consume what it produces. The equilibrium occurs on the highest indifference curve tangent to the PPC. Figure 2-2 illustrates this solution.

Figure 2-2: Closed Economy Equilibrium for England.

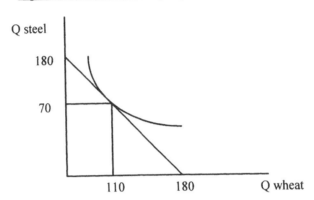

In the pre-trade environment, England produces and consumes 110 bushels of wheat and 70 tons of steel. The tangency point between the production-possibilities curve and the highest community indifference curve indicates this point. Only at this point are the slope of the PPC and the slope of the indifference curve equal.

Trade based on comparative advantage suggests that England has a comparative advantage in the production of steel. If England specializes in steel, moving all of its resources into steel production, it will be willing to export steel in exchange for wheat only if the price of wheat with trade is cheaper than without trade. Without trade, the price of wheat equals the opportunity cost of wheat production. In order for England to trade with France, the price of wheat must be less than 1 ton of steel. If the price of wheat is greater than 1 ton of steel, England will not trade, since trade makes wheat more expensive.

France has a comparative advantage in the production of wheat. With trade, this country would want to export wheat to England in exchange for steel. It will sell wheat to England only if the price of wheat increases with trade (remember, they are selling the good). Without trade, wheat sells for 1/4 ton of steel. With trade, France must receive at least 1/4 ton of steel for every bushel of wheat exported. Equilibrium occurs at that barter ratio where the value of exports of wheat from France equals the value of imports of wheat to England.

Tables 2-5 and 2-6 highlight possible consumption and production changes resulting from the introduction of trade. (Please refer to Tables 2-3 and 2-4 for production information.) Each country benefits from trade since total consumption rises in both countries. Both England and France increase consumption of steel by 30 tons while wheat consumption in England and France rises by 50 bushels and 40 bushels, respectively.

Table 2-5: Wheat Production and Consumption

	Wheat				
	Production	- Exports	+ Imports	=	Consumption
Pre-trade					
•England	110				110
•France	160				160
•Total World	270				270
Post-trade					
•England	0	- 0	+ 160	=	160
•France	360	- 160	+ 0	=	200
•Total World	360				360
Gain from Trade					
•England					+ 50
•France					+ 40
•Total World					+ 90

Table 2-6: Steel Production and Consumption

	Steel				
	Production	- Exports	+ Imports	=	Consumption
Pre-trade					
•England	70				70
•France	50				50
•Total World	120				120
Post-trade					
•England	180	- 80	+ 0	=	100
•France	0	- 0	+ 80	=	80
•Total World	180				180
Gain from Trade					
•England					+ 30
•France					+ 30
•Total World					+ 60

7.   The information provided in Tables 2-5 and 2-6 can be illustrated graphically. Figure 2-3 shows the open economy equilibrium for England.

Figure 2-3: Open Economy Equilibrium for England

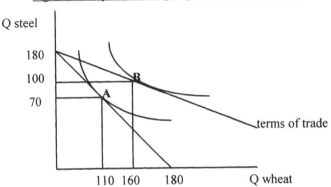

Point A represents the closed economy equilibrium. With trade, England produces 180 tons of steel, exports 80 tons of steel to France in exchange for 160 bushels of wheat. Consumption occurs at point B.

8. The previous example assumed that the opportunity cost remained constant for all possible output combinations. Realistically, some resources are better suited for producing a particular good than others and thus have different opportunity costs associated with them. In England, as more resources are drawn from wheat production into steel production, the steel production efficiency of these declines. Workers skilled in the planting and harvesting of wheat may not be as productive in the manufacturing of steel. The existence of increasing costs causes the production-possibilities curve to be bowed out (convex from above). The slope of this curve is not constant; reflecting the increasing costs embodied in the production process.

Trade equilibrium is determined in the same fashion as the constant cost case. The existence of different pre-trade cost ratios causes production to shift toward the comparative advantage good. England would shift production along the PPC toward the steel axis. Unlike the constant cost example, England does not completely specialize in steel production due to increasing costs. As more steel is produced, the opportunity cost of producing steel increases. The terms-of-trade still must lie between the pre-trade cost ratios, with the consumption equilibrium determined by the tangency between the terms-of-trade and the highest community indifference curve. At this point, the ratio of goods prices, the MRT, and the MRS in England equals the ratio of goods prices, the MRT, and the MRS in France. $(P_W/P_S^E = MC_W/MC_S^E = MU_W/MU_S^E = P_W/P_S^F = MC_W/MC_S^F = MU_W/MU_S^F)$

Each country prefers to trade a small amount of its export good for a large amount of its import good. The terms-of-trade, which are determined by the elasticities of demand and supply curves in each country, determine which country benefits most from trade. The country with relatively inelastic supply and demand curves for a particular good will benefit the most. An inelastic demand curve means that a large change in the price of a good generates a small decrease in the quantity demanded. An inelastic supply curve means that a large change in the price of a good generates a small change in the quantity supplied.

9. The offer curve shows the various combinations of the quantity of exports supplied and imports demanded at different price ratios. The shape of the offer curve depends

upon the shape of the community indifference curves and the production-possibilities curve. The offer curve does not have a constant elasticity. The intersection of two trading partners' offer curves determines the equilibrium terms-of-trade.

10.   The constant-cost and increasing-cost models assume only two goods exist and these goods are shipped without incurring transportation costs. These models can be extended to include more than two goods. In this case, a country would rank the goods it produces according to the marginal cost of production. If labor is assumed to the only input, the marginal cost of producing wheat in country A, for example, equals:

$$MC_{wheat} = (\frac{L}{Q})^A_{wheat} \cdot w^A$$

The first term on the right hand side of the equation is the amount of labor required to produce one bushel of wheat. For example, if one bushel of wheat required 10 hours of labor and the wage rate equals $10, the marginal cost of producing the bushel of wheat is $100. Comparing relative marginal cost values across countries determines comparative advantage

Appendix

1.   The concept of differing opportunity costs can be applied to price ratios defined in terms of money. In Tables 2-3 and 2-4, England had an opportunity cost of steel equal to one bushel of wheat. This implies that the price of steel equals the price of wheat. In France, the price of steel is four times the price of wheat. Using this information, relative money prices are derived in Table 2-7.

Table 2-7: Relative Money Prices Example

	England	France
Steel (per ton)	£200	Fr.400
Wheat (per ton)	£200	Fr.100
Price Ratio $(\frac{P_{steel}}{P_{wheat}})$	1:1	4:1

The price of steel in England is £200 while in France, one ton of steel costs Fr.400. Before trade can occur, the value of the exchange rate must be determined. If the one British pound exchanges for six French francs, France will not purchase any steel from England. British steel costs Fr.1200 (£200 x [Fr.6/£] = Fr.1200) which exceeds the domestic price. With this exchange rate, imported steel is too expensive. In order for two-way trade to exist, the exchange rate must make British steel relatively cheaper than French steel and French wheat relatively cheaper than British wheat. The boundaries for this example are one pound for one-half of a French franc and one pound for two French francs. At ranges outside these limits, both goods are cheaper in one country.

CHAPTER OBJECTIVES

After studying the concepts presented in Chapter 2, you should be able to answer the following questions:

1.   How does the labor theory of value explain trading patterns between countries? What assumptions are embodied in this theory? Do any problems exist with models based on this concept?

2.   What is the importance of opportunity cost when analyzing production? What implications do these costs have for international trade?

3.   In addition to consumption and production gains, what are other benefits from trade?

4.   Explain why, in the absence of trade, the marginal rate of transformation is not identical across countries.

5.   What information does the shape of the production-possibilities curve give concerning the cost structure within an economy? How are trading equilibrium points represented using the PPC framework?

6.   How can the theory of comparative advantage explain international trade? How do you determine which goods a country exports and imports? How do the conclusions from comparative advantage differ from those from the theory of absolute advantage? What are the limitations of this model?

7.   How are the terms-of-trade calculated? What is the relevance of this world price ratio?

8.   How are the gains from trade determined? How can these benefits be illustrated graphically and mathematically?

9.   What information does the shape of the production-possibilities curve give concerning the cost structure within an economy? How are trading equilibrium points represented using the PPC framework?

10. What does the offer curve represent? How can these curves show the equilibrium terms-of-trade between trading partners?

GLOSSARY TERMS

- absolute advantage
- community indifference curves
- comparative advantage
- offer curves
- opportunity cost
- terms of trade

CHAPTER 2 STUDY QUESTIONS

Multiple Choice Questions

1. The concept of absolute advantage is based on

   a. the labor theory of value.
   b. differences in wages rates across countries.
   c. the theory of comparative advantage.
   d. differences in labor endowments across countries.

2. The concept of comparative advantage is based on

   a. the labor theory of value.
   b. differences in relative costs across countries.
   c. the barter terms of trade.
   d. the law of diminishing returns.

3. Differences in wage rates between countries reflect

   a. the fact that one country may have more powerful labor unions which negotiate for higher wages.
   b. differences in labor endowments across countries.
   c. differences in transportation costs.
   d. differences in labor productivity.

Use the information in Table A to answer questions 4 through 8:

Table A: Production Information

Days of Labor Required to Produce	Country	
	England	France
Wine (1 barrel)	5	6
Cloth (1 bolt)	10	2

4. England has an absolute advantage in the production of

   a. cloth.
   b. wine.
   c. both goods.
   d. neither good.

5. France has an absolute advantage in the production of

    a. cloth.
    b. wine.
    c. both goods.
    d. neither good.

6. England has a comparative advantage in the production of

    a. cloth.
    b. wine.
    c. both goods.
    d. neither good.

7. France has a comparative advantage in the production of

    a. cloth.
    b. wine.
    c. both goods.
    d. neither good.

8. For England to export wine and France to export cloth, the equilibrium terms of trade could be

    a. 1W: 4C
    b. 1W: 1C
    c. 1W:¼C
    d. It does not matter since England never exports wine and Italy never exports cloth.

9. According to the theory of comparative advantage, if country A has a relative advantage in the production of wheat and country B has a relative advantage in the production of wine, each country should export its relative advantage good. This means that

    a. the price of wheat in country B and the price of wine in country A fall as a result of trade.
    b. the price of wheat in country A and the price of wine in country B fall as a result of trade.
    c. the price of wheat in country B and the price of wine in country A rise as a result of trade.
    d. the price of wheat falls both in country A and country B.

10. Indifference curves represent

    a.   all combinations of two goods that yield the same level of utility.
    b.   all goods that have the same price.
    c.   all goods that yield the same level of profit to firms within a particular country.
    d.   the opportunity cost theory.

True, False, Uncertain and Why Questions

When answering the following questions, be sure to support your assertion of true, false, or uncertain with two or three sentences.

1. If one country has an absolute advantage in the production of all goods, this country should not engage in international trade.

2. If two countries have different comparative advantage goods, trade will always occur regardless of the value of the terms of trade.

3. Suppose Mexico needs 15 hours to produce a bolt of cloth and 10 hours to produce a television set. Brazil needs 5 hours to produce a bolt of cloth and 10 hours to produce a television set. Brazil has a comparative advantage in the production of televisions.

4. After trade, the new consumption equilibrium occurs where terms of trade is tangent to the highest community indifference curve.

5. A country gains more from trade when the equilibrium terms-of-trade is closer to its pre-trade price ratio.

Short Answer Questions

Use the information in Table B to answer questions 1 through 4.

Table B: Production Information

Days of Labor	Country	
Required to Produce	England	Italy
Wine (1 barrel)	10	8
Cloth (1 bolt)	5	2

1. In what good does England have a comparative advantage? Why? Calculate the pre-trade price ratio for this country.

2. In what good does Italy have a comparative advantage? Why? Calculate the pre-trade price ratio for this country.

3. Using the information in Table B, construct the production possibilities curve for England, assuming that 100 labor days exist. Show possible pre-trade equilibrium production points.

4. If the terms of trade is 1W:1C, show the new equilibrium production point. Use your graph from question 3. Show possible post-trade equilibrium consumption points.

Use the information in Table C to answer question 5:

Table C: Production Information

Days of Labor	Country	
Required to Produce	United States	Canada
Golf Clubs (1 set)	5	1
Running Shoes (1 pair)	1	4

5. Which country has an absolute advantage in running shoes? Calculate the opportunity cost of producing golf clubs in each country? Which country has a comparative advantage in golf club production?

ANSWERS TO CHAPTER 2 STUDY GUIDE QUESTIONS

Multiple Choice Questions

1. a
   Each country benefits from trade by specializing in commodities that it can produce at lower real cost than another country. Real cost is measured in terms of the amount of labor hours required to produce a commodity.

2. b
   Countries will benefit from trade provided that their relative costs (the ratio of their real costs) differ.

3. d
   When workers producing wine in one country are more productive than workers producing wine in another country, wage rates will differ across countries.

4.   b
England needs less time (5 hours) to produce a barrel of wine than France (6 hours). Therefore, England has a comparative advantage in the production of wine.

5.   a
France needs less time (2 hours) to produce a bolt of cloth than England (10 hours). Therefore, France has a comparative advantage in the production of cloth.

6.   b
In order to produce one barrel of wine, England must give up 1/2 bolt of cloth while France gives up 3 bolts of cloth. Since England's opportunity cost is lower, it has a comparative advantage in wine production.

7.   a
In order to produce one bolt of cloth, England must give up 2 barrels of wine while France gives up 1/3 barrel of wine. Since France's opportunity cost is lower, it has a comparative advantage in cloth production.

8.   b
England will be willing to trade only if it can export one barrel of wine for more than 1/2 bolt of cloth. France will be willing to trade only if it can import one barrel of wine for less than 3 bolts of cloth. If the terms of trade is 1W:4C or 1W:¼C, both goods are cheaper in one country and two-way trade will not occur.

9.   a
As a result of trade, country B exports wine to country A, increasing the supply of wine in country A and decreasing the price of wine in country A. In country B the price of wheat falls because wheat imported from country A increases domestic supply.

10.   a
These curves represent all combinations of goods between which a consumer is indifferent. This means each combination yields the same level of utility.

True, False, Uncertain and Why Questions

1.   False. Even when a country can produce all goods at a lower absolute cost, the country may gain from trade. When a country specializes in the good or goods it can produce at a lower relative cost, total production of all goods increases and all nations benefit.

2.   False. If the terms of trade lies outside the pre-trade price ratios, two-way trade will not occur since both goods would be cheaper in one country.

3.   True. While neither country has an absolute advantage in the production of television sets, Brazil has a lower opportunity cost in television production. In Brazil, 1/2 bolt of cloth must be given up to produce one television. In Mexico, 2/3 bolt of cloth must be given up to produce one television. Therefore, comparative advantage suggests that Brazil export televisions to Mexico.

4.   True. After trade, the new consumption equilibrium is found where the terms-of-trade line or barter line is tangent to the highest community indifference curve. With trade, the country can consume more of a good than it produces.

5.   False. The farther away the terms-of-trade is from a country's pre-trade price ratio, the larger the gains from trade.

Short Answer Questions

1.   England has a comparative advantage in the production of wine since it only has to give up 2 bolts of cloth to produce a barrel of wine. Italy has to give up 4 bolts of cloth to produce a barrel of wine. The pre-trade price ratio in England is one bolt of cloth for 1/2 barrel of wine (or one barrel of wine for 2 bolts of cloth).

2.   Italy has a comparative advantage in the production of cloth since it only has to give up 1/4 barrel of wine to produce a bolt of cloth. England has to give up 1/2 barrel of wine to produce a bolt of cloth. The pre-trade price ratio is one barrel of wine for 4 bolts of cloth (or one bolt of cloth for 1/4 barrel of wine).

3.   and
4.

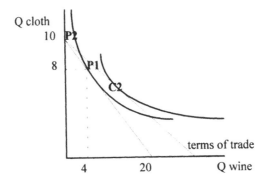

Point P1 represents a possible pre-trade equilibrium production point. If the terms of trade is 1W:1C, England specializes in the production of cloth, at point P2. Consumption occurs along the terms of trade line, at a point such as C2.

5. The United States has an absolute and comparative advantage in golf club production since it can produce this good at a lower absolute and relative cost than Canada. In the United States the opportunity cost of golf clubs in terms of running shoes is one golf club for 5 running shoes. In Canada, this ratio is one golf club for 1/4 running shoe. The United States has an absolute and comparative advantage in golf club production since it can produce this good at a lower absolute and relative cost than Canada.

TRADE AMONG DISSIMILAR COUNTRIES: INSIGHTS FROM THE FACTOR-PROPORTIONS THEORY

IMPORTANT POINTS

1. Chapter 3 develops a theory to explain why relative costs and prices differ across countries and how these differences lead to mutually beneficial trade when more than one factor of production exists. The Heckscher-Ohlin theory and its related theorems make several assumptions about the trading environment. A 2x2x2 framework characterizes the model. This means that two countries, two goods, and two factors of production exist. Technology differs between the two goods but is identical across countries. The model also assumes the level of technology to be fixed. Constant returns to scale exist in both industries, meaning if labor and capital inputs are exactly doubled, total output exactly doubles. Factor intensity reversals do not exist. In other words, commodities can be unambiguously ranked according to factor intensity. For example, if wheat production requires a higher ratio of labor to land than does the manufacture of cloth, we can conclude that wheat is labor intensive. A lack of factor intensity reversals implies wheat's greater labor intensity relative to steel holds for all possible wage rate to land price ratios.

    This theory also assumes identical demand conditions for all consumers indicating that indifference curves are the same. Perfect competition exists in both the factor and the goods market. Trade between countries occurs without any transportation costs or barriers to trade (no tariffs or quotas). These assumptions are identical to those made in Chapter 2.

2. Before trade, relative commodity prices and factor prices differ between the two countries. Suppose Mexico is labor abundant while Canada is land abundant, and that cloth production is relatively labor-intensive while wheat production is relatively land-intensive. This means that the land to labor (LN/LB) ratio in Canada is greater than the land to labor ratio in Mexico. Because of these differences, the wage rate and rental rate paid to factors of production will differ across Mexico and Canada. Since land is relatively scarce in Mexico, the rental rate paid to this land will be high while

the wage rate will be low, making the labor-intensive good (cloth) relatively cheap to produce and the land-intensive good (wheat) relatively expensive to produce. Thus, Mexico, with a large amount of labor and little land, produces a large quantity of cloth and little wheat, causing the price ratio between cloth and wheat (P_{cloth}/P_{wheat}) to be less than the same price ratio in Canada. As the countries trade, Mexico exports cloth to Canada causing P_{cloth} in Mexico to rise (as the quantity supplied domestically decreases because of exports) and P_{cloth} in Canada to fall (as the quantity supplied increases via imports). Through trade, goods prices become equalized (assuming zero transportation costs and a lack of trade impediments).

According the H-O theory, a country will have a comparative advantage in the good that uses its relatively abundant factor intensively. For the previous example, Mexico is relatively labor abundant and exports cloth, the relatively labor intensive good. Canada, the relatively land abundant country exports the relatively land intensive good.

Relative factor endowments, the source of comparative advantage in the Heckscher-Ohlin theory, can change over time. For example, if a country implements policies designed to increase the educational background of its citizens, that policy also increases the amount of human capital with which the country is endowed. Also, new technology can change which goods are labor or capital-intensive influencing in which good a country should specialize.

3.   The discussion of factor-price equalization highlights an important point. As resources are reallocated from the import-competing sector to the export industry, the returns to the factors of production change. The Stolper-Samuelson theorem analyzes the effect of changing goods prices on factor prices. In Mexico, wage rates increase and land rental rates fall as resources move from the wheat industry into the cloth sector. In Canada, the opposite occurs. As Canada produces more wheat, wage rates fall and land rental rates increase. These results can be generalized. The scarce factor of production loses and the abundant factor gains from the introduction of free trade. The higher indifference curves reached through trade indicates that total income within both countries rises, but this ignores income distribution effects. All individuals would be better off from trade only if the winners compensate the losers.

4.   The previous discussion assumes that factors of production can instantaneously migrate from one region of a country to another. Obviously, this is not a realistic assumption. More likely, factors of production are fixed within an industry for the short-run. When factors cannot move, the introduction of trade hurts all factors used in the import-competing industry and benefits all those used in the export industry. In Mexico, land and labor used in cloth production gain from trade while land and labor used in the production of wheat lose. Only when the reallocation of factors from the import competing to the export industry is complete will the earlier conclusions of the Heckscher-Ohlin theory become accurate.

5.   One of the assumptions of the Heckscher-Ohlin theory is the international immobility of factors. When production inputs are allowed to migrate across national borders, factor mobility is a substitute for free trade. For example, suppose labor-abundant Mexico places a prohibitive tariff on automobiles, which are capital intensive. This policy increases the domestic price of cars. As production shifts to the automobile industry, the demand for capital rises, increasing the rental rate for the input. If factors

are allowed to move freely, capital inflows from the rest of the world result because of the higher rental rate. The larger amount of capital shifts Mexico's production possibilities curve toward automobile production. Consumption occurs at the same point as before the tariff. Thus, free trade in goods and complete international factor mobility are substitutes.

6. Empirical testing of the Heckscher-Ohlin theory, in the 1940s and 1950s, suggested that the United States' exports were more labor-intensive than its import-competing goods, a contradiction of the Heckscher-Ohlin theorem. This result is commonly known as the Leontief paradox. Several explanations could account for this result, such as categorizing all products as either labor or capital-intensive when the goods actually use a third input (i.e., natural resources) intensively.

Appendix

1. Each country has a fixed endowment of labor and land to use in the production process. The production-possibilities curves are derived from the factor endowments and the production functions. Isoquants are used to represent all combinations of labor and land which yield the same amount of output. Figure 3-1 illustrates this concept.

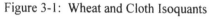

Figure 3-1: Wheat and Cloth Isoquants

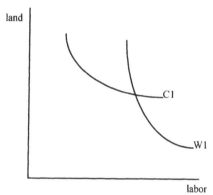

The C_1 and W_1 curves represent all combinations of land and labor that produce a specific amount of cloth and wheat respectively. The different shapes of the wheat and cloth isoquants indicate the goods use different factors intensively. More specifically, cloth is labor intensive, requiring a higher ratio of labor to land to produce one unit of cloth. Wheat, on the other hand, is land-intensive, requiring a lower labor/land (higher land/labor) ratio to produce one unit of wheat. The ratio of land to labor used in each sector depends upon the wage and rental rates of the inputs. Since firms seek to maximize profits, higher wage rates would cause both industries to substitute land for labor.

2. The production possibilities frontier is derived using an Edgeworth box diagram (See Figures 3-4 and 3-5 in the text.). The size of the box represents the country's endowment of labor and land. If country A is labor abundant, its box diagram would have long horizontal parallel lines reflecting the large amount of labor (assuming labor

is represented by the horizontal axis). If country B is land abundant, its box diagram would be thinner and taller. The isoquants for each good are drawn from the appropriate origin. The tangency points represent points on the contract line, where efficiency in production is maximized. These output combinations are also points on the PPC. Thus any point on the PPC is efficient. Any point within the PPC is not.

3. Different factor endowments between country A and country B imply non-identically shaped PPCs. Since each country possesses different relative endowments of land and labor than its trading partner, an opportunity for trade exists. The Heckscher-Ohlin theorem states that a country will export the good using its abundant factor intensively. In the previous example, this implies that country A will export cloth since it is labor abundant and cloth is labor-intensive. Country B will export wheat since wheat uses land intensively and country B is land-abundant.

4. Before trade, country A and country B produced both goods. With trade, country A incompletely specializes in the production of cloth and country B incompletely specializes in wheat production. The movement along each country's PPC toward the export-good axis generates a reallocation of resources from the import-competing sector (wheat in country A and cloth in country B) to the export industry. These changes in production patterns have implications for commodity and factor prices. As resources shift toward the export sector, factor prices change. For example, in country A resources shift from the wheat sector into the cloth industry. Since wheat is land-intensive, little labor is released as wheat production diminishes. Since cloth manufacturing requires a large amount of labor, the demand for labor increases significantly while the supply of labor rises by a lesser amount. This labor shortage causes an increase in the price of labor (the wage rate). On the other hand, since cloth production requires little land, the rental rate for land decreases. The opposite scenario occurs in country B. The expanding wheat sector requires a large amount of land and little labor. The shrinking cloth sector in country B releases an abundance of labor but little land. This increases the rental rate and decreases the wage rate. Through trade, factor prices become equalized.

CHAPTER OBJECTIVES

After studying the concepts presented in Chapter 3, you should be able to answer the following questions:

1. What are the assumptions of the Heckscher-Ohlin theory? How do they differ from those made in the previous chapters? Why is the assumption of the absence of factor-intensity reversals important?

2. How is the production-possibilities curve derived? How does a country's factor endowment influence the shape of the PPC? Why are all points along the PPC technically efficient?

3. How are factor prices equalized through trade? What happens if one country completely specializes in the production of one commodity?

4. How are goods' prices equalized through trade? What assumptions must be made to ensure equalization?

5. What predictions does this model make for the winners and losers from trade? Why? What role does the time frame of adjustment play in your answer?

GLOSSARY TERMS

- factor-price equalization
- factor intensity reversal
- Heckscher-Ohlin theorem
- Isoquant
- Leontief paradox
- relative factor endowments
- relative factor intensities
- Rybczynski theorem
- specific factors model
- Stolper-Samuelson theorem

CHAPTER 3 STUDY QUESTIONS

Multiple Choice Questions

1. According to the Heckscher-Ohlin theorem, international trade arises because of

   a. differences in technology.
   b. differences in relative factor endowments and intensities.
   c. differences in tastes and preferences.
   d. the existence of economies of scale in production.

2. International trade tends to

   a. have no effect on the prices of production inputs.
   b. cause all prices of production inputs to increase.
   c. cause the price of the scarce factor of production to increase and the price of the abundant factor of production to decrease.
   d. cause the price of the scarce factor of production to decrease and the price of the abundant factor of production to increase.

3.   According to the Heckscher-Ohlin theorem, production functions

    a.   differ across countries.
    b.   are identical across countries.
    c.   exhibit decreasing returns to scale.
    d.   constantly change in response to changes in technology.

4.   The production possibilities curve is derived from

    a.   individual and community indifference curves.
    b.   isoincome functions.
    c.   isoquants and the Edgeworth box diagram.
    d.   indifference curves and the Edgeworth box diagram.

5.   According to the Heckscher-Ohlin theory, countries will export

    a.   the good using its relatively abundant factor intensively.
    b.   the good using its relatively scarce factor intensively.
    c.   the good in which it has an absolute advantage.
    d.   the good with the lowest transportation cost.

6.   In order for factor price equalization to occur, the following conditions must hold:

    a.   factor intensity reversals and complete specialization.
    b.   factor intensity reversals and incomplete specialization.
    c.   no factor intensity reversals and complete specialization.
    d.   no factor intensity reversals and incomplete specialization.

7.   If labor is scarce in country B (and abundant in A), trade results in

    a.   an increase in the wage rate in country B and a decrease in the wage rate in country A.
    b.   an increase in the wage rate in country A and country B.
    c.   a decrease in the wage rate in country B and an increase in the wage rate in country A.
    d.   a decrease in the wage rate in country A and country B.

8.   After trade, total income in both countries increases. However, the distribution of income within each country changes. More specifically,

    a.   the scarce factor of production gains and the abundant factor loses.

    b.   the scarce factor of production loses and the abundant factor gains.

    c.   both factors of production gain from trade, but the abundant factor gains more than the scarce factor.

    d.   both factors of production gain from trade, but the scarce factor gains more than the abundant factor.

9.   If production inputs are considered internally immobile in the short-run (assuming capital and labor are the only factors of production and this country is labor abundant),

    a.   both capital and labor employed in the labor-intensive industry lose while capital and labor employed in the capital-intensive industry gain from trade.

    b.   both capital and labor employed in the labor-intensive industry gain while capital and labor employed in the capital-intensive industry lose from trade.

    c.   capital employed in both sectors loses while labor employed in both sectors gains from trade.

    d.   capital employed in both sectors wins while labor employed in both sectors loses from trade.

10.   The Leontief paradox

    a.   showed that U.S. exports were relatively more capital-intensive, which does not support the Heckscher-Ohlin theorem.

    b.   showed that U.S. exports were relatively more labor-intensive, which does not support the Heckscher-Ohlin theorem.

    c.   showed that U.S. exports were relatively more labor-intensive, which supports the Heckscher-Ohlin theorem.

    d.   showed that U.S. exports were relatively more capital-intensive, which supports the Heckscher-Ohlin theorem.

True, False, Uncertain and Why Questions

When answering the following questions, be sure to support your assertion of true, false, or uncertain with two or three sentences.

1.   All points inside the production possibility frontier correspond to points along the efficiency locus in the Edgeworth box diagram.

2.   If trade in goods is prohibited through trade barriers, no alternative to trade exists and countries return to the pre-trade equilibrium production and consumption points.

3. Trade results in a reallocation of income from the scarce factor of production to the abundant factor. By comparing utility functions across groups within a country, we can determine whether the gains exceed the losses.

4. A country's pattern of comparative advantage is fixed over time.

5. In the very short-run, trade makes all factor of production employed in the export sector better off.

Short Answer Questions

1. Computer production is relatively capital intensive while the production of corn is relatively labor-intensive. Country A has 250 million dollars worth of capital and 750 workers while country B has 100 million dollars worth of capital and 700 workers. What pattern of trade does the Heckscher-Ohlin theory predict for these countries? Why?

2. What are the effects on both goods and factor prices if a country places a tariff on its imported good?

Use the following information to answer questions 3 through 5:

Country A is labor abundant and capital scarce, while country B has the opposite pattern of factor endowments. Each produces food and clothing, the latter being more capital-intensive than the former.

3. Before trade, what pattern of goods and factor price would you expect to prevail in each country? Why?

4. Assuming that tastes are similar in each country, what pattern of trade would you expect to develop? Why? Illustrate with two relevant graphs.

5. How would the internal prices of clothing and food change in each country? What do these changes imply about factor prices?

ANSWERS TO CHAPTER 3 STUDY GUIDE QUESTIONS

Multiple Choice Questions

1. b
    When countries have different relative endowments of factors of production, specializing in the production of the good using the country's relatively abundant factor intensively will benefit the country as a whole if it engages in international trade.

2.   d

International trade reallocates resources from the import-competing sector to the export sector. This means that the return to the factor used in the export industry increases while the return to the factor used in the import-competing sector decreases.

3.   b

Unlike the Ricardian model, technology is the same between countries but differs across goods.

4.   c

The Edgeworth box shows the country's endowment of production inputs while the isoquants represent the production process (technology). The production possibilities frontier is derived from efficiency points located at the tangencies of the isoquants in the Edgeworth box.

5.   a

According to Heckscher-Ohlin, each country has a comparative advantage in the good using its relatively abundant factor intensively.

6.   d

When a country is completely specialized in the production of a good, international trade will cause goods prices to equal each other but factor prices will not be equalized. Factor intensity reversals also prevent factor price equalization.

7.   c

As the labor-intensive industry expands in country A, labor demand increases, causing the wage rate to rise. The labor-intensive industry in country B is shrinking, generating an excess supply of labor which decreases the wage rate in country B.

8.   b

As resources are reallocated from the import-competing to the export sector, the demand for the abundant factor of production increases (increasing its return) while the demand for the scarce factor decreases (decreasing its return).

9.   b

When factors are immobile, factors (both capital and labor) employed in the expanding export sector gain while factors employed in the shrinking import-competing sector lose.

10.   b

The United States is considered a capital-abundant country. According to the Heckscher-Ohlin theory, this means that the U.S. should export capital-intensive goods. Leontief showed that U.S. exports were relatively more labor-intensive, which does not support the Heckscher-Ohlin theorem.

True, False, Uncertain and Why Questions

1.   False. Any point located on the interior of the production possibilities curve is not on the efficiency locus in the Edgeworth box diagram. Any point along the production

possibilities curve is efficient since these points represent the combination of goods which minimizes costs, assuming technology and the prices of the factors of production are fixed.

2. False. If trade in goods is prohibited due to tariffs, quotas, or other trade barriers, the country can maintain its free trade consumption pattern if factors of production become internationally mobile.

3. False. While trade does result in a reallocation of incomes, interpersonal utility comparisons are not possible due to the nature of utility functions. It is not possible to be certain that total utility rises.

4. False. A country's area of comparative advantage can change over time as technology and relative endowments of production inputs change.

5. True. In the very short-run, factors of production are fixed and cannot move from one sector to the other. As a result of this immobility, trade increases the price of the exported good, increasing the returns to both factors employed in this sector.

Short Answer Questions

1. Even though country A has more of both production inputs, trade still occurs between the two countries. According to the Heckscher-Ohlin theory, a country should export that good using its relatively abundant factor intensively. Since country B is relatively abundant in workers, it should export the labor-intensive good (corn) while country A should export the capital-intensive good (computers).

2. When a country places a tariff on its imported good, the price of this good increases, which increases the return to the factor used intensively in the production of the imported good.

3. Since labor is scarce in country B, the wage rate in this nation is relatively higher than the wage rate in country A (where labor is abundant). Since capital is scarce in country A, the rental rate of capital is relatively higher in country A than in country B. Assuming similar tastes and preferences across countries, cheap labor in country A means a relatively lower price for food (the labor-intensive good) in country A than in country B. Since capital is cheaper in country B, this corresponds to a lower price for clothing in country B than in country A.

4. Assuming that tastes and preferences are similar across countries, the Heckscher-Ohlin theorem states that country A should export food and import clothing while country B should export clothing and import food.

    The following graph shows the pre-trade and trade environment for country A. In the absence of trade, country A produces at P1 and consumes at C1 with prices equal to $(Pf/Pc)1$. With trade, country A specializes in food production and produces at P2, where the new price ratio $(Pf/Pc)2$ is tangent to the PPC. Consumption occurs at C2, where the new price line $(Pf/Pc)2$ is tangent to the highest indifference curve.

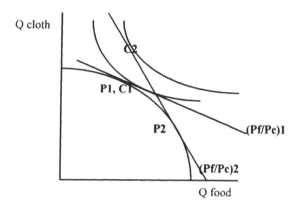

5.   As country B exports clothing to country A, the domestic price of clothing in B
       increases as the domestic amount of clothing available decreases (due to export sales).
       As a result of imports, the amount of food available in country B increases, which
       drives down the domestic price of food. The opposite movement in goods' prices
       occurs in country A. The domestic price of food rises as country A exports this good
       to country B. As a result of imports, the domestic price of clothing in country A
       decreases.

       Factor prices also change. In country B, the clothing industry expands,
       demanding a large amount of capital and little labor. As the food sector shrinks, a
       large amount of labor and little capital is released. The excess supply of labor lowers
       the wage rate while the excess demand for capital increases the rental rate. The
       opposite result occurs in country A.

CHAPTER 4

TRADE AMONG SIMILAR COUNTRIES: IMPLICATIONS OF DECREASING COSTS AND IMPERFECT COMPETITION

IMPORTANT POINTS

1. The Ricardian and Heckscher-Ohlin theories of international trade imply that trade occurs between countries with dissimilar technologies (Ricardo) or factor endowments (Heckscher-Ohlin). The Heckscher-Ohlin theory discussed in Chapter 3 suggests that mutually beneficial trade occurs between nations with differing factor endowments. Assuming wheat production is relatively land-intensive and cloth production is relatively labor-intensive, a land-abundant country exports wheat and imports cloth while the labor-abundant nation exports cloth and imports wheat. While some trade patterns adhere to this theory, others do not.

2. Economies of scale and imperfect competition provide another reason for the existence of international trade. Certain industries are characterized by large, fixed costs, particularly research and development expenditures, which lead to declining average total costs as output expands. Trade provides an additional route for output expansion. For example, manufacturing aircraft involves large, fixed R&D costs. If the firm produces only for domestic consumption, the market size may not be large enough to sustain a single firm. The introduction of trade provides additional consumers to whom the firm can sell aircraft, thus spreading R&D costs over a larger sales volume and decreasing average costs.

3. Economies of scale exist at the firm level and the industry-level. Firm level economies of scale occur when firm costs fall as its own output increases. Industry-level economies of scale (also called external economies of scale) exist when all firms within an industry have lower production costs as the industry as a whole becomes larger. Especially with external economies, the level of output at which economies of scale exist may only be attainable through export. In other words, the size of the

domestic market may be insufficient to achieve the cost reductions while the size of the world market is sufficient.

4.   External economies of scale may exist for several reasons. When most firms within an industry are concentrated in the same geographic region, these firms may benefit from spillover effects and a greater specialized labor pool. Internal economies of scale occur in several cases such as when a firm faces significant fixed costs or increasing returns to scale characterize the production process.

5.   Introducing external economies of scale to the PPC changes the shape of the curve. Figure 4-1 illustrates a PPC with external economies of scale. As the country produces more computers, its costs of production decrease, implying decreasing opportunity cost. As an economy trades, increasing production of its export good, it is able to reach a higher indifference curve than without trade.

Figure 4-1: PPC with External Economies of Scale

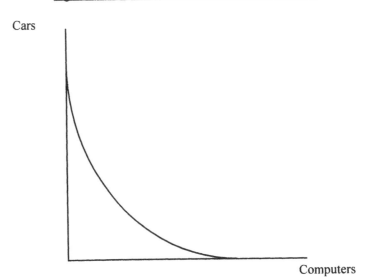

6.   The Vernon Product Cycle explains how comparative advantage changes over time. In other words, as time progresses, the good in which a country has a relative advantage changes. The product cycle theory divides this production change into four stages. New products are developed in one country and sold domestically (Stage I). As domestic production increases, the good is exported to the rest of the world (Stage II). As patents expire and technology escapes via other routes, the original monopoly of the original country is lost. As foreign firms produce this good, the market share of the country that initiated the product declines (Stage III). This country eventually becomes a net importer of the product (Stage IV).

The eventual loss of market share has implications for future research and development (R&D) expenditures. If firms believe the length of time between stages I and III is decreasing, these companies may be less likely to initiate risky product development strategies. The earnings from stages I and II sales may not be enough to recoup investment costs. The dynamic nature of comparative advantage has important implications for commercial and trade policy.

7.   The preference similarity hypothesis, also known as Linder trade, suggests that countries with goods that have an active domestic market that enables firms in these industries to exploit economies of scale. International trade occurs in differentiated products such as automobiles. For example, Germany exports BMWs to England and imports Jaguars from England. Sweden exports Saabs to England and Germany and imports Italian Fiats. Trade occurs between these countries because of consumer tastes and internal economies of scale, not because of different relative factor endowments (Heckscher-Ohlin theory) or differences in technology (Ricardian comparative advantage). Such trade is known as intraindustry trade.

8.   Imperfect competition provides another reason for trade. When industries characterized by monopolistic competition are opened to trade, consumers benefit from greater variety and lower prices. With Cournot competition, production decisions by firms recognize the interdependence of output levels. Since firms in these industries earn positive economic profit, countries can be better off if they can shift profit from a foreign competitor to a domestic firm.

9.   In an imperfectly competitive environment, firms have an incentive to collude. Collusive behavior takes many forms, the formation of a cartel being the most explicit. These firms or countries act together, pooling their market share in order to reap monopoly profits. The most widely known cartel is the Organization of Petroleum Exporting Countries (OPEC). During part of the 1970s and 1980s, member countries were able to increase the price of oil sharply by restricting supply. Not all cartels have been successful. In order to influence the price, certain conditions must hold. The commodity must have few, if any, substitutes in consumption. This means that when the price increases, the quantity demanded does not decline sharply. The cartel must consist of the majority of actual and potential suppliers of the commodity. If this is not the case, the price rise generated by the production cut cannot be maintained since outside suppliers have an incentive to increase their quantity supplied to the market.

10.   Frequently, exporting firms are accused of dumping. Dumping may take several forms. When the elasticity of demand differs across markets, a firm maximizes profits by selling its product for a lower price in the more elastic market and a higher price in a less elastic market. Firms may also practice predatory dumping. This strategy means that the firm sells the product for a lower price in its export markets than in its domestic market. The domestic market may be protected from competition by high tariffs and other barriers to trade. By undercutting domestic import-competing firms, the foreign firm is able to gain a larger market share in its export market, driving import-competing firms out of business. The foreign firm is able to charge artificially low prices since losses from export sales are balanced by monopoly/oligopoly profits from its domestic market. Once competition in the export market is eliminated, the foreign firm operates in a monopoly or oligopoly environment, able to increase price above cost and recoup previous losses.

CHAPTER OBJECTIVES

After studying the concepts presented in Chapter 4, you should be able to answer the following questions:

1. Explain how comparative advantage can change over time and implications these changes have on firms' incentives to invest in research and development activities.

2. How can the existence of economies of scale provide a reason for international trade?

3. Explain the differences between intraindustry trade and interindustry trade.

4. Why is dumping illegal? How does a foreign firm that dumps imports on the local market affect domestic firms?

5. Why are some cartels successful while others are not? What roles do the price elasticity of demand and price elasticity of supply play in your answer?

GLOSSARY TERMS

- border trade
- cartel
- dumping
- economies of scale
- intellectual property
- intra-industry trade
- predatory dumping
- preference similarity hypothesis (Linder trade)
- principle of second best
- strategic trade policy
- Vernon product cycle
- World Trade Organization

CHAPTER 4 STUDY GUIDE QUESTIONS

Multiple Choice Questions

1. The factor proportions or Heckscher-Ohlin theorem is successful in explaining trade

    a. among only industrialized countries.
    b. among only developing countries.
    c. between industrialized and developing countries.
    d. among all countries.

2.   According to the Vernon product cycle theory, trade between countries occurs

a.   because of differences in tastes and preferences.
b.   because of increasing returns to scale.
c.   because of the existence of monopolies and oligopolies.
d.   because of changing areas of comparative advantage.

3.   Recent U.S. export performance suggests that the performance of U.S. products abroad has weakened. The Vernon product cycle theory would explain this occurrence as

a.   a decrease in the length of Stages I and II.
b.   a decrease in the length of Stages II and III.
c.   a decrease in the length of Stages III and IV.
d.   a decrease in the length of Stages I and III.

4.   Utilizing _____ is/are one way to forestall Stages III and IV of the product cycle.

a.   factor abundance.
b.   natural resources.
c.   economies of scale.
d.   protectionist trade policies.

5.   According to Linder trade theory, trade occurs because of

a.   differences in tastes and preferences.
b.   differences in relative factor endowments.
c.   preference similarity.
d.   differences in technology.

6.   Dumping includes all of the following practices except

a.   setting marginal revenue equal to marginal cost when demand elasticities differ across markets.
b.   charging a price lower than cost.
c.   charging a price lower than marginal revenue
d.   charging a higher price in one market than another market.

7.   With monopolistic competition

a.   firms do not have any price setting ability
b.   firms set prices without any threat of competition
c.   firms set prices and are constrained by the existence of close substitutes for their product.
d.   firms produce identical goods.

8.   Economies of scale exist when

    a.   average costs of production increase as more output is produced.
    b.   more than one product can be produced using the same production process.
    c.   average costs of production decrease as more output is produced.
    d.   resources become more productive.

9.   Successful cartels tend to have

    a.   relatively inelastic demand and low elasticity of supply from non-cartel members.
    b.   relatively elastic demand and low elasticity of supply from non-cartel members.
    c.   relatively inelastic demand and high elasticity of supply from non-cartel members.
    d.   relatively elastic demand and high elasticity of supply from non-cartel members.

10.   With external economies of scale, the PPC is characterized by

    a.   the absence of opportunity costs.
    b.   decreasing opportunity costs
    c.   constant opportunity costs.
    d.   increasing opportunity costs

True, False, Uncertain and Why Questions

When answering the following questions, be sure to support your assertion of true, false, or uncertain with two or three sentences.

1.   A cartel will be successful when the elasticity of supply for the product from outside the cartel is low.

2.   Dumping is usually defined as the sale of a commodity in a foreign market at a price above that charged in the domestic market.

3.   Trade in monopolistically competitive industries tends to increase the amount of product variety and lower prices.

4.   When economies of scale are present in production, a firm's total costs fall as its production levels increase.

5.   Technological advancement affects the duration of the different stages in the Vernon product cycle.

Short Answer Questions

1.   Suppose Firm A sells athletic shoes in several countries. The demand for these shoes in MacroLand is more elastic than demand in MicroLand. What type of prices will you expect Firm A to charge in these two markets? Is this an example of predatory dumping?

2.   Using the PPC graph, illustrate the following events: Country A produces computers and cars. Economies of scale characterized production of both goods. Without trade, country A produces and consumes both goods. With trade, it specializes in computers and imports cars. Explain what happens to opportunity cost as specialization occurs.

3.   Using the graph for monopolistic competition, illustrate how trade can erode a firm's economic profit, lowering price and increasing product variety.

4.   Suppose the Brazilian computer industry has lower average total costs than the Peruvian computer industry. If the Peruvian industry is established first, why might the Brazilian industry be unable to compete? Illustrate with the appropriate graph.

5.   Why does the value of the elasticity of demand play an important role in the success of a cartel? Why might this value change over time?

ANSWERS TO CHAPTER 4 STUDY GUIDE QUESTIONS

Multiple Choice Questions

1.   c
Heckscher-Ohlin predicts that trade should occur between countries with different factor endowments. This theory is successful in explaining trade between developing nations and industrialized countries.

2.   d
According to the Vernon product cycle, areas of comparative advantage change over time. A country that initially exported a product to the rest of the world could eventually become a net importer of the good, as the technological monopoly is lost.

3.   a
A decrease in the length of Stages I and II means that the amount of time the U.S. is the sole producer of a product is decreasing. Technological monopolies are more short-lived.

4.   c
Economies of scale infer a significant cost advantage on existing firms in the market and may create substantial entry barriers making foreign production more difficult.

5.   c

Linder trade suggests the countries with similar income levels have similar tastes. Each country will produce primarily for its home market, but part of the output will be exported to other countries.

6.   c

Dumping, by definition, occurs when a firm charges different price in different markets (for the same good) or sells the product for less than fair market value. The former may occur if demand elasticity differs across markets. The latter occurs when the firm sets price below average cost or marginal cost.

7.   c

With monopolistic competition, each firm has monopoly power for its good. However, unlike a monopoly, close substitutes exist. If the firm earns positive economic profit, entry occurs, decreasing demand for existing products, causing a decrease in price.

8.   c

If economies of scale exist, average costs fall as the amount produced increases.

9.   a

With inelastic demand, consumers are not very sensitive to price changes. When price increases, quantity demanded falls by a small amount. With low elasticity of outside supply, higher prices do not generate a large increase in production by firms outside the cartel. These conditions are necessary for the cartel to be successful.

10.   b

With economies of scale, average total costs fall as production levels increase, leading to decreasing opportunity costs.

True, False, Uncertain and Why Questions

1.   True. When the price of the product increases, firms outside the cartel have an incentive to increase quantity supplied. If this supply response is large enough, the price would decline. Therefore, the outside supply response must be low as the price increases.

2.   False. Dumping is usually defined as the sale of a commodity in a foreign market at a price below that changed in the domestic market. High tariff barriers usually protect the domestic market.

3.   True. With trade, the size of the market increases, allowing some firms to exploit economies of scale, lowering price to consumers. Since both foreign and domestic firms serve the market, product variety increases.

4.   False. As production increases, the firm's total cost increase and average total cost fall with economies of scale.

5.   True. With improvements in technology, the duration of the monopoly stage is
       shortened.

Short Answer Questions

1.   The price for the shoes in the more inelastic market (MicroLand) would exceed the
       price for the same shoes in the more elastic market (assuming equal marginal cost in
       both markets). If the firm maximizes profit, it should set marginal revenue equal to
       marginal cost in each market to determine the optimal level of output. Different types
       of consumers will lead to different prices. Since the firm is not selling the product for
       less than cost, this example is not a predatory dumping case.

2.   The shape of the PPC reflects the existence of economies of scale (see thicker curve).
       Without trade, country A produces and consumes at point 1. With trade, it specializes
       in the production of computers, moving along the PPC toward the horizontal axis.
       Assuming the country exports computers and imports cars, it produces at point 2 and
       consumes at point 3. The country is better off as a whole since it reaches a higher
       indifference curve.

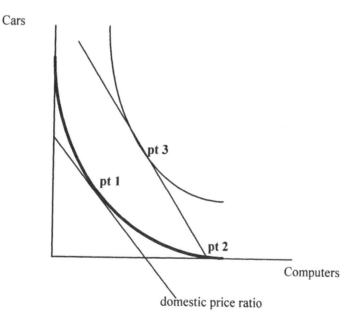

3.   With monopolistic competition, each firm sets marginal revenue equal to marginal
       cost. With little competition, these firms may earn a positive economic profit. With
       trade, more firms produce similar products, which decreases each individual firm's
       demand curve (shifting demand inward). As this decrease in demand occurs, prices
       fall, eroding firm profit.

4.   If the Peruvian produces on a smaller scale than the Brazilian industry, its average
       costs may be higher, even though the Peruvian industry is more efficient. For

example, if Peru produces Q1 units, its average cost equal AC1. If Brazil produces on a larger scale at Q2, its average costs are lower (equal to AC2).

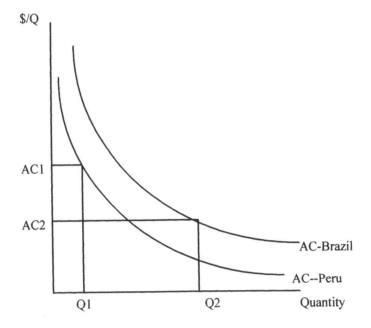

5.   When demand is inelastic, total revenue increases as price increases. Over time, consumers will look for substitute goods, making demand more elastic. Over time, higher prices may lead to lower total revenue.

CHAPTER 5

THE THEORY OF PROTECTION: TARIFFS AND OTHER BARRIERS TO TRADE

IMPORTANT POINTS

1.   Two modes of analysis are used to study barriers-to-trade. The partial equilibrium framework focuses on the sector of the economy on which the tariff or quota is imposed. Linkages to other areas of the economy are ignored. The general equilibrium approach attempts to analyze broader effects across an economy by abstracting to a two-good model with two factors of production and two countries.

2.   A country unable to influence its terms-of-trade is labeled a small country. In other words, these nations lack any degree of monopoly or monopsony power in trade. If country A is small and wants to reduce the quantity of imported goods within the economy, several policies can be selected.

        A tariff affects the price of the good on which it is imposed. This tax is either specific (i.e., $0.20 per unit) or ad valorem (i.e., 20 percent of the value of the good). The specific tariff is used unless otherwise specified. Suppose Mexico places a tariff on automobiles imported from the United States. Figure 5-1 shows the effects of this trade policy on the Mexican economy.

Figure 5-1: Partial Equilibrium Tariff Analysis, Small Country Case

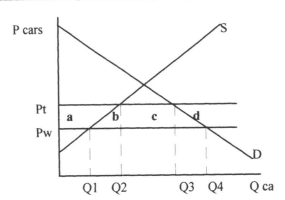

With free trade, Mexico imports (Q4-Q1) cars at a price equal to P_w. The tariff increases the domestic price of autos in Mexico from P_w to P_t. Since Mexico is assumed to be a small country, the tariff does not affect the world terms-of-trade. As a result of the domestic price increase, the quantity of cars demanded decreases from Q4 to Q3 and the quantity of cars produced by Mexican firms increases from Q1 to Q2. Consumers lose area A+B+C+D because of the higher price and lower consumption (loss of consumer surplus). Mexican producers gain area A (increase in producer surplus) while the government collects tariff revenue equal to C (tariff rate times the number of imports). The dead-weight loss from the tariff is area B (production inefficiency) plus D (consumption inefficiency).

3. If Mexico places a quota on the importation of cars made in the U.S., the Mexican price also increases, while the world price remains unchanged. The changes in consumer and producer surplus are identical to those in Figure 5-1. Area C differs. The higher price under the quota generates higher profits for those firms or governments who own the quota rights. In the case of a Voluntary Export Restraint (VER), foreign firms agree to reduce imports. The reduction in supply causes a higher price and results in greater profits for foreign firms. If foreign firms had to bid for the right to export the commodity to Mexico, the Mexican government receives the quota rents.

    If the Mexican government auctions the quota rents, the partial equilibrium analysis is identical to the tariff discussion. If foreign governments determine which firms will export, the home country is worse off under the quota since the foreign firms or government receives area C. When the domestic firm is a monopoly, tariff and quotas do not generate the same results.

4. If Mexico is considered a large country, the assumption of the absence of market power in trade is removed. Mexican trade policies influence the world price for the particular commodity on which a tariff, quota or some other barrier to trade is imposed. When a large country places a tariff on an imported good, both domestic and world prices change. Suppose Mexico places a tariff on imported cars from the United States. The tariff causes the supply of cars in Mexico to decrease, increasing the domestic price of cars. Since the United States can no longer export as many cars into Mexico, the supply of cars in the U.S. increases, reducing the price of cars in the

U.S. Two conditions must be satisfied after the imposition of the tariff: the United States' exports of automobiles must equal Mexico's imports and the price of cars in Mexico must deviate from the price of cars in the U.S. by the amount of the tariff. The values of the elasticities of supply and demand for both countries determine how much the price in the United States and the price in Mexico deviate from the pre-tariff price. Figure 5-2 illustrates the effects of a tariff by Mexico on imported U.S. cars if Mexico is a large importing country.

Figure 5-2: Partial Equilibrium Tariff Analysis, Large Country Case

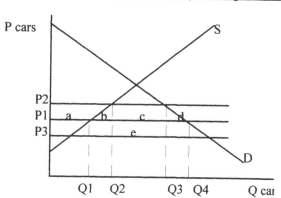

Before the tariff, Mexico imports (Q4-Q1) cars at a price equal to P1. The tariff increases the domestic price in Mexico from P1 to P2 while the world price fall from P1 to P3. P2 and P3 differ by the amount of the tariff. The quantity of cars demanded falls to Q3 while the quantity of cars produced by Mexican firms increases to Q2. The quantity of imports decreases from (Q4-Q1) to (Q3-Q2).

The price changes have implications for national welfare. Consumer surplus decreases by area A+B+C+D while producer surplus increases by area A. The government receives area C+E in tariff revenue. The net change in net welfare is E (terms-of-trade gain) minus B minus D (both areas are dead-weight losses). Whenever E exceeds (B+D), country A is better off with the tariff.

5. The effects of tariffs and quotas can be illustrated using a general equilibrium framework. This method uses the production possibilities curve and community indifference curves to show the effect of trade policy on the economy. The small country case is examined first. In Figure 5-4 (in the text), the free trade equilibrium is shown by line TT and indifference curve i_2. Production occurs at point P_1 where the domestic price ratio (TT) is tangent to the PPC. Consumption occurs at C_1, where the world price ratio TT (which equals the domestic price ratio) is tangent to community indifference curve i_2. A tariff on food creates a wedge between domestic and world prices. Since Mexico is assumed to be a small country, the world price ratio remains TT. The domestic price ratio becomes flatter due to the higher price of food. Production occurs at the point P_2 where the domestic price ratio (DD) is tangent to the PPC. Consumption occurs at C_2 where the domestic price ratio is tangent to community indifference curve i_1 along the world price line. Since consumption occurs on a lower indifference curve, the tariff decreases net welfare in Mexico.

6.   In the large country case, the tariff causes both the domestic and world price ratios to change. The domestic price line becomes flatter (as domestic supply of the imported good decreases), while the world terms-of-trade becomes steeper. After the tariff, the country reaches a higher community indifference curve because of the change in the world price of the imported good. For a large country, a small tariff may improve national welfare. This improvement can be illustrated using either a production possibilities diagram or an offer curve. (Refer to Figures 5-8 and 5-9 in the text.)

7.   Trade policy is not limited to the area of imported goods. Governments also focus on export-good industries, encouraging firms to increase production or expand into new fields in the hope of capturing a large share of an export market. The structure of export subsidies varies from the explicit to the subtle. One form would be a strategy in which producers receive a payment for the production of exported goods. This differs from the production subsidy in that the export policy is not designed to increase domestic consumption. The export subsidy reallocates goods from the domestic market toward foreign ones. This increases domestic prices while depressing the world price (if we assume a large country case). If the country is small, the world price of the good remains unchanged.

Export taxes, assuming the exporting country is small, cause the domestic price to decrease, which benefits consumers at the expense of producers. Consumer surplus and government revenue increase while producer surplus decreases.

8.   The previous tariff analysis assumed that the good was produced entirely within the boundaries of a specific country. The possibility of inputs that could be imported has been ignored. When this assumption is dropped, the difference between nominal and effective tariff rates is important. The effective tariff rate is defined as the percentage increase in an industry's value-added per unit of output resulting from the tariff. The formula for the effective tariff uses a comparison between value-added with the tariff and the value under free trade:

$$Effective \; tariff \; rate = \frac{Value \; added_{Country \; A} - Value \; added_{free \; trade}}{Value \; added_{free \; trade}}. \qquad (5.1)$$

The effective tariff rate can also be calculated using the following formula:

$$e_j = \frac{t_j - \Sigma a_{ij} \, t_i}{1 - \Sigma a_{ij}} \qquad (5.2)$$

where $e_j =$ the effective tariff in industry j
       $t_j =$ the nominal tariff rate in industry j
       $t_i =$ the nominal tariff rate in industry i
       $a_{ij} =$ the share of inputs from industry i in the value of output from industry j, measured at free trade prices.

CHAPTER OBJECTIVES

After studying the concepts represented in Chapter 5, you should be able to answer the following questions:

1. Explain the difference between the large country and small country tariff cases. Can a single country be classified as both small and large?

2. What are the effects of a tariff placed on a small country's imported good? How do the graphical representations of the tariff differ between the partial equilibrium framework and the general equilibrium model?

3. How does the implementation of a quota by a small country differ from the tariff case? Why is the ownership of quota rents so important?

4. How do the effects of a quota and tariff change when the country is assumed to be large? What causes the country to potentially gain from the imposition of the tariff? How can the value for the optimal tariff be determined?

5. What trade policy can be used to target the export sector? Is this policy more difficult to implement than the tariffs or quotas?

GLOSSARY TERMS

- ad valorem tariff
- consumer surplus
- countervailing duty
- deadweight loss
- effective tariff
- non-tariff barrier
- optimum tariff
- producer surplus
- quota
- quota rents
- specific tariff
- tariff
- terms-of-trade
- voluntary export restraint (VER)

CHAPTER 5 STUDY QUESTIONS

Multiple Choice Questions

Use the information in Figure A to answer questions 1 through 7.

Figure A: Partial Equilibrium Tariff Analysis

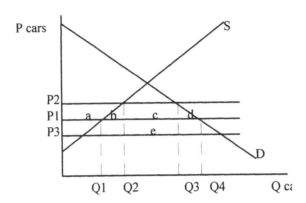

Assume that before the tariff that Mexico imports autos at a price of P1.

1. If Mexico is a large country and places a tariff on imported cars, the domestic price of cars _____ while the foreign (world) price of cars _____ .

    a. decreases to P3; increases to P2.
    b. decreases to P3; remains unchanged.
    c. increases to P2; decreases to P3.
    d. increases to P2; remains unchanged.

2. If Mexico is a small country and places a tariff on imported cars, the domestic price of cars _____ while the foreign (world) price of cars _____.

    a. decreases to P3; increases to P2.
    b. decreases to P3; remains unchanged.
    c. increases to P2; decreases to P3.
    d. increases to P2; remains unchanged.

3. If Mexico places a tariff on imported cars, the change in consumer surplus is

    a. loss of area A.
    b. loss of areas A + C.
    c. loss of areas A + B + C + D.
    d. loss of areas B + D.

4.   If Mexico is a small country, the amount of revenue generated by the tariff is equal to

    a.   areas A + C.
    b.   area C.
    c.   area E.
    d.   areas C + E.

5.   If Mexico is a large country, the amount of revenue generated by the tariff is equal to

    a.   areas A + C.
    b.   area C.
    c.   area E.
    d.   areas C + E.

6.   The terms-of-trade gain from the tariff (assuming Mexico is a small country) is

    a.   area A.
    b.   area C.
    c.   area E.
    d.   No terms-of-trade gain exists.

7.   The terms-of-trade gain from the tariff (assuming Mexico is a large country) is

    a.   area A.
    b.   area C.
    c.   area E.
    d.   No terms-of-trade gain exists.

8.   When a country can influence the terms-of-trade, price elasticities of demand and supply determine who bears the burden of the tariff. If country A implements a tariff on products from country B causing the terms-of-trade to turn against country B, it must be the case that

    a.   country A's supply curve is relatively elastic.
    b.   country B's supply curve has an elasticity of less than infinity.
    c.   country A's demand curve is relatively elastic.
    d.   country B's demand curve is relatively elastic.

9.   Of the four trade policies discussed (subsidies, tariffs, quotas, and VERs), _____ are the least inefficient means of encouraging domestic output.

    a.   tariffs.
    b.   quotas.
    c.   subsidies.
    d.   VERs.

10.   Of the four trade policies discussed (subsidies, tariffs, quotas, and VERs),
_____generates an increase in the price domestic firms receive.

   a.   tariffs.
   b.   quotas.
   c.   all of the policies.
   d.   none of the policies.

True, False, Uncertain and Why Questions

When answering the following questions, be sure to support your assertion of true, false or
uncertain with two or three sentences.

1.   A tariff always results in a net loss for the country imposing the tariff. Therefore,
tariffs should not be used to try to increase domestic production.

2.   When a country uses imported inputs, the appropriate measure of the rate of protection
is the effective tariff.

3.   Ad valorem tariffs are always preferred over specific tariffs.

4.   For a small country, the welfare effects of a tariff, quota, and VER are the same.

5.   A production subsidy is preferred to a tariff on welfare grounds since it generates a
smaller dead weight loss and leaves consumption unchanged.

Short Answer Questions

1.   Suppose the nominal tariff on steel is 30% and the nominal tariff on cars is 40%. The
amount of steel in the value of cars at free trade prices ($P_{cars} = \$10,000$) is 70%.
Calculate the effective tariff rate.

2.   Using the information in Table A, calculate the effective tariff rate for the truck
industry.

Table A: Effective Tariff Example:

	Firm in Country A	Free-Trade Firm
Truck Price	$12,000	$10,000
Steel Input	$ 6,000	$ 5,000
Value Added	$ 6,000	$ 5,000

3.   Using the appropriate graphs, compare and contrast the effects of a tariff in the small
and large country cases.

4.   Using the general equilibrium framework, show the effect of a tariff on food if country A is a large importing country.

5.   Using offer curve analysis, show the effects of a tariff war assuming that country A initially places a tariff on food imports and country B responds by placing a tariff on cloth imports.

ANSWERS TO CHAPTER 5 STUDY GUIDE QUESTIONS

Multiple Choice Questions

1.   c
     If Mexico places a tariff on imported cars (and is a large country), the price of cars in Mexico rises to P2 because the supply of cars in Mexico decreases. The world price of cars falls to P3 since the supply of cars in the rest of the world increases.

2.   d
     If Mexico places an tariff on imported cars (and is a small country), the price of cars in Mexico rises to P2 because the supply of cars in Mexico decreases. The world price of cars remains unchanged because Mexico is a small country.

3.   c
     Consumers lose the area beneath the demand curve equal to A+B+C+D because of the higher domestic price.

4.   b
     Tariff revenue equals the amount of the tariff (P2-P1) times the number of imports.

5.   d
     Tariff revenue equals the amount of the tariff (P2-P3) times the number of imports.

6.   d
     If Mexico is a small country, it cannot influence the terms-of-trade.

7.   c
     The number of imports times the world price decrease (P1-P3) measures the terms-of-trade gain.

8.   b
     When country B's supply curve is less than infinitely elastic, the terms-of-trade shift more toward country A's favor.

9.   c
     Subsidies are the most efficient way to increase domestic production since they do not generate a consumption inefficiency. There is only one dead-weight loss triangle.

10. c

All of the policies increase the price domestic firms receive. The tariff, quota and VER generate higher prices for both consumers and firms while the subsidy increases the price received.

True, False, Uncertain and Why Questions

1. False. If the country is a large country and implements an optimal tariff, the terms-of-trade effects will outweigh the consumption and production losses and result in a net welfare gain.

2. True. When some inputs are imported, the most efficient means of measuring the rate of protection is the effective, not the nominal, tariff.

3. False. Ad valorem tariffs create the incentive for transfer pricing as a way of circumventing the trade policy.

4. False. The welfare effects of the tariff, quota, and VER are identical only if the trading rights are auctioned off for the VER or the quota.

5. True. A production subsidy does not distort the price that consumers pay for a product. Instead, it creates a wedge between what consumers pay and what producers receive. The area of dead weight loss is smaller with the subsidy than the tariff.

Short Answer Questions

1. The effective tariff rate is calculated using the following formula:

$$e_j = \frac{t_j - \Sigma a_{ij}\, t_i}{1 - \Sigma a_{ij}}$$

where

e_j = the effective tariff in industry j
t_j = the nominal tariff rate in industry j = 0.40
t_i = the nominal tariff rate in industry i = 0.30
a_{ij} = the share of inputs from industry i in the value of output from industry j, measured at free trade prices = 0.70

$$e_j = \frac{0.40 - (0.70)0.30}{1 - 0.70} = 0.633$$

2.   The effective tariff rate is calculated using the following formula:

$$Effective\ tariff\ rate = \frac{Value\ added_{Country\ A} - Value\ added_{free\ trade}}{Value\ added_{free\ trade}}.$$

$$e_j = \frac{\$6,000 - \$5,000}{\$5,000}$$

$$e_j = 0.20$$

3, 4.   The small country case does not generate a terms-of-trade gain. Therefore, for a small country, a tariff reduces welfare.

welfare changes for a small country:
- consumer surplus $-(A + B + C + D)$
- producer surplus $+A$
- government revenue $+C$
- net welfare change $-(B + D)$

For a large country, a tariff on food will change the terms-of-trade. Depending on the size of the tariff, the country may be better off as a result of the tariff.

welfare changes for a large country
- consumer surplus $-(A + B + C + D)$
- producer surplus $+A$
- government revenue $+(C + E)$
- net welfare change $+E - (B + D)$

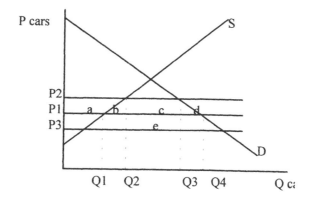

5.

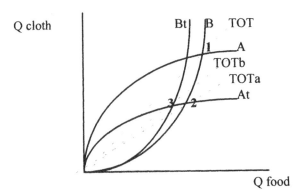

When country A places a tariff on its imported good, its offer curve shifts from A to
At. The terms-of-trade also change (assuming A is a large country) from TOT to
TOTa as the world price of food falls (pt. 2). If country B responds by placing a tariff
on its imports, its offer curve shifts from B to Bt. The terms-of-trade changes from
TOTa to TOTb (pt. 3). The total volume of trade has decreased.

CHAPTER 6

ARGUMENTS FOR PROTECTION AND THE POLITICAL ECONOMY OF TRADE POLICY

IMPORTANT POINTS

1.   There are many reasons some individuals, firms, or countries advocate protection over free trade. This chapter highlights the more popular arguments for trade barriers, with an emphasis on the problems and flaws of each approach.

2.   The use of protectionist policies, it is argued, can increase output and employment. By reducing imports and increasing domestic production to prevent any shortage, national product rises through the Keynesian multiplier effect. This argument has a number of problems. The decrease in imports will not be completely offset by an increase in domestic production. For example, if prices rise and imports decline by $1 billion, domestic production will expand by less than $1 billion, because consumption will fall. While the tariff generates positive production effects, consumption will fall as a result of higher prices caused by the tariff or quota.

        Other policies may be more effective in increasing employment and production. If the government's goal is to reduce the unemployment rate, the first-best policy is one that directly targets the root of the problem, such as expansionary fiscal and monetary policies. Tariffs might increase production and employment but are not the most efficient means of achieving these goals.

        This argument also ignores the possibility of retaliation by trading partners. The tariff causes the country's import bill to fall, but the amount of exports could decline as other nations implement similar strategies. If a tariff war begins, the volume of international trade dramatically declines, and countries approach the production and consumption patterns associated with autarky.

3.   The Pauper labor approach argues that free trade places import-competing firms at an unfair disadvantage due to differing costs of labor. Protectionist policies will help correct this cost bias. While the percentage of total cost due to labor expenses differs across countries, a firm's cost advantage may exist for other reasons. For example, labor is not the only input into production. While one country may have a lower wage bill, another country may have a cheaper rental rate of capital. Thus, to conclude that differences in wages are the sole source of cost differences is erroneous.

4.   The Heckscher-Ohlin theorem states that a country will export the good that uses its abundant factor intensively. The introduction of trade causes the abundant factor to gain and the scarce factor to lose, as resources are reallocated from the import-competing sector to the export industry. This implies that the scarce factor of production has an incentive to push for protection for the import-competing good. A tariff or quota drives a wedge between domestic and world prices. This prevents the equalization of goods and hence factor prices, and implies that labor will support protection in labor-scarce countries but oppose it in labor-abundant countries.

     This argument assumes that factors of production are fully mobile within the country. In the short-run, labor and capital may not be able to easily move from one sector to another. Allowing for specific factors alters the conclusions of the model. When factors of production are immobile in the short run, capital and labor used in the labor-intensive industry would support trade barriers on labor-intensive goods. Capital and labor used to produce capital-intensive goods would favor protection in the capital-intensive industry.

5.   A large country's ability to influence the terms-of-trade is the basis for the optimum tariff argument. Chapter 5 outlined the effects of a tariff on the national welfare of a country. In the large country case, the tariff generates a change in both domestic and world prices. When country A places a tariff on imported goods, it decreases the world price of its imports, improving its terms-of-trade. As long as the rest of the world does not retaliate, the tariff-imposing country can improve its terms-of-trade and reach a higher community indifference curve. The gains in national welfare depend upon the size of the tariff. The optimal tariff defines the amount of the import tax that generates the largest net national welfare gain. If the rest of the world retaliates, the value of the optimal tariff changes. The value of the tariff depends upon the elasticity of the offer curves. If countries engage in a tariff war, the optimal tariff may not be optimal after all, since the tariff cycle could cause both countries to move to a lower level of welfare.

6.   The infant-industry argument is based on the fact that when domestic firms enter an existing market, they usually are less efficient and smaller than their pre-existing rivals. Inefficiencies arise for several reasons. Production technology may include scale-economies or learning-by-doing cost advantages. Initially, the domestic firms will produce a higher cost, lower quality product that is unable to compete with foreign imports. The infant industry argument asserts that tariffs provide the

temporary protection domestic firms need in order to develop into competitive entities. Tariffs and quotas can be used to raise the price of the imported good to a level that allows the domestic product to be competitive. This argument has appeal for developing countries that want to diversify the range of goods domestically produced. By targeting areas of potential efficiency, governments can use trade policy to develop future comparative advantage sectors. Despite the appeal of this argument, the infant-industry model has some controversy.

The concept of opportunity cost explains one troubling area associated with this argument. A country cannot erect high tariff walls around all sectors of the economy. Protecting one sector means resources may be diverted from another promising area. In other words, the infant-industry argument assumes that the government can determine which sectors of the economy are the future comparative advantage areas. This is often not the case. Also, if the government is able to determine the sector in which growth potentially exists, why can private entrepreneurs not make the same calculations? Thus, infant-industry advocated protection assumes the government has perfect foresight and that tariffs, quotas, and other barriers to trade are the most efficient means of creating investment opportunities.

Even if the government successfully selects the industries in which future advantage lies, another problem develops. Once tariffs and quotas are implemented, it is politically difficult to remove the trade barriers once the industry achieves a competitive size. Thus, in a sense, the infant has no incentive to become a self-supporting adult.

7.   A recent argument for protection focuses on industrial strategy. Drawing from theories of industrial organization, protection gives domestic firms an edge over foreign rivals and may discourage entry by foreign firms. Suppose a particular market consists of two firms, home and foreign. Both firms are considering whether to produce in a specific domestic market. Table 6-1 shows the payoff matrix associated with this game. The market is such that production by both firms results in losses for each firm. Because of the payoff structure, each firm has an incentive to be the first firm producing in this market. Suppose the foreign firm starts production in the first period. When the domestic firm contemplates entry, the payoff to both firms is negative, which deters entry by the domestic firm. Without government intervention, whichever firm moves first gains the entire market.

Table 6-1: Payoff Matrix without Entry Deterrence

FOREIGN FIRM

		produce	do not produce
DOMESTIC FIRM	produce	-$10m, -$10m	+$100m, $0
	do not produce	$0, +$100m	$0, $0

If the government places a tariff on imported goods, the payoff matrix can change to favor the home firm. Table 6-2 shows one possible payoff matrix.

If both firms enter the market, the foreign firm loses $30 million while the home firm gains $20 million. Assuming the foreign firm has complete information regarding the tariff structure and the payoff matrix, it is deterred from entering the market. Strategic government policy can also target the export industry, using export subsidies or taxes to achieve a higher level of profit for the home firm. An important point needs to be made. The preceding analysis assumed the foreign government did not duplicate the home government's trade policy. The possibility of tariff wars has not been considered.

Table 6-2: Payoff Matrix with Entry Deterrence

FOREIGN FIRM

		produce	do not produce
DOMESTIC FIRM	produce	+$20m, -$30m	+$200m, $0
	do not produce	$0, +$100m	$0, $0

8. Cournot analysis from Chapter 4 illustrates two benefits from government intervention. A production subsidy shifts a firm's reaction function, increasing the domestic firm's profit, often at the expense of the foreign firm. When spillovers exist in an industry, interventionist policy can generate positive welfare effects.

9. Another common argument for protection is the existence of domestic market imperfections. A production or consumption externality may exist within an industry. Firms may produce at suboptimal points along the production possibilities frontier or individuals may consume combinations of goods which do not maximize utility. Also, firms may be producing at points located in the interior region of the production possibilities frontier (perhaps due to minimum wage legislation). While tariffs can correct these distortions, they are not the most efficient policy. A tariff does not correct the source of the imperfection and creates new distortions. The first-best policy, in the case of a production externality, would be a production tax (for a negative externality) or a subsidy (for a positive externality).

10.   Theories from political economy help explain why governments implement various trade policies. The median voter model suggests that government officials determine policies based on the preferences of the median voter. These results suggest that the intensity of a voter's preference does not matter. For example, if a country is relatively labor intensive, implying more labor-owners than capital-owners, policies benefiting labor owners would be implemented, regardless of the intensity of the capital-owners preferences.

CHAPTER OBJECTIVES

After studying the concepts presented in Chapter 6, you should be able to answer the following questions:

1.   Explain the Pauper-labor theory. Why is it erroneous to conclude that differences in wage differentials give one country a cost advantage over another?

2.   Using the results of Heckscher-Ohlin, explain why the definition of time frame is important when explaining why some factors of production support protectionist policies.

3.   Is it ever to the advantage of a large country to impose a tariff on imports? Why or why not?

4.   Explain the infant industry argument. Why is the temporary element of protection important in this theory? What role does opportunity cost play in this model?

5.   Is it possible for government trade policy to help firms compete against foreign rivals? Why or why not?

6.   Why is trade policy not the first-best policy if a domestic production or consumption externality exists? What is the optimal policy?

GLOSSARY TERMS

- industrial strategy
- infant-industry protection
- International Monetary Fund
- Pauper-labor theory
- strategic trade policy
- trade adjustment assistance

CHAPTER 6 STUDY QUESTIONS

Multiple Choice Questions

1. Protectionism, it is argued, can increase output, incomes, and employment through

    a.   a change in factor endowments.
    b.   the Keynesian multiplier effect.
    c.   Ricardian comparative advantage.
    d.   a change in the terms-of-trade.

2. The Pauper labor argument asserts that protection is justified since domestic firms face higher labor costs than their foreign competitors. Wage differentials may exist for several reasons, one of which is

    a.   differences in labor productivity.
    b.   differences in the length of the workday.
    c.   differences in the standard of living between countries.
    d.   differences in countries' areas of comparative advantage.

3. The Factor-Price Equalization and Heckscher-Ohlin theorems suggest another reason for protection on the grounds that

    a.   comparative advantage sectors change over time.
    b.   the scarce factor of production gains while the abundant factor loses from trade.
    c.   the scarce factor of production loses while the abundant factor gains from trade.
    d.   interpersonal utility comparisons are difficult to make.

4. The optimum tariff argument holds for

    a.   a small country.
    b.   a large country.
    c.   a small country and no retaliation by the rest of the world.
    d.   a large country and no retaliation by the rest of the world.

5. According to the infant industry argument, the government should protect those industries

    a.   that are currently exporting goods to the rest of the world.
    b.   that are currently importing goods from the rest of the world.
    c.   that face low-cost foreign rivals.
    d.   that face high-cost foreign rivals.

6.   The industrial strategy approach is viewed as an extension of

    a.   the Vernon product cycle and Ricardian models.
    b.   the Ricardian and Heckscher-Ohlin models.
    c.   the Heckscher-Ohlin and infant industry models.
    d.   the Vernon product cycle and infant industry models.

7.   When a negative production externality exists, the most efficient means of correcting the distortion is a

    a.   tariff.
    b.   quota.
    c.   production subsidy.
    d.   production tax.

Use the information in Table A to answer questions 8 through 10.

Table A: Payoff Matrix from Production in Market X.

		FIRM A	
		produce	do not produce
FIRM B	produce	-$20, -$20	+$100, $0
	do not produce	$0, +$100	$0, $0

8.   If firm A produces and firm B does not, the payoff to firm B is
    a.   -20.
    b.   -100.
    c.   +100.
    d.   +0.

9.   If firm A produces first, the solution to this game is where

    a.   firm A and firm B both produce.
    b.   firm A and firm B both do not produce.
    c.   firm A produces and firm B does not produce.
    d.   firm A does not produce and firm B produces.

10. If the government of firm B wishes to change the payoff matrix to better benefit firm B, the government should

    a.   adopt a tariff making it profitable to both firms if both produce in the market.

    b.   adopt a tariff making it profitable to firm B if both firms produce in the market.

    c.   adopt a subsidy making it profitable to both firms if both produce in the market.

    d.   adopt a subsidy making it profitable to both firms if both firms do not produce in the market.

True, False, Uncertain and Why Questions

When answering the following questions, be sure to support your assertion of true, false, or uncertain with two or three sentences.

1. Protectionist policies are justified if home country firms face foreign competitors with significantly lower wage bills, since lower wages give the foreign firms an unfair advantage in the market.

2. The infant industry argument contradicts the theory of comparative advantage.

3. A country should never impose a tariff since it generates a net loss of welfare because of consumption and production distortions.

4. Large research and development costs are one possible justification for protection from foreign competition.

5. Subsidies are always preferred to tariffs as a means of protecting domestic producers.

Short Answer Questions

1. Using offer curves, illustrate the optimal tariff argument. State any assumptions you make when answering the question.

2. Using the information in Table B, determine the solution if firm B moves first and neither governments decide to intervene.

Table B: Payoff Matrix from Production in Market X

		FIRM A	
		produce	do not produce
FIRM B	produce	-$30, -$30	+$50, $0
	do not produce	$0, +$50	$0, $0

3.   Using the information in Table B, construct a payoff matrix that might result if the government of firm A decides to place a tariff on good X.

4.   In addition to the infant industry, optimal tariff, and industrial strategy arguments, what are some additional reasons that are used to justify protection?

5.   Explain why trade policies are considered second-best policies when correcting domestic distortions.

ANSWERS TO CHAPTER 6 STUDY GUIDE QUESTIONS

Multiple Choice Questions

1.   b
Protectionism decreases imports and increases production of import substitutes that, according to the Keynesian model, increases incomes through the multiplier effect.

2.   a
According to microeconomic theory, wages are related to the marginal productivity of workers. Countries with relatively low wages may have low labor productivity.

3.   c
According to the Heckscher-Ohlin theory, factor price equalization means the return to the scarce factor of production decreases. Thus, the scarce factor will support protection.

4.   d
Only a large country can influence the terms-of-trade. The optimum tariff argument holds only if the rest of the world does not retaliate.

5.   c

According to the infant-industry argument, the government should protect firms that may be viable in the future that face rigorous competition from lower cost foreign firms.

6.   d

The industrial strategy approach advocates protectionism for emerging industries while expensive research and development is carried out and until sufficient economies-of-scale are reached to reduce average costs.

7.   d

The first-best policy targets the source of the externality. A production tax would reduce production of the good without creating as much inefficiency as trade policy.

8.   d

The lower left cell represents the relevant payoff matrix when firm A produces and firm B does not.

9.   c

Firm A gains a first-mover advantage. Firm A's best option is to produce. Firm B's best response, given firm A's production, is not to produce (assuming this is a sequential game).

10.   b

A tariff making production profitable to firm B if both firms produce would change the payoff matrix to firm B's advantage.

True, False, Uncertain and Why Questions

1.   False. Wage differences could exist for several reasons such as differences in labor productivity. If wages in one country are higher than in another, firms may or may not face higher production costs. If labor in the higher wage country is more productive than labor in the lower wage country, domestic firms are not at a disadvantage because of the higher wage rates. The value of the exchange rate can also influence wage rate differentials.

2.   False. The infant industry argument supports the theory of comparative advantage. A country following this approach would protect those industries in which it believes a future comparative advantage exists.

3.   Uncertain. If a country is a large country, the terms-of-trade gains from the tariff may outweigh the consumption and production distortions.

4.   True. The industrial strategy approach advocates using protectionist policies to encourage domestic firms to undertake research and development costs.

5.   False. While subsidies generate smaller dead weight loss effects and do not distort
       consumption, subsidies are often unpopular. Subsidies also are a cost to the
       government while tariffs are a source of revenue.

Short Answer Questions

1.   If country A places a tariff on imports, its offer curve shifts from A to At. Since
       country A is considered large, the terms-of-trade change from TOT to TOTt, which
       benefits country A at the expense of country B. In order for this tariff to be optimal,
       the rest of the world must not retaliate.

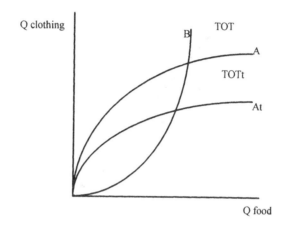

2.   If firm B decides to move first, the equilibrium solution is where firm B produces and
       firm A does not produce.

3.   The payoff matrix should be altered to allow a positive payoff for firm A even if both
       firms decide to produce. One such possibility is:

		FIRM A produce	do not produce
FIRM B	produce	-30, +10	+50, 0
	do not produce	0, +60	0, 0

4.   Other arguments for protection include national defense, protection of social or
       cultural values, and the scientific tariff.

5.   Trade policies affect both consumers and producers of a product. If the government wants to encourage domestic consumption and places a tariff on the good, domestic consumers are also affected since they pay a higher price for the good.

CHAPTER 7

INTERNATIONAL MOBILITY OF LABOR AND CAPITAL

IMPORTANT POINTS

1.   The theories presented in previous chapters assumed that goods were internationally mobile and factors of production were internationally immobile. Before trade, the labor-abundant country had a relatively lower wage rate than the capital-abundant country. Through trade, wage and rental differentials disappeared. If country A is labor-abundant and country B is capital abundant, before trade labor in country A is relatively cheaper than labor in country B. Country A exports the labor-intensive good, causing an increase in the domestic price of this good. The wage rate in country A also increases while the rental rate for capital declines. Country B exports the capital-intensive good, causing the domestic price for this good to increase. The rental rate for capital rises and the wage rate falls. Through trade in goods, differentials in factor prices diminish. The identical result occurs when trade in goods is prohibited (through the use of a tariff, for example) but factor mobility is allowed. When labor and capital are internationally mobile, abundant labor in country A would migrate to country B because of the higher wage. As labor flows from country A to country B and capital moves the opposite direction, the wage rate in A increases as labor becomes scarce. Capital would move from country B, where its abundance generates a low return, to country A, where its scarcity yields a higher return. In other words, international mobility of factors also generates an equalization of prices.

    Although labor and capital are unable to move freely across national borders because of immigration laws, capital controls, and other measures, quite a bit of factor mobility does occur. Labor migration has become politically controversial. Thus, the discussion of the implications of some factor mobility is important, especially because of growing pressure on industrialized countries by people from developing nations to migrate.

2.   The process of international capital and labor flows is analogous to the arbitraging process that occurs within regions of a country. People migrate from areas of the United States with low wages or high unemployment rates to those regions where incomes or job prospects are better. As labor moves from one sector to another, the wage differential decreases. The wage rates in areas from which labor is moving increase as the regional labor force falls. As more individuals move to the higher wage-rate states, incomes in this area begin to fall. Obviously, wages do not become uniform for several reasons. Moving from one area to another incurs transportation costs which may exceed the wage differential. Also, people may have geographic preferences. Even though job prospects are better in the South, some people may prefer a cooler climate in the North. Thus, factor mobility does not ensure that the factor's return is the same across all regions.

3.   International factor mobility and free trade in goods are substitutes. When factors are immobile, the flow of goods from one country to another causes factor and goods' prices to become equalized. In the absence of commodity trade, factor and goods' prices also become equal. These two theories also have another commonality. Under Heckscher-Ohlin, the scarce factor of production loses and the abundant factor gains as resources are reallocated from the import competing to the export sector. If country A exports the capital-intensive good (country A is capital abundant), the Heckscher-Ohlin theory predicts that labor will lose from free trade since the real wage rate declines as factor price differentials are eliminated. Thus, labor will favor protectionism that hinders the equalization of goods and factor prices. When factors are mobile and goods are not, the identical situation results. The higher pre-trade wage rate in country A causes an inflow of labor from the rest of the world. As this migration occurs, the wage rate declines. Thus, labor in country A will oppose looser immigration laws or any other legislation increasing the rate at which the labor force expands via international migration.

4.   One of the major problems facing the United States and other industrialized countries in the area of international factor mobility centers on migration of unskilled workers from developing countries. Although immigration into the U.S. increases total income, it may not increase per capita income. The classical growth model illustrates the effect of migration on income levels:

$$\overset{+\ \ +\ \ +\ \ +}{Y = f(K, LB, LN, T)} \qquad\qquad (7.1)$$

where
       Y = income
       K = capital stock
       LB = labor force
       LN = land stock
       T = technology.

Thus, income is a positive function of the capital stock, labor force, land stock, and technology. Migration into the U.S., according to this model, will increase income.

The classical growth model can also show the level of per capita income. Dividing each of the terms in the above expression by the labor force yields (assuming that a constant percentage of the population is in the labor force):

$$Y/LB = f(\overset{+}{K/LB}, \overset{+}{LN/LB}, \overset{+}{T}) \tag{7.2}$$

The level of per capita income (Y/LB) is positively related to the capital to labor ratio (K/LB), the land to labor ratio (LN/LB), and technology. When the size of the labor force increases due to immigration, the capital to labor and land to labor ratios decline, lowering output per capita. If the increase in the size of the labor force is accompanied by an increase in the stock of capital, per capita income does not have to fall.

5.   One of the more important means through which capital flows from one country to another is through multinational corporations (MNCs). These firms have played an important role in the integration of the world economy. MNCs reallocate resources (such as capital and technology) from areas where they may be abundant to areas where they are scarce. However, the actions of these firms are not without controversy. MNCs can use foreign subsidiaries (using transfer pricing, for example) in order to reduce the amount of profit the firm's home country can tax.

Within the source country, several issues regarding MNC investment are debated. For example, the impact of MNC investment on the distribution of income within the source country is of particular concern. Foreign investment may reduce the capital to labor ratio that tends to lower wages relative to the return on capital. Foreign investment also incurs an opportunity cost. Since firms are expanding foreign operations, they may be unable to expand domestic production, meaning the loss of potential domestic jobs

For the host country, MNC investment in the domestic economy has both positive and negative aspects. The inflow of investment can increase the capital stock and level of technology within the economy. The host country's capacity to export may also increase. However, the introduction of new technology may not be suitable for use in other sectors of the economy. The technology used by the MNC may also be inappropriate when considering the host country's endowment of factors of production. MNCs may also repatriate most of the profits earned by the investment.

CHAPTER OBJECTIVES

After studying the concepts presented in Chapter 7, you should be able to answer the following questions:

1.   Why are trade in goods and international factor mobility considered substitutes?

2.   Using the classical growth model, explain why per capita income in the United States may increase or decrease as a result of international migration into the United States.

3. Why would an Internal Revenue Service auditor be concerned with the foreign subsidiaries of a U.S.-based multinational firm?

4. What are the pros and cons of foreign investment by MNCs from the point of view of the source country? the host country?

GLOSSARY TERMS

- brain drain
- European Economic Community

CHAPTER 7 STUDY QUESTIONS

Multiple Choice Questions

1. According to the Heckscher-Ohlin theory, factor prices between countries differ before trade. This implies that

    a. capital is internationally mobile while labor is internationally immobile.
    b. capital is internationally immobile while labor is internationally mobile.
    c. capital and labor are both internationally immobile.
    d. capital and labor are both internationally mobile.

2. Factor mobility increases efficiency and total output because

    a. it involves a reallocation of abundant resources from the export area to the import-competing sector.
    b. it involves a reallocation of abundant resources from the import-competing area to the export sector.
    c. it involves the movement of scarce production assets from less productive to more productive locations and uses.
    d. it involves the movement of abundant production assets from less productive to more productive locations and uses.

3. The marginal product of capital function is downward sloping because

    a. of the law of diminishing returns.
    b. of increasing returns to scale.
    c. of constant returns to scale.
    d. capital is a scarce resource.

4.   If the interest rates are 12% in Canada and 10% in the United States while
      transportation costs for financial capital are zero, international factor mobility implies
      that

      a.   capital will flow out of Canada and into the United States.
      b.   capital will flow out of the United States and into Canada.
      c.   existing capital in Canada benefits from the international capital inflow into
              Canada while existing capital in the United States loses from the transfer.
      d.   existing capital in the United States benefits from the international capital
              inflow into the United States while existing capital in Canada loses from the
              transfer.

Use the information in Table A to answer questions 5 through 7.

Table A

Profit:	United States	Canada
pre-tax	10.0%	15.0%
tax paid	5.0%	7.5%
net to investors	5.0%	7.5%

The tax rate in the U.S. and Canada is 50%.

5.   A U.S. firm decides to invest equity in the U.S. or in its Canadian subsidiary. This
      firm should invest in

      a.   Canada, since its return to investors is 15.0%.
      b.   Canada, since its return to investors is 7.5%
      c.   the United States, since it has to pay a smaller percentage of profits in tax
              (5.0% versus 7.5%).
      d.   neither country.

6.   If the firm invests in Canada, the total return to the United States is

      a.   7.5%.
      b.   15.0%.
      c.   5.0%.
      d.   10.0%.

7.   If the firm invests in the United States, the total return to the United States is

      a.   7.5%.
      b.   15.0%.
      c.   5.0%.
      d.   10.0%.

8. Immigration into the United States

    a. increases both total and per capita incomes in the United States.
    b. increases total income and decreases per capita income in the United States.
    c. decreases total income and may decrease per capita income in the United States.
    d. increases total income and may increase or decrease per capita income in the United States.

9. If labor immigrates from Mexico to the United States

    a. the marginal productivity of capital in the U.S. will increase, assuming the capital stock remains unchanged.
    b. the marginal productivity of capital in the U.S. will fall, assuming the capital stock remains unchanged.
    c. the marginal productivity of capital in the U.S. will fall.
    d. the marginal productivity of capital in the U.S. will increase.

10. If labor immigrates from Mexico to the United States

    a. the marginal productivity of capital in Mexico will increase, assuming the capital stock remains unchanged.
    b. the marginal productivity of capital in Mexico will fall, assuming the capital stock remains unchanged.
    c. the marginal productivity of capital in the Mexico will fall.
    d. the marginal productivity of capital in the Mexico will increase.

True, False, Uncertain and Why Questions

When answering the following questions, be sure to support your assertion of true, false, or uncertain with two or three sentences.

1. Factor mobility is a substitute for Heckscher-Ohlin trade in goods.

2. Suppose wage rates in country A are, on average, 50% higher than wage rates in country B. If country A allows free mobility of labor between the two countries, labor will flow out of country B and into country A until the wage differential disappears.

3. Increases in the population of a country, without corresponding increases in the stocks of capital and land, will cause GNP per capita to fall.

4. Direct foreign investment by multinational corporations unambiguously benefits the host country.

5. Using the conclusions of the Heckscher-Ohlin theorem, unskilled and semi-skilled labor in the U.S. and capital in Mexico should support international factor mobility.

Short Answer Questions

1. Explain how MNCs can bring about a more efficient allocation of world resources and an increase in world output.

2. Why does organized labor in the United States often oppose direct foreign investment?

3. Suppose the interest rate in Canada is 10% and in the United States is 14%. Explain how international capital mobility affects the returns to capital and labor in each country.

4. How could the existence of transportation costs affect your answer to question 3?

5. If a developing country seeking sources for external capital is unable to borrow money from a commercial bank, what other alternatives exist for this country?

ANSWERS TO CHAPTER 7 STUDY GUIDE QUESTIONS

Multiple Choice Questions

1. c
   When labor and capital are internationally immobile, any difference in the wage rate or rental rate paid to labor and capital among countries will not generate any immigration.

2. c
   Factor mobility moves resources to the area where they are most productively used.

3. a
   The law of diminishing returns states that the productivity of capital declines as more capital is used in production (assuming all other inputs remain fixed).

4. b
   Assuming capital is mobile, the higher interest rate in Canada will generate capital flows out of the U.S. and into Canada (assuming the assets are considered to be close substitutes).

5. b
   After taxes, the firm receives the highest yield in Canada.

6. a
   If the firm invests in Canada, the return to the U.S. is 7.5%.

7.   d
        If the firm invests in the U.S., the return to the U.S. is 10% since the return to the firm and tax revenue is counted.

8.   d
        If immigrants bring enough capital with them to increase the capital to labor ratio, per capita income may increase. If immigrants do not bring capital (for example, human capital), per capita income may decrease.

9.   b
        An increase in the U.S. labor endowment decreases the productivity of capital, assuming the capital stock remains unchanged. If labor immigration affects the capital stock (i.e., human capital accumulation), the marginal productivity of capital may not decrease.

10.   a
        A decrease in the Mexican labor endowment increases the productivity of capital, assuming the capital stock remains unchanged. If labor immigration affects the capital stock (i.e., human capital accumulation), the marginal productivity of capital may not increase.

True, False, Uncertain and Why Questions

1.   True. If trade in goods is prohibited for some reason (by a prohibitive tariff, for example), the difference in factor prices generates a movement of resources to the area of highest return. If, for example, country A has a relatively higher interest rate than country B, capital would flow out of country B and into country A, causing the interest rate differential to diminish.

2.   Uncertain. Wage rates may not be equalized if transportation costs are high (i.e. the cost of moving overseas). Workers may also have a preference for living in their home country.

3.   Uncertain. If the country was under populated, the increase in the population will not necessarily cause per capita GNP to fall. If, however, the country is not under populated, the increase in population could cause GNP per capita to decline.

4.   False. MNC direct foreign investment has both positive and negative side effects for the host country.

5.   False. Using the conclusions of the Heckscher-Ohlin theorem implies that unskilled and semi-skilled labor in the United States and capital in Mexico should not support international factor mobility since the returns to these factors would fall if such mobility existed.

Short Answer Questions

1. By moving resources from countries where they are relatively abundant to countries where they are relatively scarce, MNCs tend to bring about a more efficient allocation of world resources and an increase in world output.

2. Organized labor often opposes direct foreign investment claiming it involves an export of jobs. Even though the products produced abroad are destined for foreign markets, these goods could have been produced domestically and shipped to the foreign markets.

3. The higher interest rate in the U.S. generates capital inflows, reducing the interest rate in the U.S. and increasing the interest rate in Canada. Existing capital in the U.S. loses because of the lower rate while labor in the U.S. gains as the wage rate rises because of the higher capital to labor ratio. In Canada, existing capital receives a higher interest rate while labor receives a lower wage rate since the capital to labor ratio declines.

4. If transportation costs are extremely high, Canadian investors may not transfer capital from Canada to the United States.

5. Another alternative for the country is to encourage foreign direct investment by foreign-based multinational corporations.

REGIONAL TRADING BLOCS: DISCRIMINATORY TRADE LIBERALIZATION

IMPORTANT POINTS

1. Previous discussion of protection assumed that all restrictions on imports are non-discriminatory. While such policies are the goals of GATT, most countries have several different levels of protection. Within the United States, countries are allowed differing degrees of market access. On one end are those countries with which trade is embargoed. Other nations are allowed to export commodities to U.S. markets but are subject to high tariffs. The next level are those countries that enjoy most favored nation status (MFN). These countries are guaranteed the lowest possible tariff that exists on a particular good. For example, if the United States lowers the tariff on German-made tennis rackets, the same reduction must be offered to all foreign tennis racket firms from MFN countries.

2. Regional trading blocs are a step beyond MFN status. These arrangements have various levels of cooperation between member countries. The most loosely structured arrangement is the free trade area, under which most barriers to trade are removed among the members of the bloc. Each country maintains a separate external trade policy. While the autonomous nature of the tariff and quota policy has obvious appeal, it provides the opportunity for trans-shipment. If country A and country B form a free trade area and country B maintains a higher external tariff on goods originating in country C, firms in country C may ship goods to country A because of country A's lower tariff. The products could be illegally shipped to country B without any additional tariff charge. Certificates of origin are supposed to stop such trans-shipment.

3. A customs union avoids the trans-shipment problem since members not only remove trade barriers existing between them but also impose a common external tariff. A

common market moves a step beyond the customs union by allowing mobility of labor and capital among member nations. The highest degree of cooperation among trading partners is the formation of an economic union. This level of integration combines the characteristics of a common market plus a unified taxation and expenditure system and may include jointly managed monetary policy.

4. The creation of regional trading blocs has implications for efficiency. The reduction of some trade barriers implies an increase in efficiency since consumers within the bloc are able to purchase goods at a lower price, which increases consumer surplus. This may not be the case if the bloc is trade diverting instead of trade creating. Table 8-1 depicts the effects of the formation of a customs union on the bathing suit market in Italy.

Table 8-1: The Italian Market for Bathing Suits

	Source:		
	Italy	France	United States
Manufacturer's Price	$140	$120	$110
Applicable Tariff	$ 0	$ 25	$ 25
Italian Wholesale Price	$140	$145	$135

With a common tariff for all foreign firms, Italy imports bathing suits from the United States since these suits are the lowest priced. If Italy and France form a trading bloc and eliminate the tariff between the two countries, Italians no longer purchase bathing suits imported from the United States. The applicable tariff for France goes to zero, reducing the cost of French bathing suits to $120. Suits made in the United States still sell for $135. Italian consumers benefit from the lower priced product. However, one cannot conclude that the trading bloc is beneficial. France is not the lowest cost producer. When consumers substitute higher priced U.S. suits for the cheaper French product, efficiency declines since the lowest-cost producer no longer supplies the market. When France and the United States faced identical tariffs, domestic consumers purchased suits from the lowest cost producer. The loss in efficiency from the production shift is $10 (the difference between the manufacturers price of French and U.S. suits) times the amount of suit production diverted from the United States to France.

When increasing costs exist, trade diverting and trade creating effects can occur in the same market. Trade diversion occurs whenever the lowest cost producer is not able to supply the market due to tariffs, quotas, or other barriers to trade. Trade creation results from an increase in production generated by the lower domestic price for bathing suits. If countries having similar factor endowments, levels of development, and internal structures form a trade bloc, the agreement will tend to be trade creating. When countries are very dissimilar and do not have overlapping industries, regional trade areas tend to create inefficiencies through trade diversion.

5.   Regional trade blocs also enable countries to develop industries that exploit economies-of-scale. Some of the benefits from economies of scale include lower production costs, greater product variety, and higher profit.

6.   The European Economic Community (EEC) evolved from a free trade area to an agreement to establish a single European market with a common currency. The EEC faces several challenges such as reducing CAP expenditures, stimulating slower growing economies of member nations, and the coordination of government policies.

7.   The North American Free Trade Agreement (NAFTA) forms a free trade area among the United States, Mexico, and Canada, as well liberalizing investment restrictions. To avoid the problem of trans-shipment, strict rules of origin are imposed on goods flowing duty-free among the three countries.

CHAPTER OBJECTIVES

After studying the concepts presented in Chapter 8, you should be able to answer the following questions:

1.   What are most-favored nation clauses? Why are they commonly used in international trade negotiations?

2.   Explain the various degrees of integration that can exist between members of a regional trading bloc. What are some of the problems associated with a free trade area? Why might countries have difficulty moving from a common market to an economic union?

3.   What are the possible effects of the creation of a regional trading bloc on efficiency? When will a trade bloc tend to be trade creating? When will the bloc tend to be trade diverting? Can these two effects result from the creation of the same trade agreement?

4.   What role do economies-of-scale play in the formation of regional trading blocs?

GLOSSARY TERMS

- common market
- customs union
- economic union
- embargo
- European Economic Community
- European Monetary System
- free trade area
- trade creation
- trade diversion

CHAPTER 8 STUDY QUESTIONS

Multiple Choice Questions

1. One problem associated with the formation of a free trade area is

    a. trade promotion.
    b. trans-shipment.
    c. transfer pricing.
    d. trade creation.

2. A customs union incorporates

    a. a free trade area without a common external tariff.
    b. an economic union without a common external tariff.
    c. a free trade area with a common external tariff.
    d. an economic union with a common external tariff.

3. A regional trading bloc is trade creating if

    a. supply functions are horizontal, implying constant costs of production.
    b. supply functions are upward sloping, implying changing costs of production.
    c. the country was previously importing a product from a country that does not become a member of the bloc.
    d. inefficient local production is replaced by more efficient output from another member country.

4. Trade diversion will tend to occur when member countries are

    a. very different in terms of their factor endowments and industrial structures.
    b. very similar in terms of their factor endowments and industrial structures.
    c. very different in terms of their political structure.
    d. very similar in terms of their political structure.

5. When countries form a regional trading bloc that eliminates tariffs between members, adopts a common external tariff structure, allows for free mobility of labor and capital, and integrates fiscal and monetary policies, they have formed a

    a. customs union.
    b. free trade area.
    c. common market.
    d. economic union.

Use the information in Figure A to answer questions 6 through 10.

Figure A: The Canadian automobile market:

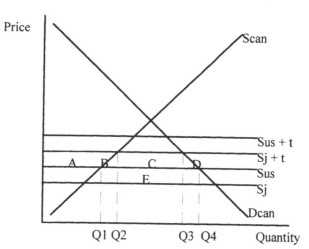

Sx represents the supply curve for country X. Sx + t represents the supply curve for country X when its goods face a specific tariff equal to t. ("X" is equal to Japan (j) or the United States (us).)

6.   With free trade, Canada should import the cars from

      a.   both the United States and Japan.
      b.   the United States.
      c.   Japan.
      d.   no other country (produce all cars domestically).

7.   In the absence of free trade, all imported cars face a tariff equal to t. Suppose Canada and the United States form a free trade area, eliminating the tariff on cars imported from the United States. The tariff amount on Japanese cars is represented by

      a.   the horizontal difference between Q1 and Q2.
      b.   the horizontal difference between Q2 and Q3.
      c.   the vertical difference between Sj and Sus.
      d.   the vertical difference between Sj and Sj + t.

8.   The trade creation effects of the bloc are represented by

      a.   areas A + B + C + D.
      b.   area C.
      c.   area E.
      d.   areas B + D.

9. The trade distorting effects of the bloc are represented by

    a. areas A + B + C + D.
    b. area C.
    c. area E.
    d. areas B + D.

10. The increase in consumer surplus is represented by

    a. areas A + B + C + D.
    b. area C.
    c. area E.
    d. areas B + C.

True, False, Uncertain and Why Questions

When answering the following questions, be sure to support your assertion of true, false, or uncertain with two or three sentences.

1. The creation of a regional trading bloc always increases economic efficiency.

2. A customs union eliminates the problem of trans-shipment.

3. Countries with similar endowments and industrial structures will tend to form trade creating regional blocs.

4. Trade creation and trade diversion cannot occur in the same regional bloc.

5. In a free trade area, tariffs are removed from trade between members while a common external tariff structure is maintained.

Short Answer Questions

1. England imports televisions from either Germany and France. Show the trade creation and diversion effects of the formation of a free trade area between England and Germany if costs are increasing and France is the lowest cost producer.

2. If England and France form a free trade area (and France is the lowest cost producer), show the trade creation and diversion effects of this bloc.

3. The information in Table A describes the British market for wine.

Table A

	England	France	Italy
Manufacturers Price	$50	$30	$20
Applicable Tariff	$ 0	$20	$20
British Wholesale Price	$50	$50	$40

Describe the effects of the formation of a free trade area between France and England. Be sure to describe any trade distorting effects of the bloc.

4.   Suppose England and Italy form a free trade area. How do the results of this agreement differ from your answer in question 3?

5.   Explain why the formation of a customs union may not increase welfare.

ANSWERS TO CHAPTER 8 STUDY GUIDE QUESTIONS

Multiple Choice Questions

1.   b

Since countries forming a free trade area do not maintain a common external tariff, non-member countries have an incentive to ship products to the country with the lowest external tariff and move the products to other members of the trade bloc without paying higher tariff rates.

2.   c

A customs union is similar to a free trade area except customs union members also maintain a common external tariff.

3.   d

Whenever inefficient production is replaced by more efficient sources, the trade bloc is efficiency enhancing.

4.   a

With different factor endowments and industrial structures, countries will produce a vastly different array of goods which increases the chance that the bloc will be trade diverting.

5.   d

An economic union is the highest degree of economic integration that maintains national sovereignty.

6.   c

With free trade, Canada would import cars from the lowest cost producer, which is Japan.

7.   d

A tariff shifts the supply curve for Japanese cars up by the amount of the tariff. This is represented by a shift from Sj to Sj+t.

8.   d

Without the free trade area, Canada imports cars from Japan since Japan is the lowest cost producer. The relevant supply curve is Sj+t. Removing the tariff on U.S. goods results in an increase in efficiency in the amount of areas B+D (since the relevant supply curve is now Sus).

9.   c

Since Canada is not importing cars from the lowest cost producer once the free trade area is implemented, an inefficiency in the form of area E arises.

10.   a

Areas A+B+C+D measure the increase in consumer surplus which represent the benefit of lower prices and more output.

True, False, Uncertain and Why Questions

1.   False. A regional trading bloc can have both trade creating and diverting effects. If the trade diverting effects outweigh the trade creating effects, the regional trading bloc may be efficiency decreasing.

2.   True. The adoption of a common external tariff eliminates the incentive for transshipment.

3.   True. Countries with similar factor endowments and industrial structures will tend to form trading blocs that are trade creating.

4.   False. When costs of production are increasing, trade creating and diverting effects can occur within the same bloc.

5.   False. With a free trade area, each member country maintains its own external tariff system.

Short Answer Questions

1. If England and Germany form a free trade area, England will import televisions from Germany. Total domestic consumption of televisions increases from Q3 to Q4 while domestic production decreases from Q2 to Q1. Consumer surplus increases while producer surplus falls. Areas B and D represent the trade creation effects. Since France is the lowest cost producer, the free trade area creates a distortion since the lowest cost producer does not supply the market. This distortion is represented by area E.

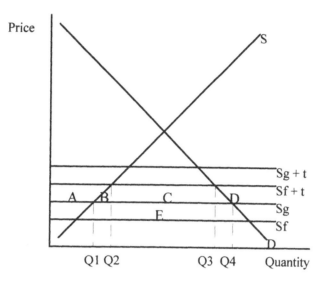

2. If England and France form a free trade area, total domestic consumption increases without generating any efficiency loss. Trade creation gains equal area (B+D).

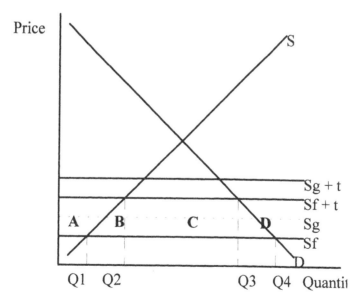

3.   If France and England form a free trade area, the $20 tariff on German wine is eliminated, reducing the British wholesale price of German wine to $30. Since German wine is cheaper than Italian wine (which still faces the tariff), England will import German wine. The movement away from the lowest-cost Italian wine creates an inefficiency since trade no longer occurs with the most efficient producer.

4.   If England and Italy form a free trade area, the British wholesale price of Italian wine falls to $20. England continues to import wine from the lowest-cost producer and the trade diverting effects that occurred with the England-German bloc are absent.

5.   Since trade diverting and creating effects can exist in the same bloc, the formation of a customs union will increase efficiency only if the trade creating effects outweigh the trade distorting effects.

CHAPTER 9

COMMERCIAL POLICY: HISTORY AND RECENT CONTROVERSIES

IMPORTANT POINTS

1. This chapter provides an historical analysis of the use of tariffs and other barriers to trade and of the effects of these polices on the world economy. Throughout history, the sentiment has fluctuated concerning protectionism versus free trade. The rise of mercantilism and the establishment of colonies in the New World were closely tied to regulated trade. During this period (1500-1800) nations used a variety of measures to control the quantity and composition of imports and exports. The theory of comparative advantage, suggesting that two-way trade is mutually beneficial, contradicted the assumptions of a mercantilist world. The notion that imports were actually a good idea was a shocking concept.

2. As emerging industries in France and other European countries demanded protection against British firms, barriers to trade were resurrected. The rise of colonialism also fueled the protectionist fire. In the early years of the U.S., domestic production centered on agricultural goods and raw materials. Manufactured goods were imported in exchange for these products. During the Napoleonic War and the War of 1812, the level of international trade drastically declined, and infant industries developed in the United States in order to supply those goods previously imported. When the war ended in 1815 and trade reopened with Britain, domestic firms demanded protection. In 1828, Congress passed the "Tariff of Abominations", which favored some geographic regions of the country over others. More specifically, agricultural states favored low rates of protection for imported manufactured goods while the northern and mid-Atlantic regions of the United States sought high tariffs to support their industries. The tariff of 1828 included high rates of protection for both manufactured and raw material goods. In 1833 tariff rates were lowered and continued to drift down for the next 30 years.

3.   During the Civil War, tariff rates were increased and they remained at high levels until the turn of the century. Support for protectionism still varied regionally, with Southern states favoring free trade. In the aftermath of the Civil War, the former Confederate states had little political weight and were unable to stem the tide of protectionism. The outbreak of World War I disrupted trade for several years, diminishing the need for tariffs and quotas. During the 1920s, unemployment was low and the economy appeared strong. Manufacturing sectors did not lobby Congress for tariffs. Most barriers to trade focused on the agricultural sector. The crash of the stock market and the beginning of the Great Depression generated new cries for protection. Congress passed the Smoot-Hawley Tariff Act in 1930 that drastically reduced the volume of imports into the United States. The legislation had another related effect. During World War I and the rebuilding period, many European countries borrowed money from the United States. In order to meet interest payments and repay the principal, these nations needed export revenues. In order to sell goods abroad, export markets must exist with sufficient levels of aggregate demand. With limited access to the consumers in the United States, these European countries encountered difficulty in loan repayment. In retaliation, many European nations erected similar tariff rates, further diminishing the volume of international trade.

4.   As the depression persisted, the Roosevelt administration sought ways to increase employment and expand production. The Reciprocal Trade Agreements Act authorized the President to negotiate bilateral trade agreements designed to reduce the worldwide level of protection on specific commodities. Two important concepts were incorporated in these trade agreements. First, each one contained a most-favored nation clause in order to achieve non-discriminatory tariff rates. Second, the United States initiated the negotiations with the nation that was the primary supplier of the product. The U.S. followed this policy in order to prevent one-way tariff reductions. Through these agreements, trade liberalization slowly evolved.

5.   Until World War II, trade negotiations tended to be bilateral. After World War II, the emphasis shifted toward multilateralism. In 1947, the General Agreement on Tariffs and Trade (GATT) was adopted. This agreement includes a code of conduct for international trade and guidelines for multinational trade negotiations. The primary objective of GATT is the perpetuation of non-discriminatory trading practices. Signatory countries adhere to the most-favored nation clause, ensuring that tariff reductions between two countries are extended to all members. Two exceptions to the MFN clause need to be explained. Countries forming a regional trading bloc can eliminate tariffs between themselves and not be required to extend the reduction to all GATT countries. Also, a provision known as the Generalized System of Preferences was included, allowing developing countries to apply for lower tariff rates than those faced by developed nations.

        One key feature of GATT is its opposition to the use of quotas. If a country uses trade barriers, an explicit tariff is the preferred tool since it is more easily observed and the trade effects more easily determined. Quotas are usually discriminatory and the effects are not as clearly seen. While GATT frowns upon quotas, countries are permitted to use them in particular situations. Quotas are used to complement domestic price support programs for agricultural goods. Also, quotas are allowed to aid a country's economic development plan. Finally, a large loophole exists in the form of quotas to rectify balance-of-payment problems.

6.   GATT sponsors periodic tariff negotiations between member countries. During the past 20 years, three GATT rounds occurred. The most recent is the Uruguay round, begun in 1986, and passed by the U.S. Congress in 1994. The focus of the most recent round is on trade in services, agricultural export subsidies, intellectual property rights, and voluntary-export restraints. As a result of these negotiations, industrialized countries have agreed to reduce tariffs on manufactured goods by over one-third. Agricultural export subsidies and tariffs are also targeted for reduction. The Multi-Fiber Arrangement quota system for textiles and garments is to be phased out over 10 years.

7.   The Uruguay Round of negotiations established the World Trade Organization (WTO) as its successor. While countries found to be in violation of WTO policies cannot be forced to comply, the complaining country is allowed to retaliate.

The WTO faces several challenges in the future. Many countries wish to join WTO. Some of these nations, such as China and Russia, have limited free markets. Another area of concern focuses on domestic policy autonomy. In areas such as environmental regulations, WTO policies may conflict with a country's domestic agenda.

CHAPTER OBJECTIVES

After studying the concepts presented in Chapter 9, you should be able to answer the following questions:

1.   Why was the infant industry argument popular in the United States during the late 1700s and 1800s? Why was the tariff package passed in 1828 considered the Tariff of Abominations? Which geographical regions in the United States favored free trade? Why?

2.   What impact did the Great Depression have on the popularity of protectionism? What effects did the rising fever for high tariffs have on European countries?

3.   Explain the shift from bilateral to multilateral trade negotiations. How did GATT differ from previous tariff reductions? What are the important components of GATT?

4.   Explain the problems and controversy surrounding the Uruguay round agreement. Why did countries finding it difficult to reach consensus on the key issues?

5.   Explain the benefits and costs associated with WTO membership.

GLOSSARY TERMS

- commercial policy
- General Agreement on Tariffs and Trade (GATT)
- Generalized System of Preferences
- intellectual property
- mercantilism
- most-favored nation status (MFN)
- Section 301
- Smoot-Hawley Tariff
- Tariff of Abominations
- U.S. Trade Representative
- World Trade Organization (WTO)

CHAPTER 9 STUDY QUESTIONS

Multiple Choice Questions

1. The first tariff in the United States (1789) was designed primarily

    a. to protect fledgling industries.
    b. to protect agricultural commodities.
    c. to raise revenue for the government.
    d. in response to unfair British trading practices.

2. The Tariff Act of 1828 was controversial because

    a. it favored certain geographic areas over others; southern and western states wanted low tariff rates on imported manufactured goods while the northern and Mid-Atlantic States desired heavy protection.
    b. it favored certain geographic areas over others; southern and western states wanted high tariff rates on imported manufactured goods while the northern and Mid-Atlantic States desired little protection.
    c. it favored certain geographic areas over others; southern and western states wanted high tariff rates on imported agricultural goods while the northern and Mid-Atlantic States desired little protection.
    d. it favored certain geographic areas over others; southern and western states wanted low tariff rates on imported agricultural goods while the northern and Mid-Atlantic States desired heavy protection.

3. After the Civil War, southern states

    a. continued to favor protectionism for imported goods.
    b. continued to favor free trade.
    c. favored protectionism for imported goods, which differed from their pre-war stance.
    d. favored free trade, which differed from their pre-war stance.

4.   The Smoot- Hawley Tariff Act (1930)

   a.   reduced the level of protection to the lowest level since the mid 1800s.
   b.   reduced the level of protection to the lowest level since the late 1800s.
   c.   increased the level of protection to the highest level since the mid 1800s.
   d.   increased the level of protection to the highest level since the late 1800s.

5.   The Reciprocal Trade Agreements Act

   a.   authorized the President to raise tariffs without the approval of Congress.
   b.   authorized Congress to raise tariffs without the approval of the President.
   c.   authorized the President to negotiate bilateral trade agreement in order to reduce tariff rates.
   d.   authorized Congress to negotiate bilateral trade agreement in order to reduce tariff rates.

6.   The effect of the most-favored-nation clause is to

   a.   maintain a discriminatory tariff structure.
   b.   maintain a non-discriminatory tariff structure.
   c.   eliminate all tariffs between countries.
   d.   increase all tariff rates between countries.

7.   The Generalized System of Preferences

   a.   allows members of a regional trading bloc to violate the most-favored-nation clause.
   b.   allows any country to violate the most-favored-nation clause.
   c.   allows developing countries' exports to receive preferential tariff treatment.
   d.   allows developing countries' imports to receive preferential tariff treatment.

8.   According to GATT, quotas on manufactured goods

   a.   are permitted since they generate similar welfare effects as tariffs.
   b.   are not permitted since they are difficult to administer.
   c.   are not permitted since they are almost always discriminatory.
   d.   are permitted as long as the country adheres to the most-favored-nation clause.

9.   Until the Uruguay Round, GATT agreements had excluded the following areas:

   a.   agriculture and textiles.
   b.   consumer durable goods.
   c.   consumer non-durable goods.
   d.   non-tradable goods

10.   Suppose Canada and Japan form a free trade area. Under the most-favored nation clause:

   a.   Canada must extend any tariff or quota reductions to any other country.
   b.   Canada does not have to extend the tariff or quota reductions to any other country.
   c.   Canada must extend any tariff or quota reductions to Mexico and the United States since Canada also has a free trade area with these countries.
   d.   Canada must extend any tariff or quota reductions to all WTO members since Canada is a part of the WTO.

True, False, Uncertain and Why Questions

When answering the following questions, be sure to support your assertion of true, false, or uncertain with two or three sentences.

1.   The theories of Adam Smith and David Ricardo support the mercantilist point of view.

2.   The Napoleonic War and the War of 1812 severely hurt young industries in the United States.

3.   The Generalized System of Preferences is an example of a discriminatory trading practice.

4.   According to GATT, quotas are prohibited under any circumstances.

5.   A country can pick and choose which WTO findings to which it will adhere.

Short Answer Questions

1.   Why was the Smoot-Hawley tariff act considered to be an example of irresponsible economic policy? What were the effects of this policy on the volume of world trade?

2.   What is the purpose of a most-favored-nation clause? Why are members of a regional trading bloc exempt from this statute?

3.   Why is intellectual property theft of great concern to the United States? What counter-arguments do countries charged with intellectual property theft make?

4.   Why is agriculture a difficult issue in trade negotiations? What is the importance of the Common Agricultural Policy?

5.   What trade strategies are considered unfair trading practices? Why?

ANSWERS TO CHAPTER 9 STUDY GUIDE QUESTIONS

Multiple Choice Questions

1. c

    The first tariff (1789) was designed to raise revenue for the federal government. Some manufactured products had higher rates than other areas to stimulate and protect specific domestic industries.

2. a

    The Tariff Act of 1828 favored the northern industrial areas of the country over the more agricultural southern and western states. This led to tension between regions of the nation.

3. b

    Southern states continued to favor free trade so that they could purchase cheaper foreign manufactured products in exchange for their agricultural goods.

4. c

    The Smoot-Hawley Tariff increased rates to the highest level since the Tariff of 1828.

5. c

    The Reciprocal Trade Agreements Act empowered the President to negotiate bilateral trade agreements to lower tariff rates. Until this point, the ability to set tariff rates was under the control of the Congress.

6. b

    The MFN clause is non-discriminatory in nature.

7. c

    The GSP is designed to help the export performance of a developing country's goods. These products receive preferential treatment over goods from industrialized countries.

8. c

    One of the goals of GATT is to encourage a non-discriminatory trade environment. Quotas in manufacturing goods are almost always discriminatory.

9. a

    Previous GATT negotiations were unable to make progress on reducing trade restrictions on agriculture and textiles. The Uruguay Round agreements include a reduction in agricultural subsidies and import restrictions. The MFA quotas will be phased out over a 10-year time span.

10. b

    Free trade areas and other regional trading blocs are excluded from the mfn-clause. Therefore, Canada does not have to extend the tariff/quota reductions to any other trading partners.

True, False, Uncertain and Why Questions

1. False. The theories of Adam Smith and David Ricardo suggest that two-way trade is beneficial, which is not a mercantilist view.

2. False. The interruption of international trade helped domestic industries. Without competition from cheaper foreign imports, these industries were able to fully develop quickly.

3. True. According to the GSP, exports from developing countries face a lower tariff rate than goods from industrialized countries (with certain limitations). Since this policy favors certain countries over others, it is an example of a discriminatory trading practice.

4. False. Quotas are allowed in certain areas such as agricultural goods in order to balance any effects of different subsidy programs and deal wit seasonal import needs.

5. False. A WTO member cannot pick and choose among different statutes and must adhere to all WTO policies.

Short Answer Questions

1. The Smoot- Hawley tariff resulted in a drastic reduction in the volume of international trade as foreign governments responded in kind to the tariff. The high tariff rates hampered the attempts of European countries to repay World War I debts.

2. A most-favored nation clause ensures that tariff reductions given to one member country are extended to all members. Members of trading blocs are exempt from this statute since one of the benefits of a trading bloc is reducing trade barriers among members, not the entire world.

3. Since the United States has a comparative advantage in high-technology goods, intellectual property theft reduces its gains from trade, and also diminishes the incentive for future research and development efforts. Nations accused of this practice often claim that copyrights and patents make certain goods such as medicines too expensive to purchase legally.

4. Several countries have large agricultural subsidy programs that generate large agricultural surpluses. One outlet for the excess supply is dumping it on export markets. Domestic firms facing subsidized foreign competition may have difficulty competing.

5.   Some unfair trading practices include export subsidies, dumping, and intellectual property theft. Export subsidies are considered unfair since firms receiving these subsidies can charge lower prices (which may be lower than marginal or average cost) than the domestic firms. Predatory dumping is one way a large firm may be able to force local firms out of the market, creating a monopoly. Intellectual property theft creates a disincentive for firms to invest in research and development activities since some of the benefits from R&D accrue to the firm's competitors.

CHAPTER 10

TRADE AND GROWTH

IMPORTANT POINTS

1. In previous chapters, factor growth and technological change has been assumed to be zero. Allowing resources to expand and technology to improve suggests several implications for patterns of trade. An equal increase in both inputs generates an even outward shift of the production possibilities curve, indicating that larger amounts of both goods can be produced. When growth occurs in only one input, however, the PPC shifts but the change is biased toward the good using the increased factor intensively. For example, suppose the labor force participation rate of women in country A increases. This shifts the PPC toward the labor-intensive good, cloth. Country A's production of cloth increases. With unchanged demand conditions, the additional supply of cloth causes a decline in the price of cloth. If cloth is A's export good, the growth in the labor force decreases the price of the export good and worsens country A's terms-of-trade.

    A change in technology is similar to growth of a production input. An improvement in technology means that more cloth or wheat can be produced with the same amount of inputs. If technological change is biased toward the export good, the terms-of-trade could worsen.

2. Developing countries can be classified into two broad categories: ones that currently export mainly labor-intensive manufactured goods and those more focused on the export of primary products. When exports are not greatly diversified, export revenues can fluctuate greatly. Countries falling in the second category have experienced such volatility.

3. Primary product prices have been more volatile than the prices for manufactured goods. Several possible reasons exist for this difference. Demand and supply elasticities for primary products tend to be lower than for manufactured goods. Price stabilization programs and commodity futures markets are possible ways to help reduce price fluctuations, although a long-term strategy is export diversification.

4.   Another problem that primary product exporters face is declining export prices. International price data suggests that the terms-of-trade for primary product producers have declined in recent years, which somewhat supports the Singer-Prebisch hypothesis. Several explanations for the decline in the terms-of-trade exist. Engel's law suggests that the income elasticity of demand for food is less than one, meaning that as incomes rise by one percent, quantity demanded increases by less than one percent. Technology has produced substitutes for some primary products; artificial fibers and fiber optics are examples.

5.   Import substitution and export promotion are two alternative development strategies. Import substitution attempts to replace the imports of manufactured goods with domestically made products. To maximize economic growth, tariffs and quotas are used to choke off foreign supply of manufactured products. Domestic firms, unable to compete with foreign rivals without the tariffs, enter the market and provide the previously imported products for domestic consumers. This argument is closely tied to the infant industry theory discussed in Chapter 6. The country hopes the new domestic firms will eventually be able to expand production beyond the scope of the domestic market, allowing the nation to diversify its export goods.

     Through the process of trial and error, import substitution has been found to cause several negative effects. Tariffs generate higher domestic prices. If the protected goods are used as inputs into production of other goods, the costs of production rise. If industries using protected inputs are export firms, they are able to compete less efficiently on the world market. When using an import substitution strategy, it is important to remember the concept of the effective tariff, presented in Chapter 6. When tariffs are imposed on inputs for the export industry, the effective tariff rate for the export industry is negative.

     The use of import-substitution strategies also may cause LDCs to use inappropriate technology as production in the import-competing sector expands. Often, firms in LDCs will import technology from companies in the developed world. If the LDC has a similar factor endowment as that of the developed country in which the foreign firm produces, adopting the same technology does not generate any inefficiency. However, LDCs tend to be capital-scarce while developed countries are usually capital-abundant. Implementing technology designed with capital-abundance in mind is not a wise decision. The result has been the development of manufacturing sectors in LDCs that are inefficient, depend on high rates of protection, and employ little labor. Import substitution can be successful if used as a temporary policy in industries with clear promise of developing an export potential. It has failed when used in capital or human capital-intensive industries, which are not competitive at world prices.

6.   Free trade zones are a way to encourage exports of products requiring inputs the country produces inefficiently. A free trade zone establishes a geographic area, such as an airport, in which inputs can be imported duty-free and used to produce goods that are then exported.

7. An alternative to inward-looking strategies is the export-led approach that promotes the development of areas of comparative advantage. These policies emphasize diversification of exports as a way to reduce risk. The crucial question is how to select the potential comparative advantage sector. Proponents of export promotion suggest using market prices as a guide in allocating resources. Instead of sheltering the developing industries with high tariffs, export promotion forces firms to meet the world market price. To survive, these firms must be efficient and reduce cost in order to compete internationally. Advocates of this approach point to Thailand, South Korea, and Taiwan as success stories. Proponents of the import-substitution strategy point out that most of these countries followed inward looking polices in the period preceding the export-oriented push.

CHAPTER OBJECTIVES

After studying the concepts presented in Chapter 10, you should be able to answer the following questions:

1. How does factor growth affect an economy?

2. What is the relevance of the terms-of-trade when discussing the effects of trade on the economic development of a country? In other words, why do countries care about this price ratio?

3. What is the income elasticity of demand? What are the implications of differing income elasticities for manufactured and primary product goods?

4. How do inward-looking and outward-looking growth strategies differ? Which approach has been more successful?

5. What is import substitution? What are some of the problems associated with this strategy? What is export promotion? What are some of the problems associated with this strategy?

GLOSSARY TERMS

- export-led growth
- import-substitution strategy
- infant industry promotion
- trade-adjustment assistance
- trade-related investment measures (TRIMs)

CHAPTER 10 STUDY GUIDE QUESTIONS

Multiple Choice Questions

1. Some LDCs argue that

    a. the prices of their imports relative to their exports have declined, worsening the terms-of-trade.
    b. the prices of their imports relative to their exports have declined, improving the terms-of-trade.
    c. the prices of their exports relative to their imports have declined, improving the terms-of-trade.
    d. the prices of their exports relative to their imports have declined, worsening the terms-of-trade.

2. Prebisch argued that the income elasticity of demand

    a. was lower for manufactured goods than for primary products.
    b. was higher for manufactured goods than for primary products.
    c. was the same for both manufactured goods and primary products.
    d. was unit elastic for manufactured goods.

3. The geographical pattern of trade flows shows that the majority of world trade takes place

    a. between LDCs and developed countries.
    b. among LDC countries.
    c. among developed countries.
    d. between regional trade blocs.

4. Import substitution is an example of

    a. an outward-looking growth strategy.
    b. an inward-looking growth strategy.
    c. absolute advantage.
    d. the Vernon product cycle.

5. Outward-looking growth strategies emphasize

    a. protection for export-competing industries.
    b. protection for import-competing industries.
    c. resource allocation based on the principle of comparative advantage.
    d. resource allocation based on the principle of absolute advantage.

6. The compensation principle suggests

   a. since the winners from free trade gain more than the losers lose, free trade is beneficial.
   b. since some individuals lose from trade, outward-looking growth strategies may hurt a developing country.
   c. since the winners from free trade gain more than the losers lose, the winners could compensate the losers and still retain net gains.
   d. since some individuals lose from trade, the losers should bribe the potential winners not to support free trade.

7. Comparing per capita incomes between developed countries and LDCs illustrates

   a. the widening disparity in income levels of developed countries and LDCs.
   b. that income growth rates among developed countries have stagnated.
   c. that income growth rates among all developing countries have stagnated.
   d. that income differences between developed countries and LDCs have decreased.

8. Suppose a country experiences growth in all factors of production (at the same rate), while constant returns to scale exist and technology remains unchanged. The production possibilities curve

   a. does not shift.
   b. shifts outward, biased toward the export good.
   c. shifts outward, biased toward the import good.
   d. shifts evenly outward.

9. Suppose country A is a small country and experiences a population boom. If country A is labor abundant, this increase in labor causes

   a. the terms-of-trade for country A to worsen since the price of its export good will fall in world markets.
   b. the terms-of-trade for country A to improve since the price of its export good will increase in world markets.
   c. the terms-of-trade for country A to worsen since the price of its imported good will rise in world markets.
   d. the terms-of-trade to remain unchanged.

10. Suppose country A is a large country and experiences a population boom. If country A is labor abundant, this increase in labor causes

   a. the terms-of-trade for country A to worsen since the price of its export good will fall in world markets.
   b. the terms-of-trade for country A to improve since the price of its export good will increase in world markets.
   c. the terms-of-trade for country A to worsen since the price of its imported good will rise in world markets.
   d. the terms-of-trade to remain unchanged.

True, False, Uncertain and Why Questions

When answering the following questions, be sure to support your assertion of true, false, or uncertain with two or three sentences.

1. Import substitution does not have any negative side effects on other sectors of the economy.

2. Developed countries should support free trade policies designed to encourage growth in the economies of the developing world.

8. If a LDC follows an import-substitution strategy, it should not automatically use the same production technology used in the developed world.

9. Developing countries are not concerned about commodity price instability.

10. The growth in one or more production inputs is unambiguously beneficial for a country.

Short Answer Questions

1. Briefly explain the benefits and problems associated with import substitution. Why have some countries successfully implemented this strategy while other countries have not?

2. Explain the major differences between import-substitution and export-promotion growth strategies.

3. How should countries pursuing outward-looking growth strategies select potential comparative advantage areas?

Use the following information to answer questions 4 and 5.

Suppose country A experiences an increase in the labor force participation rate of women. Country A produces two goods, food and clothing, the latter of which is capital-intensive. Assume country A is labor-abundant.

4. Analyze the effects of the labor force expansion if country A is considered a large country. Be sure to include any changes in relative goods and factor prices.

5. How does your analysis change if country A is capital abundant?

ANSWERS TO CHAPTER 10 STUDY GUIDE QUESTIONS

Multiple Choice Questions

1.   d

    Many LDCs argue that they face worsening terms-of-trade since the prices they receive for exports have declined while import prices have remained stable or increased.

2.   b

    Arguing for worsening terms-of-trade, Prebisch asserted that the income elasticity of demand was higher for manufactured goods than for primary products.

3.   c

    Evidence suggests that the largest volume of trade occurs between developed countries.

4.   b

    Import substitution stresses reducing reliance on international trade by developing import-competing sectors.

5.   c

    Outward-looking strategies emphasize allocating resources based on the theory of comparative advantage.

6.   c

    Since free trade does not benefit everyone, the compensation principle can be used to reallocate some of the gains from the winners to the losers from trade.

7.   a

    Comparing per capita GNP figures between developed countries and LDCs shows that the income gap between these groups has increased.

8.   d

    With constant returns to scale, a 10 percent increase in all inputs yields a 10 percent increase in output. This means the PPC shifts evenly outward.

9.   d

    Since country A is a small country, it is unable to influence its terms-of-trade.

10.   a

    If country A is a large country, an increase in the labor endowment causes an increase in production of the labor intensive good. Since A is a large country, the price of this good will fall on the world market. Since A is relatively labor abundant, it exports the labor intensive good. This implies that the price of country A's export good falls.

True, False, Uncertain and Why Questions

1. False. If a country is a large country, the growth in one factor of production will influence its terms-of-trade. If growth occurs in the factor used intensively in the export sector, the increased supply of the export good will decrease the price of the good, which worsens that country's terms-of-trade. The increase in inputs may result in immiserizing growth.

2. Uncertain. On paper, all countries benefit from free trade since the amount of total world income increases. Realistically, free trade hurts certain groups within the economy that may dampen enthusiasm for free trade.

3. True. A country should implement the technology that is appropriate for its resource endowments. If a developing country wishes to produce a product that is also produced in a capital-abundant country, it should use the same technology only if it is also capital-abundant.

4. False. Commodity price instability is of great concern to developing countries, because it causes their total export revenues, which means their ability to pay for imports, to be unstable.

5. False. If a large, labor abundant country exporting the labor-intensive good experiences an increase in its labor endowment, the country may not be better off. When factor growth results in a decrease in the price of the country's export good, immizerizing growth occurs.

Short Answer Questions

1. Import substitution provides protection for industries unable to compete with more advanced foreign rivals. However, such protection must be short-term and evidence suggests that protection is difficult to remove once it is implemented. The protection must also be in industries where a clear potential comparative advantage exists.

2. Import-substitution policies attempt to replace imported goods with domestic production while export promotion seeks to encourage production of goods for sale abroad, which generates additional export earnings.

3. Countries should use the market to determine the allocation of resources within a country. Countries that are relatively labor abundant should shift resources into labor-intensive industries.

4. The increase in the labor force shifts production towards the labor-intensive good, food. Since country A is labor abundant, this increases the supply of the export good, decreasing the price of the good in world markets and worsening the terms-of-trade. The wage rate in country A also declines.

5. If country A is capital abundant, the increase in the labor force still generates an outward shift in the production possibilities curve. Since food is the import-competing good, the increased supply of food decreases the price of country A's imported good, which improves its terms-of-trade (assuming country A is a large country).

CHAPTER 11

ISSUES OF INTERNATIONAL PUBLIC ECONOMICS

IMPORTANT POINTS

1. An externality occurs when all the benefits or costs associated with the production or consumption of a good are not reflected in the market price. Pollution is an example of a negative externality. When a firm produces paper, emitting pollutants into the air, the firm's costs would not include the effects of this pollution on the economy. The existence of externalities implies additional costs and benefits associated with trade. If a country begins importing a good with a negative production externality, the decrease in domestic production reduces pollution, providing a benefit to the economy. If the good in question is an export good, trade encourages production and greater pollution.

2. Cost-benefit analysis can be applied to pollution without cross-border effects. Suppose a negative production externality exists and the pollution is limited to a specific geographic region. One solution to this problem is to set the marginal benefit of pollution abatement equal to the marginal cost of the cleanup. Figure 11-1 shows these curves.

Figure 11-1: Marginal Analysis of Pollution Abatement

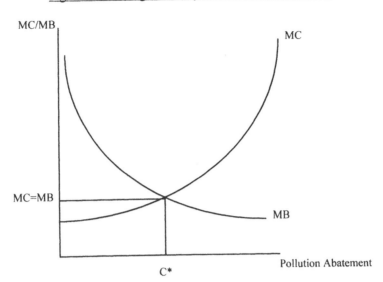

The upward slope of the marginal cost (MC) function suggests that the costs of abatement increase at an increasing rate while the marginal benefit (MB) decreases at a decreasing rate. The optimal solution occurs at C*, where MB=MC. For any amount of cleanup greater than C*, the extra cost of cleaning up exceeds the benefit. For any amount of cleanup less than C*, the extra benefit from additional abatement exceeds the cost.

Grossman and Krueger estimate the relationship between a country's income level and environmental quality. The authors determine that an inverted-U relationship exists. As income increases, pollution increases to a certain point and then begins to decline. This implies that poorer countries will have more environmental degradation.

3. When pollution transcends borders, environmental policies are more difficult to implement. The Coase theorem suggests that the same level of pollution will be attained regardless of the allocation of property rights, assuming low transactions costs. For example, suppose firms in Country A dump chemicals into a river with a basin in Country B and that the cost of reducing pollution in country A is $10,000 while the value of clean water in country B is $15,000. If country A is assigned the property rights, country B will have to pay firms in country A not to pollute. Firms in country A would be willing to accept $10,000 from country B. When the property rights are assigned to country B, firms in country A would have to pay to pollute. Since the cost of cleaning up ($10,000) is less than the transfer payment required to allow pollution ($15,000), firms in country A will not pollute. Thus, regardless of the allocation of property rights, pollution will not occur.

4. The problems of ozone layer depletion and global warming are examples of the tragedy of the commons, which occurs when no one has an incentive to change behavior unless everyone does so. The Montreal Protocol, which bans the use of CFCs, is one example of a successful attempt to correct cross-border pollution.

Attempts to develop a similar agreement targeting greenhouse gas emissions have been less successful.

5. Taxes on goods, such as sales and value-added (VAT) taxes have implications for trade and investment flows. VAT, which is used by European and Latin American countries, is examined in detail. Table 11-1 provides information for a VAT example.

Table 11-1: VAT Example	
Purchased car inputs	$10,000
Additional labor and other activities	$6,000
Purchase price of the car	$16,000

The value-added by the car manufacturer is the difference between the purchase price of the car and the cost of the intermediate inputs ($6,000=$16,000-$10,000). If the VAT rate is 20 percent, the VAT is $1,200 (0.20 x $6,000).

In practice, VAT is calculated on the final purchase price of the car, allowing for rebates on intermediate input taxes. Table 11-2 represents this case. The VAT would be $3,200 (=0.20 x $16,000) less the $2,000 VAT paid on the intermediate input ($12,000-$10,000).

Table 11-2: VAT Example		
	No VAT	VAT = 20%
Purchased car inputs	$10,000	$12,000
Additional labor and other activities	$6,000	$6,000
Purchase price of the car	$16,000	$16,000

VAT taxes may be applied according to the destination or origin principle. The former occurs when the VAT is levied at the point of consumption while the latter is imposed at the point of production. Thus, with the destination principle, exports do not have a VAT while imports are subject to VAT.

6. Taxes on factor income affect factor migration. When countries have different tax rates, mobile factors of production will move to the area of highest after-tax return. For example, if the after tax wage rate in country A is greater than in country B, workers living in country B have an incentive to move to country A, arbitraging these two wage rates. As wages change, goods' prices are also affected. The elasticity of demand for these goods determines whether the country benefits from any price change. If the price of the country's export good increases and demand is inelastic, the country may benefit from the price increase.

Portfolio capital also responds to differences in tax rates. If a country increases the tax on capital, investors may move these resources to an area of higher return. Since the amount of capital in a country affects the productivity of other factors of production, higher taxes not only generate capital outflows, but also reduce the productivity of the immobile factors of production.

CHAPTER OBJECTIVES

After studying the concepts in Chapter 11, you should be able to answer the following questions:

1.   In the presence of an externality, why does the market price not reflect all the costs and benefits associated with the production or consumption of goods?

2.   Why are externalities with cross-border effects harder to correct than externalities with localized effects?

3.   How do taxes on production resources affect the location of these resources?

4.   Explain how income levels differ across countries and what problems arise when countries attempt to solve this problem.

GLOSSARY TERMS

- externality
- destination principle
- indirect taxes
- origin principle
- residence principle

CHAPTER 11 STUDY GUIDE QUESTIONS

Multiple Choice Questions

1.   When pollution generated by a firm in the United States affects people living in Mexico, this pollution is labeled

   a.   intra-industry pollution
   b.   inter-industry pollution
   c.   cross-border pollution
   d.   trans-firm pollution

2.   A negative production externality reflects the fact that

   a.   private costs of producing the good reflect all the costs associated with the production of that good.
   b.   private benefits from consuming the good reflect all the costs associated with the consumption of that good.
   c.   private costs of producing the good are less than the total societal costs associated with the production of that good.
   d.   private costs of producing the good are greater than the total societal costs associated with the production of that good.

3.   A positive production externality reflects the fact that

   a.   private costs of producing the good reflect all the costs associated with the production of that good.
   b.   private benefits from consuming the good reflect all the costs associated with the consumption of that good.
   c.   private costs of producing the good are less than the total societal costs associated with the production of that good.
   d.   private costs of producing the good are greater than the total societal costs associated with the production of that good.

4.   With portfolio capital flows, a country wishing to attract more capital inflows should set its tax rate so that

   a.   its tax rate is greater than the rate in other countries.
   b.   its tax rate is less than the rate in other countries
   c.   its tax rate is zero, regardless of the rate in other countries.
   d.   its tax rate is zero, only if the rate in other countries is very high.

5.   When countries implement policies targeting reductions in greenhouse gas emissions or chlorofluorocarbon use, a free-rider problem exists since

   a.   other countries cannot be excluded from the benefits of this environmental policy, regardless of whether they implemented any reductions.
   b.   other countries can be excluded from the benefits of this environmental policy if they have not implemented any reductions.
   c.   no one benefits from the reductions unless everyone pays for the cleanup.
   d.   countries with borders adjacent to countries reducing these gains will gain the most.

6.   _____ are classified as commonly owned international goods.

   a.   The oceans and the air mass
   b.   The oceans and Glacier National Park
   c.   Glacier National Park and the Grand Canyon
   d.   None of the above

7. The destination principle ensures that imported goods sold in Country A

   a. face the same tax burden as goods consumed in the importing country.
   b. face a higher tax burden than goods produced domestically.
   c. face a lower tax burden than goods produced domestically.
   d. face the same tax burden as goods produced domestically.

8. When a country increases the tax on labor income and the labor force does not remain constant,

   a. output in the taxing nation will remain unchanged.
   b. output in the taxing nation will increase.
   c. output in the taxing nation will decrease.
   d. output in the taxing nation will increase and then decrease.

9. When a country increases the tax on labor income and the labor force remains constant,

   a. output in the taxing nation will remain unchanged.
   b. output in the taxing nation will increase.
   c. output in the taxing nation will decrease.
   d. output in the taxing nation will increase and then decrease.

10. The marginal benefit and marginal cost curves for pollution abatement will

   a. differ across countries with similar levels of development.
   b. be similar across countries.
   c. be identical across countries.
   d. differ across countries with different levels of development.

True, False, Uncertain and Why Questions
Support your statement of true, false, or uncertain with a few sentences.

1. Engaging in trade does not affect any environmental issues.

2. A country's tax structure affects its international competitive position.

3. The distribution of income across countries is less equal than the distribution of income within a country.

4. The polluter pays principle assumes that individuals own the property rights to water and air.

5. According to WTO rules, a country cannot impose trade restrictions on a country for environmental reasons.

Short Answer Questions

1. Explain why common-use property is more likely to be inefficiently used than private property.

2. Why do industrialized countries tend to have a greater preference for higher levels of environmental quality?

3. Why did the WTO rule against US restrictions on imported shrimp caught using sea turtle unfriendly nets?

4. Why would reducing greenhouse gas emission be easier if all nations had identical costs and benefits of pollution?

5. What is capital export neutrality?

ANSWERS TO CHAPTER 11 STUDY GUIDE QUESTIONS

Multiple Choice Questions

1. c
When the effects of pollution affect regions in different countries, the pollution is called cross-border pollution.

2. c
When the private costs of producing do not equal the costs incurred by society, an externality exists. If social costs are greater than firm costs, a negative production externality exists.

3. d
When the private costs of producing do not equal the costs incurred by society, an externality exists. If social costs are less than firm costs, a positive production externality exists.

4. b
To attract portfolio capital, a country has an incentive to offer lower tax rates than its competition for that capital.

5. a
With a free-rider problem, a country benefits from the reduction of greenhouse gases and CFCs regardless of whether any reductions originated in that country.

6. a
The oceans and the air mass are international common-use goods that are subject to the tragedy of the commons.

7.   d
      According to the destination principle, all goods consumed in a country are taxed at the same rate, regardless of whether the good is domestically produced or imported.

8.   c
      Increasing the tax on labor income generates labor migration, which reduces output.

9.   a
      Increasing the tax on labor income does not generate labor migration, leaving output unchanged.

10.   d
      Countries will different levels of development will have different costs and benefits associated with pollution abatement.

True, False, Uncertain and Why Questions

1.   False. Depending on the type of externality and comparative advantage, trade creates costs and benefits for a country. For example, suppose trade reduces domestic output in the import-competing sector, which has a negative production externality. The economy benefits from lower domestic production since less pollution is created.

2.   True. A country's taxes on factors of production affects the location of those resources, which affects production and efficiency of domestic industries.

3.   True. Policies targeting income redistribution are easier to implement within a country than across countries.

4.   True. The polluter pays principle forces the polluter to compensate the individual for the right to pollute. This policy assumes that the individual owns the right to the common resource (i.e., air).

5.   False. WTO law permits the non-discriminatory application of trade restrictions to enforce environmental policy.

Short Answer Questions

1.   Common use resources are subject to the tragedy of the commons. With private property, the owner of the property has an incentive to use the resource efficiently. With common use resources, each user of the resource does not have an incentive to protect the resource from overuse.

2.   Environmental quality can be interpreted as a luxury good. Increases in income generate greater increases in demand for environmental quality. Grossman and Krueger estimate an inverted-U shaped relationship between pollution and income, suggesting that poorer countries will have different tastes and preferences for environmental quality than wealthier nations.

3.   The WTO ruled that the endangered species could be protected using trade policy. However, the implementation of the policy must be non-discriminatory in nature. The US ban on imported shrimp was determined to be unfairly and unevenly applied.

4.   When countries value pollution abatement differently and face different cleanup costs, unanimous support for reducing greenhouse emissions will be difficult. Adding the free-rider problem makes cooperation even less likely.

5.   Capital export neutrality occurs when a country's tax rates do not influence a firm's decision to invest domestically or abroad (investment in this case is foreign direct investment). Using the residence principle and tax credit for foreign taxes paid, a firm will incur the same tax liability regardless of the location of the investment.

CHAPTER 12

BALANCE OF PAYMENTS ACCOUNTING

IMPORTANT POINTS

1. The balance of payments accounts record estimates of all international financial and commercial transactions that occur within a given time period, usually one year. These accounts include all interactions between domestic agents (individuals, companies, and the government) and the outside world. Thus, transactions between two domestic firms are not included in the balance of payments accounts. The balance of payments differs from a corporate balance sheet since the former represents flows of transactions over a period of time and the latter presents the stocks of assets and liabilities at a point in time.

   Items included in the balance of payments accounts are assigned positive or negative signs. Credit transactions have a positive sign and represent transactions in which a domestic resident receives payment from a foreigner. A debit entry has a negative sign and indicates that a domestic resident has made a payment to the rest of the world. For example, when someone in the United States purchases Italian shoes, this transaction is recorded as a debit in the United States' balance of payments and a credit in the accounts for Italy. Thus, the sum of any item for all countries in the world should be zero. Due to statistical and measurement errors and differences in calculating shipping costs, the world balance may not equal zero.

2. The balance of payments accounts distinguish between financial and commercial transactions. The current account includes imports (debit), exports (credit), net services, dividend payments (a debit if sent to the rest of the world, a credit if received from the rest of the world), and unilateral transfers such as gifts, foreign aid, and remittances from workers back to their families abroad. The capital account measures international capital flows (except for foreign exchange reserve transactions) and is often divided into short-run and long run components. For example, when funds flow from the United States to Italy to purchase a financial asset, the transaction is a negative (debit) entry for the United States and a positive (credit) entry for Italy. If someone in the United States maintains a foreign bank account, withdrawing funds from the account to pay for imports from Italy results in a short-term capital flow into

the United States (credit) and an outflow from Italy. The imports generate a debit entry in the current account for the United States and a credit entry in Italy's balance of payments account.

Foreign direct investment is a source of long-term capital flows. When foreign firms invest in the United States, a credit entry in the capital account for this country and a debit entry for the foreign country occurs. When U.S. firms build plants abroad, capital flows out of the United States and into the foreign country, generating a debit entry for the U.S. and a credit entry for the foreign country.

3.   Another source of capital flows are changes in foreign exchange reserves. Such reserves are held by central banks and are used to offset balance of payments deficits or surpluses. When foreign central banks increase holdings of dollar reserves, U.S. official reserve liabilities increase, resulting in a transaction which is a credit for the United States and a debit for the foreign country. Thus, increases in a country's reserve assets or reductions in its reserve liabilities are debit entries, and decreases in its assets or increases in its liabilities are credit entries. A country may hold its reserves in the form of foreign currency, gold, and IMF related assets such as SDRs. Reserves held in the form of foreign currency earn interest while gold reserves do not earn interest.

4.   The balances of the capital and current accounts are important. The current account balance represents the change in the country's investment position relative to the rest of the world. A current account surplus means that the country has increased its net creditor position or decreased its level of indebtedness over the relevant time period. If the sum of the current and capital accounts differs from zero, an offsetting foreign exchange reserve transaction occurs. For example, if the United States' current and capital accounts sum to a negative number, U.S. foreign exchange reserve assets should decrease (or reserve liabilities increase) to offset the negative number. In other words, the following relationship must hold:

$$CA + KA - \Delta FXR = 0 \qquad\qquad (12.1)$$

where
CA   = the current account
KA   = the capital account
ΔFXR   = change in the country's foreign reserve position.

Since a gain in a country's reserve position is recorded as a debit and vice versa, the sum of the current account, the capital account and the change in foreign exchange reserve transactions must exactly equal zero. The balance of payments must balance at zero.

Due to estimation error, illegal imports, and a variety of other omissions, the balance of payments accounts also include an entry for errors and omissions (statistical discrepancy with floating exchange rates). All of the items in the current and capital accounts are estimates and subject to error. Only the value for net errors and omissions is known since some mistakes may offset each other. The value for errors and omissions is calculated by summing the values for the current and capital accounts, and comparing the figure to the change in foreign exchange reserve position.

The errors and omissions entry is the number making the foreign exchange reserve transactions plus the sum of the capital and current accounts equal to zero.

5.   A payments surplus or deficit can be measured as the Official Reserve Transactions balance, which is the sum of all current and capital transactions. The "basic balance" of payments includes all current account and long-term capital account transactions, and thus excludes short-term capital as well as foreign exchange reserve transactions. Using the "basic balance" of payments calculation allows for the differentiation between short-term and long-term capital flows and the potential side effects of using short-run capital to finance current account deficits.

6.   The format of balance-of-payment accounting in the IMF's International Financial Statistics differs from the method described above. The term "Financial Account" refers to the capital account in the previous section without any differentiation between short and long-term capital. The term "Capital Account" captures some foreign aid and debt forgiveness.

7.   The previous discussion assumed that the exchange rate was fixed. When exchange rates are flexible, the presentation of the accounts is different. If a country has a clean float, no transactions in foreign exchange reserves occur. This implies that the capital and current accounts must sum to zero and that the official reserve transactions balance is always zero. Equilibrium in the balance of payments is maintained by adjustments in the value of the exchange rate. If a country has a tendency toward a balance of payments deficit, the domestic currency depreciates, making imports more expensive, forcing the balance of payments to equilibrium.

       Many industrialized countries maintain a dirty or managed float. This means that countries   allow exchange rates to fluctuate over some range. If the exchange rate moves too far or too rapidly, the central bank will intervene to slow or stop the movement. Thus, foreign exchange reserves can change under the floating system.

       The structure of the U.S. balance of payments under a floating exchange rate regime differs from the way the accounts are organized under a fixed-parity. The current account is the same except the floating rate version does not include a balance for the current account. The capital account is the area in which most differences occur. The account is divided into two sections, changes in U.S. assets abroad and changes in Foreign assets in the U.S.. Both long-term and short-term capital are included, as are changes in foreign exchange reserves. The statistical discrepancy, which is another name for errors and omissions, is added after the capital account.

8.   Many countries also publish a table depicting their net creditor or debtor situation relative to the rest of the world. A country's net investment position should change each year by the amount of its current account balance. A current account deficit of $2 billion dollars implies the country's foreign assets have decreased and/or its liabilities to foreigners increased by $2 billion.

       The net creditor tables for the United States in recent years shows that the United States' net creditor position has been replaced by a large net debtor position. Before this conclusion is reached, the process of evaluating the assets whose values are used to compute the relative creditor/debtor position must be considered. More specifically, direct investments have been carried at historic value, which may undervalue certain assets. Considering inflation or common stock price increases suggests that the value of some assets may greatly exceed the value calculated using the historic value method. Allowing for unrealized capital gains suggests that the United States is not as large a debtor as had been thought, but this method of valuation remains controversial.

9. National income identities can be used to represent the impact of trade surpluses and deficits on the rest of the economy. Gross national product (GNP) consists of consumption, investment, government expenditures and net imports. GNP can be represented by the identity (assuming there is no government sector):

$$Y = C + I + (X - M) \qquad (12.2)$$

Income is either consumed or saved:
$$Y = C + S_p \qquad (12.3)$$

where:
Y= GNP
C= consumption
I = investment
X= exports
M = imports
S_p= private savings.

Setting equations (12.2) and (12.3) equal to each other yields:

$$I - S_p = M - X \qquad (12.4)$$

If a country runs a current account deficit $(X < M)$, it must invest more than it saves $(S_p < I)$.

Including the government sector introduces another source of possible saving (or dissaving):

$$I - (S_p + (T - G)) = M - X \qquad (12.5)$$

$$I - (S_p + S_g) = M - X \qquad (12.6)$$

where:
T = taxes
G = government spending
S_g= T - G.

If a country runs a current account deficit $(M > X)$, investment must exceed total savings, S_T, which is the sum of personal and government savings. When private savings are low and the government has a budget deficit $(G > T$ so S_g is negative), a large volume of investment is financed by savings originating from the rest of the world.

10. The national income accounting framework can be used to illustrate typical stages of development. A developing country tends to start out with a small capital stock relative to the size of the labor force and/or land mass. The small capital stock implies a high marginal productivity of capital, which should be reflected in high interest or profit rates. In the absence of capital controls or excessive risks, international capital will flow into the economy. The imported capital allows for investment rates well beyond the savings rate of the country, allowing the capital stock to grow beyond limits implied by the domestic rate of savings. During this stage of development, countries tend to run current account deficits. The level of net indebtedness increases yearly by the amount of its current account deficit.

As the capital stock grows relative to the labor force, the marginal productivity of capital falls while the marginal productivity of labor increases. This implies that interest rates decline and wage rates rise. Higher domestic incomes lead to higher savings rates which help to maintain the level of investment as international capital flows decline, due to the falling interest rates. The country is able to export more and import less, pushing the current account toward surplus. This period is known as the late debtor stage. The level of indebtedness declines each year by the amount of the current account surplus until it reaches zero, beginning what is known as the early creditor stage. During this period, the country continues to run current account surpluses, accumulating net financial claims on the rest of the world. The fourth and final stage is the late creditor stage and refers to that time period where countries use income from dividends and interest payments to finance trade deficits.

Appendix

1. When a country runs a trade deficit, absorption is greater than income. This deficit must be offset by a surplus elsewhere in the world. Adding the element of time to this model implies that deficit countries are consuming in the current period and will pay for by consuming less in the future. Surplus countries are postponing consumption in the current period for more consumption in the future.

2. This intertemporal model can be expressed graphically. In Figure 12-1, the (I-S) function for country A and country B are represented. Without international capital flows, the interest rate in country A equals ra and the interest rate in country B equals rb. With international capital flows, the interest rates will arbitrage together, allowing country B to save more than it invests and country A to invest more than it saves (and consume more than it produces).

Figure 12-1: Intertemporal Model

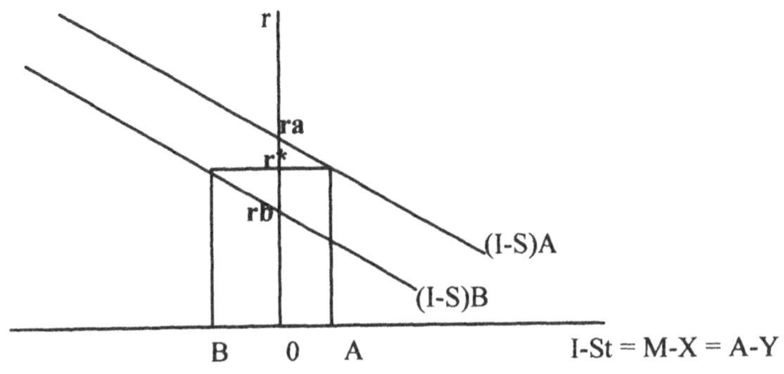

CHAPTER OBJECTIVES

After studying the concepts presented in Chapter 12, you should be able to answer the following questions:

1.   What types of transactions are credit entries for the United States in its balance of payments accounts? What type of transactions are debit entries?

2.   What are the components of the current account? What makes up the capital account? What is the significance of the balances on the current and capital accounts?

3.   Will the sum capital and current accounts exactly equal the change in foreign exchange reserves? Why or why not?

4.   Contrast and compare the presentation of the balance of payments accounts under fixed and flexible exchange rate systems.

5.   Explain how the IMF balance of payments format differentiates between long-term and short-term capital.

6.   What is the net creditor table? What is its significance?

7.   How can national income accounting show the relationship between the trade account and the investment/savings identity? Use this framework to explain the stages of growth model.

GLOSSARY TERMS

- balance of payments
- basic balance
- capital account balance
- C.I.F.
- credit
- current account balance
- debit
- F.A.S.
- F.O.B.
- foreign exchange reserves
- official reserve transactions balance
- trade balance
- transfer pricing

CHAPTER 12 STUDY QUESTIONS

Multiple Choice Questions

1. A credit transaction in the balance of payments accounts of Argentina reflects

    a. the fact that a resident of Argentina receives a payment from a foreigner. This transaction carries a negative sign in the balance of payments for Argentina.

    b. the fact that a resident of Argentina receives a payment from a foreigner. This transaction carries a positive sign in the balance of payments for Argentina.

    c. the fact that a resident of Argentina makes a payment to a foreigner. This transaction carries a negative sign in the balance of payments for Argentina.

    d. the fact that a resident of Argentina makes a payment to a foreigner. This transaction carries a positive sign in the balance of payments for Argentina.

2. If an American deposits funds in a Canadian bank, that transaction

    a. is a minus for both Canada and the United States in the balance of payments accounts

    b. is a plus for both Canada and the United States in the balance of payments accounts.

    c. is a minus for the United States and a plus for Canada in the balance of payments accounts.

    d. is a plus for the United States and a minus for Canada in the balance of payments accounts.

3. If Canada increases its holding of foreign exchange reserves in the form of U.S. dollars,

    a. U.S. official reserve liabilities to foreigners increase, and that transaction is a minus for the United States and a plus for Canada.
    b. U.S. official reserve liabilities to foreigners increase, and that transaction is a plus for the United States and a minus for Canada.
    c. U.S. official reserve liabilities to foreigners decrease, and that transaction is a plus for the United States and a minus for Canada.
    d. U.S. official reserve liabilities to foreigners decrease, and that transaction is a minus for the United States and a plus for Canada.

4. Short-term capital includes all of the following except

    a. Treasury bills.
    b. bank accounts.
    c. direct investment by multinational firms.
    d. short-term export financing.

5. If a country's current and capital accounts sum to a negative number,

    a. its foreign exchange liabilities should decrease.
    b. its foreign exchange assets should increase.
    c. its foreign exchange liabilities and assets should decrease.
    d. its foreign exchange liabilities should increase or its foreign exchange assets should decrease.

6. The basic balance of payments approach measures

    a. surpluses or deficits as the sum of the current account and of the long-term capital account.
    b. surpluses or deficits as the sum of the current account, and the short-run and long run capital accounts.
    c. surpluses or deficits as the sum of the current account.
    d. surpluses or deficits as the sum of the short-run and long run capital accounts.

7. If a country has a current account deficit,

    a. its domestic investment exceeds total domestic savings.
    b. total investment exceeds total savings.
    c. its domestic savings exceeds domestic investment.
    d. total savings exceeds total investment.

8.   During the early debtor stage, it is normal for countries to

    a.   run current account deficits in order to invest more than they save.
    b.   run trade account surpluses and current account deficits.
    c.   run current account surpluses.
    d.   run capital account deficits.

9.   An increase in U.S. exports of cars to Mexico is

    a.   a debit entry for the United States and a credit entry for Mexico.
    b.   a debit entry for both the United States and Mexico.
    c.   a credit entry for both the United States and Mexico.
    d.   a debit entry for Mexico and a credit entry for the United States.

10.   If Goodyear opens a tire plant in China, this transaction is

    a.   a debit entry for the United States and a credit entry for China.
    b.   a debit entry for both the United States and China.
    c.   a credit entry for both the United States and China.
    d.   a debit entry for China and a credit entry for the United States.

True, False, Uncertain and Why Questions

When answering the following questions, be sure to support your assertion of true, false, or uncertain with two or three sentences.

1.   Balance of payments accounts are analogous to a balance sheet.

2.   An increase in U.S. foreign exchange reserve liabilities to the Bank of England appears as a credit on the balance of payments accounts of both countries.

3.   If an American firm writes a check on an account in a Canadian bank to pay for imports from Canada, the withdrawal of short-term capital from Canada results in a plus for the United States and a minus for Canada. The merchandise imports are a minus for the United States and a plus for Canada.

4.   The money an American tourist spends abroad is a private capital inflow for the United States.

5.   The dividend payment to foreigners on U.S. common stock is a debit in the capital account.

Short Answer Questions

1. Use the following list of transactions to construct a balance of payments table for the United States. Note that the (+) and (-) signs are not assigned to many of the transactions; part of your task is to correctly assign them. Also note that one transaction is followed by a question mark. You are to solve for that number and for its sign. Find the official settlements balance and the basic balance of payments (assume a fixed exchange rate).

Imports	60
U.S. income from foreign investment	10
Other services, net	-20
Increase in short-term foreign claims on the U.S.	20
Increase in U.S. official reserve assets	20
Errors and omissions, net	?
Exports	50
Foreign purchases of U.S. securities	25
U.S. direct investment abroad	15
Increase in official U.S. liabilities to foreign official agencies	40
U.S. purchases of foreign securities	20
Foreign income from U.S. investments	15
Foreign direct investment in the U.S.	20
U.S. gifts and remittances to foreigners	15
Foreign gifts and remittances to the United States	25

2. How does your answer to question 1 change if exchange rates are flexible?

Use the following information for questions 3 through 5:

You are in charge of the balance of payments accounts for your country. What revisions are necessary in the accounts for 1998, or any other affected year if, in 1999, you discovered the following:

3. During 1998 somebody employed by your central bank managed to steal $1 million out of your foreign exchange reserves, so actual reserves at the end of the year were $1 million less than you had previously thought. In 1999, he is caught and the money is returned.

4. During 1997 one of your exporters under-invoiced an export sale by $1 million and used the funds to buy a British company. In 1998 he sold the company for $1.5 million and used the money to buy British 90-day treasury bills.

5.   Due to the customs agent in San Francisco being ill, $5 million in imports that came in during 1997 were recorded as having arrived in 1998. These imports were financed with 18-month loans from the exporters.

ANSWERS TO CHAPTER 12 STUDY GUIDE QUESTIONS

Multiple Choice Questions

1.   b

A credit transaction in Argentina's payments accounts represents a payment into Argentina.

2.   c

The flow of funds out of the U.S. is a debit for the U.S. and a credit for Canada (since funds are flowing into Canada).

3.   b

When a foreign country increases its foreign exchange reserves in the form of dollars, U.S. foreign exchange reserve liabilities increase which is a credit for the U.S. and a debit for other country.

4.   c

Foreign direct investment is considered long-term capital.

5.   d

Since the change in foreign exchange reserve transactions must offset the change in the sum of the current and capital accounts, the negative balance of payments number implies that foreign exchange liabilities should increase or foreign exchange reserve assets decrease.

6.   a

The Basic Balance excludes short-term capital and foreign exchange reserve movements.

7.   a

A current account deficit implies that domestic investment exceeds total domestic savings.

8.   a

In the early debtor stage, countries tend to run current account deficits in order to invest more than they save.

9.   d

When a U.S. firm exports a car to Mexico, the transaction creates a flow of funds from Mexico to the U.S. An outflow of funds is a debit entry and an inflow of funds is a credit entry.

10.   a

This transaction is U.S. direct investment abroad and is a debit entry for the U.S. and a credit entry for China.

True, False, Uncertain and Why Questions

1.   False. Since the balance of payments accounts reflect flows of transactions during a year and a balance sheet presents stocks of assets at a moment in time, the two are not analogous.

2.   False. An increase in U.S. foreign exchange reserve liabilities to the Bank of England is a credit in the balance of payments accounts of the United States and a debit in the balance of payments accounts of England.

3.   True. When the U.S. firm uses funds held in a foreign commercial bank, the short term capital flows result in a credit for the United States and a debit for Canada. The merchandise imports are a debit for the U.S. since the U.S. firm is making a payment to foreigners.

4   False. The money an American tourist spends abroad is reflected in the current account as a debit entry.

5.   False. The dividend payment to foreigners on U.S. stock is a debit in the current account (as investment income).

Short Answer Questions

1.   Current Account

Exports	+50
Imports	-60
U.S. income from foreign investment	+10
Foreign income from U.S. investments	-15
U.S. gifts and remittances to foreigners	-15
Foreign gifts and remittances to the United States	+25
Other services, net	<u>-20</u>
	-25

Capital Account
Long-term

Foreign purchases of U.S. securities	+25
U.S. purchases of foreign securities	-20
U.S. direct investment abroad	-15
Foreign direct investment in the U.S.	<u>+20</u>
	+10

BASIC BALANCE OF PAYMENTS (sum of the current and long-term capital accounts)	-15

Capital Account
Short-term

Increase in short-term foreign claims on the U.S.	+20
Errors and omissions, net	-25

OFFICIAL RESERVE BALANCE OF PAYMENTS	-20

Foreign Exchange Reserves

Increase in U.S. official reserve assets	-20
Increase in official U.S. liabilities to foreign official agencies	+40

2.   With the float, the change in foreign exchange goes in the capital account. The capital account is also reorganized (as change in U.S. claims on foreigners and change in foreigners claims on the U.S.). No surpluses or deficits are shown and errors and omissions becomes statistical discrepancy.

3.	1998	change in Foreign Exchange reserves	+$1m
		Errors and omissions	-$1m
	1999	change in Foreign Exchange reserves	-$1m
		Errors and omissions	+$1m
4.	1997	Exports	+$1m
		Capital account, long-term	-$1m
	1998	Capital account, long-term	+$1.5m
		Capital account, short-term	-$1.5m
5.	1997	Trade Balance, imports	-$5m
		Capital account, long-term	+$5m
	1998	Trade balance, imports	+$5m
		Capital account, long-term	-$5m

CHAPTER 13

MARKETS FOR FOREIGN EXCHANGE

IMPORTANT POINTS

1.   Foreign exchange markets are necessary to facilitate trade and other transactions between countries with different currencies. This chapter examines foreign exchange markets. International business transactions typically involve two currencies. If a department store imports Italian shoes, it must exchange dollars for lira in order to pay the exporting firm. Debit entries in the U.S. balance of payments represent sales of dollars and purchases of foreign exchange. Credit entries indicate that dollars are purchased and foreign currency sold to complete the transaction. The only exception to this conclusion is when the same individual is involved in two international transactions of the same size and opposite sign. The transactions are self-canceling in their balance of payments effects and do not necessitate the use of the foreign exchange market. For example, if the department store purchases Italian shoes and pays for the imports with a check drawn on a lira account in an Italian bank, there would be no purchase of currency in the exchange market and there would be two offsetting balance of payments entries. Except for such offsetting transaction, every change in the balance of payments accounts is reflected in the exchange market. When a balance of payments surplus or deficit exists, a parallel disequilibria occurs in the exchange market. When a country experiences a balance of payments deficit, an excess supply of domestic currency (excess demand for foreign currency) exists in the exchange market. Under fixed exchange rates, the balance of payments deficit must be offset by central bank intervention, altering the level of foreign exchange reserves to clear the market. If exchange rates are floating, the adjustment process occurs automatically as the exchange rate changes to instantly restore equilibrium in the foreign currency market.

2.   A supply and demand diagram can represent the exchange market. The supply of foreign exchange is derived from the foreign demand for this country's goods, services, and financial assets. The demand curve for foreign exchange is derived from domestic demand for foreign goods, services, and financial assets. The supply and demand curves for foreign exchange are shown in Figure 13-1. (E denotes the

exchange rate, which is the foreign price of local money, making the local price of foreign money equal to 1/E.)

Figure 13-1: The Market for Foreign Exchange

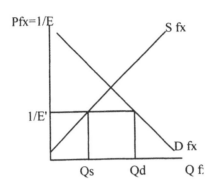

If exchange rates are pegged at 1/E', a balance of payments deficit is represented by excess demand for foreign currency at the current exchange rate (Q^D foreign exchange > Q^S foreign exchange). The central bank must sell foreign exchange and purchase local currency to restore equilibrium. If central bank intervention does not occur, the price of foreign exchange would increase until quantity of foreign exchange demanded equals the quantity supplied. If this price movement occurs, the exchange rate is no longer fixed. The floating exchange rate system used by some industrialized countries has operated since 1973.

3. Before 1914, many countries used the gold standard. Central banks did not set exchange rates directly. Instead these institutions set relative prices of gold, promising to buy or sell gold in unlimited amounts at those prices. For example, if the French government set the price of an ounce of gold at Fr.8 while the British price was £4, and the central banks of both countries agreed to buy and sell at these prices, the exchange rate would have to be approximately £1 equals Fr.2. If the exchange rate rose significantly above this value, French individuals would not sell in the exchange market since they could sell francs for gold, ship the gold to England and buy pounds. A British balance of payments surplus, which produces an excess demand for pounds and upward pressure on the exchange value of sterling, results in the loss of gold reserves by France and an increase in British reserves. Since gold cannot be transported at zero cost, the exchange rate can vary slightly around the 2:1 parity, the range of movement depending on transportation costs of gold.

4. Under the Bretton Woods system, the dollar was tied to gold at $35 per ounce, and the U.S. government agreed to buy and sell gold at that rate, dealing only with foreign governments or central banks. Other countries fixed their currencies in terms of the U.S. dollar, intervening in the exchange market to maintain the parity. If France ran a balance of payments surplus, the dollars they purchased in the exchange market would be deposited at the New York Federal Reserve Bank, increasing French reserve assets and U.S. liabilities. Any dollars not needed in the near future could be converted into interest-bearing U.S. Treasury securities or into gold.

Under this system, the United States had no control over the value of the dollar relative to the rest of the world. The U.S. could change the price of gold but could not alter any bilateral exchange rate.

5.   Some LDCs do not allow free convertibility. In other words, private residents are unable to carry out transactions requiring the exchange of domestic currency for foreign currency and vice versa, unless they have a permit to do so. These arrangements are designed to guarantee that scarce foreign currency flows into official reserves immediately. When a resident receives foreign currency, he or she is required to sell such funds to the central bank at the official exchange rate. The government allocates the   available foreign currency to those purposes that are viewed as particularly important or useful. Investments abroad or imports of luxury goods are unlikely to be approved.

This system of rationing generates several disadvantages. Individuals denied access to foreign exchange will probably look for other less legal avenues for foreign exchange. As a result, a secondary or black market will emerge, from which foreign currency is purchased and sold at a price exceeding the official rate. Foreign tourists are likely to be approached by domestic residents offering attractive rates for local money. Depending on the degree of exchange rate controls, the black market exchange rate may be viewed as the more accurate measure of expectations about what the local currency is actually worth. Transfer pricing and exporting goods without leaving an official paper trail are two ways individuals faced with exchange controls may circumvent the restrictions.

6.   The floating exchange rate system, in theory, implies an absence of central bank intervention in the exchange market. The exchange rate fluctuates in response to changes in the supply and demand of foreign and domestic currencies. Rapid changes in the exchange rate have been found to be highly disruptive, so central banks often intervene to maintain a more stable rate, producing what is known as a 'dirty' or managed float.

7.   The foreign exchange market operates through major commercial banks in cities such as New York, Tokyo, Frankfurt, and Singapore. Unlike the New York Stock Exchange where transactions occur in a single location, the foreign exchange market is a telephone market in which traders from the member banks engage in transactions electronically. The banks usually maintain trading rooms that are staffed by at least one trader for each major currency. The banks maintain inventories, of the currencies in which they trade, in the form of deposits at foreign banks. For example, Citibank purchases pounds from a customer and places them in its account in London. Sales of pounds by Citibank come from this account. As trading occurs, these currency inventories fluctuate, leaving the bank's currency portfolio open to losses if a currency quickly changes values. For example, if Citibank's sterling assets are less than its sterling liabilities and the pound appreciates, the bank loses because of its short position.

Currency prices are typically quoted in hundredths of a penny or basis points. For large transactions, the bid/asked spread is about 5 basis points. The more risky the currency is perceived to be, the larger the bid/asked spread. The spread also becomes larger as the size of transactions diminishes. The rate at which a tourist exchanges dollars for pounds differs from the exchange rate that a large multinational encounters. Banks also sell and buy currency among themselves in the inter-bank market. International currency transactions are typically completed with a two-day lag. Transactions agreed to on Wednesday would clear on Friday, with the exchange rate determined on Wednesday. If the rate changes during this time, the transaction still clears at the Wednesday rate.

Changes in technology affect the spot exchange rate market. Although stock trading is more common, internet currency trading is becoming more common. Such electronic trading benefits relatively small transactions since the bid/ask spread depends on the size of the transactions. The exchange rate difference between the price a currency is bought and sold is much greater when the volume of currency traded is small.

8. This discussion has focused on bilateral exchange rates. Using these rates, when the dollar appreciates, it rises relative to one currency. Since countries trade with more than one country, a multilateral rate provides useful information. The nominal effective exchange rate is an index of the weighted average of the bilateral exchange rates of a country's major trading partners. As more countries are included in the index, the exchange rate becomes more accurate. This statement assumes that currencies are weighted according to the percentage of trade occurring between the two countries. For example, if Canadian trade makes up 25% of total U.S. international trade with those countries included in the index, the Canadian dollar should be assigned a 0.25 weight in the nominal effective exchange rate for the United States.

Adjusting the nominal effective exchange rate for inflation yields the real effective exchange rate. This value is an indication of a country's price competitiveness in world markets. The index is constructed as follows:

$$XR_r = \frac{XN_n \cdot P_{dom}}{P_{row}} \tag{13.1}$$

where:

XR_r = the real effective exchange rate, measured as the foreign price of local money

XR_n = the nominal effective exchange rate, measured as the foreign price of local money

P_{dom} = the domestic price level, usually measured as wholesale prices

P_{row} = the price level in the rest of the world, using trade share as weights.

The real and nominal exchange rates are measured as the foreign price of local money. If inflation in the domestic economy is 10% while its trading partners experienced 12% inflation, a fixed nominal exchange rate implies a 2% improvement in that country's competitive position in world markets and a 2% real depreciation. In other words, if the real effective exchange rate falls, the country's competitive position has improved.

Another definition of the real effective exchange rate uses the price of both traded and non-trade goods:

$$XR_r = \frac{P_{NT}}{P_T} \qquad (13.2)$$

The Big Mac index provides one way to quickly determine whether a currency is over or under-valued. Since a Big Mac sold in the United States should be the same as a Big Mac sold in Warsaw, the price differential between the US Big Mac and the Polish Big Mac should reflect the exchange rate.

CHAPTER OBJECTIVES

After studying the concepts in Chapter 13, you should be able to answer the following questions:

1. Explain the relationship between credit and debit entries in the balance of payments and transactions in the foreign exchange market. What types of transactions result in a credit in the United States' payments account? What generates a debit entry?

2. How can the market for foreign exchange be represented by supply and demand curves? How is a fixed exchange rate shown in this framework?

3. Describe the spot market for foreign exchange. How does this market differ from the forward and futures markets for currency? What types of customers use each of these markets?

4. What is the real effective exchange rate? What additional information does this rate tell you that the nominal effective exchange rate does not?

5. Why can the Big Mac index provide one, albeit humorous, way to determine if a currency is over or under-valued?

GLOSSARY TERMS

- appreciation
- arbitrage
- bilateral exchange rate
- clean floating exchange rate
- Clearing House International Payments System (CHIPS)

- depreciation
- devaluation
- exchange market intervention
- floating exchange rate
- gold standard
- managed or dirty floating exchange rate
- real effective exchange rate
- real interest rate
- revaluation
- spot market

CHAPTER 13 STUDY QUESTIONS

Multiple Choice Questions

1. With a fixed exchange rate, an U.S. balance of payments surplus means

    a. an excess demand for foreign currencies exists in the exchange market.
    b. an excess demand for dollars exists in the exchange market.
    c. the rate of inflation in the United States exceeds the rate of inflation in the rest of the world.
    d. the rate of inflation in the rest of the world exceeds the rate of inflation in the United States.

2. In developing countries with foreign exchange controls, sometimes the most accurate measure of the value of the domestic currency is

    a. the official exchange rate.
    b. the prime lending rate.
    c. the illegal or street exchange rate.
    d. the rate of inflation.

3. When a country experiences a payments deficit and has a fixed exchange rate,

    a. the central bank must sell domestic currency and buy foreign exchange to restore equilibrium.
    b. the central bank must buy domestic currency and sell foreign exchange to restore equilibrium.
    c. the currency appreciates to restore equilibrium.
    d. the currency depreciates to restore equilibrium.

4. When a country (that is not a reserve currency country) experiences a large surge of imports and has a floating exchange rate,

    a. the central bank must sell domestic currency or buy foreign exchange to restore equilibrium.
    b. the central bank must buy domestic currency or sell foreign exchange to restore equilibrium.
    c. the currency appreciates to restore equilibrium.
    d. the currency depreciates to restore equilibrium.

5. The nominal effective exchange rate is

    a. an unweighted index of several bilateral exchange rates.
    b. a weighted index of several bilateral exchange rates.
    c. a bilateral exchange rate that is adjusted for inflation.
    d. a bilateral exchange rate that is unadjusted for inflation.

6. The real effective exchange rate is

    a. a weighted index of several bilateral exchange rates, adjusted for inflation.
    b. a weighted index of several bilateral exchange rates, unadjusted for inflation.
    c. a bilateral exchange rate that is adjusted for inflation.
    d. a bilateral exchange rate that is unadjusted for inflation.

7. When the real effective exchange rate declines (with a fixed nominal effective exchange rate), the country's cost competitive position relative to the rest of the world

    a. remains unchanged since the production costs and technology determine cost competitiveness.
    b. deteriorates because it has experienced less inflation than its trading partners.
    c. improves because it has experienced less inflation than its trading partners.
    d. improves because it has experienced more inflation than its trading partners.

Use the following information to answer question 8:

$$XR_n=150$$
$$Pdom=150$$
$$P_{row}=120$$

8. The real effective exchange rate equals

    a.   187.50
    b.   120
    c.   150
    d.   167.50

9. If an excess demand for dollars exists on the foreign exchange market with fixed exchange rates, the central banks must

    a.   buy dollars or sell foreign exchange in order to maintain the fixed parity value.
    b.   sell dollars or buy foreign exchange in order to maintain the fixed parity value.
    c.   buy either dollars or foreign exchange in order to maintain the fixed parity value.
    d.   sell either dollars or foreign exchange in order to maintain the fixed parity value.

10. If an excess supply of dollars exists on the foreign exchange market with fixed exchange rates, the central banks must

    a.   buy dollars or sell foreign exchange in order to maintain the fixed parity value.
    b.   sell dollars or buy foreign exchange in order to maintain the fixed parity value.
    c.   buy either dollars or foreign exchange in order to maintain the fixed parity value.
    d.   sell either dollars or foreign exchange in order to maintain the fixed parity value.

True, False, Uncertain and Why Questions

When answering the following questions, be sure to support your assertion of true, false, or uncertain with two or three sentences.

1. Most countries in the world maintain a clean floating exchange rate.

2. The foreign exchange market is similar to the New York and American Stock Exchanges.

3.   If a country experiences more inflation than its trading partners, its competitive position in the world worsens.

4.   When the real effective exchange rate rises, it must be the case that the country's price level increased.

5.   With floating exchange rates, the central bank must intervene if the value of a currency greatly changes.

Short Answer Questions

1.   What are some reasons for an excess demand for a currency on the spot market? Explain what happens to the value of the currency with fixed and flexible exchange rate systems.

2.   Why does a balance of payments surplus imply an excess supply of foreign exchange and an excess demand for dollars?

3.   With flexible exchange rates, explain what happens to the value of a currency when a tendency toward a balance of payments surplus exists.

4.   Explain how each of the following will affect the exchange rate for the Mexican peso (assume floating exchange rate):

      a.   An increase in foreign demand for Mexican textiles.
      b.   A decrease in foreign interest rates.
      c.   An increase Mexican interest rates.
      d.   A decrease in the GDP of Mexico's trading partners.

5.   You are a foreign exchange trader for a large New York bank and face infinitesimal transaction costs. You notice the following quotes on the Reuters screen.

          US$/UK sterling = $2.00
          US $/ Canadian $ = $0.76
          Canadian $/UK sterling = $2.58.

What would you do? If other traders in New York did the same thing, what would you expect to happen to the Canadian $/ UK sterling rate, assuming the other two bilateral rates remain unchanged?

ANSWERS TO CHAPTER 13 STUDY GUIDE QUESTIONS

Multiple Choice Questions

1. b

    A balance of payments surplus means that U.S. exports exceed imports and that an excess demand for dollars exists in the foreign currency market.

2. c

    Because exchange controls and other government policies can distort the value of the official exchange, the illegal market rate is often more accurate.

3. b

    In order to maintain a fixed parity, the central bank must sell foreign exchange reserves and buy domestic currency to restore equilibrium.

4. d

    A large surge of imports leads to a tendency for an excess demand for foreign currency, causing the exchange rate to depreciate.

5. b

    The nominal effective exchange rate is a weighted (by trade shares) index of several bilateral exchange rates.

6. a

    The real effective exchange rate is adjusted for inflation.

7. c

    When the real effective exchange rate falls, the country has experienced less inflation than its trading partners, meaning its cost competitive position relative to the rest of the world has improved.

8. a

    The real effective exchange rate equals the nominal effective exchange rate times the ratio of domestic to world price levels.

9. b

    An excess demand for dollars implies that the quantity of dollars supplied at the existing exchange rate is less than the quantity demanded. To maintain the value of the fixed exchange rate, the central bank must sell dollars or buy foreign exchange.

10. a

    An excess supply of dollars implies that the quantity of dollars supplied at the existing exchange rate is greater than the quantity demanded. To maintain the value of the fixed exchange rate, the central bank must buy dollars or sell foreign exchange.

True, False, Uncertain and Why Questions

1. False. Most countries that maintain a floating exchange rate frequently intervene in the exchange market to influence the value of the domestic currency. Thus, countries maintain a `dirty' float.

2. False. The foreign exchange market is a telephone market and transactions do not take place in one specific location as with the New York and American Stock Exchanges.

3. True. Assuming that the nominal effective exchange rate remains unchanged, an increase in the price level of one country relative to the rest of the world implies that its competitiveness decreases. With greater inflation than the rest of the world, the country's imports would be expected to increase and exports decrease.

4. False. The real effective exchange rate can increase for reasons other than an increase in the country's price level. For example, an increase in the nominal effective exchange rate or a decrease in the rest of the world's price level increases the real effective exchange rate

5. False or Uncertain. With a pure float, the central bank does not intervene in the foreign exchange market. With a dirty or managed float, the central bank may intervene to affect the value of the currency.

Short Answer Questions

1. An excess demand for a currency may exist for several reasons. The demand for a currency on the foreign exchange market represents foreign demand for that country's goods, services, and assets. The supply of a currency on the foreign exchange market represents that country's demand for foreign goods, services, and assets. If an excess demand for the currency exists, the foreign demand for that country's products exceeds that country's demand for foreign products, implying a payments deficit. With a fixed exchange rate, the central bank must intervene and sell dollars. With a flexible exchange rate, the currency will appreciate in value.

2. The demand for a currency on the foreign exchange market represents foreign demand for that country's goods, services, and assets. The supply of a currency on the foreign exchange market represents that country's demand for foreign goods, services, and assets. If an excess supply for the currency exists, the foreign demand for that country's products is less than that country's demand for foreign products, implying a payments surplus.

3. With flexible exchange rates and a tendency towards a payments surplus, the currency will appreciate in value, which increases the price of exports and decreases the price of imports. With a pure float, the value of the currency will change until the quantity supplied equals the quantity demanded.

4.   Holding all else constant:

    a.   An increase in foreign demand for Mexican textiles increases the demand for pesos in the foreign exchange market, which causes the peso to appreciate.

    b.   A decrease in foreign interest rates decreases demand for foreign assets (and increases demand for Mexican assets), causing the peso to appreciate.

    c.   An increase in Mexican interest rates also increases the demand for Mexican assets, increasing demand for the peso in the foreign exchange market, causing a peso appreciation.

    d.   A decrease in the GDP of Mexico's trading partners would decrease foreign demand for Mexican products and result in a depreciation of the peso.

5.   Since sterling = US$2.00 and Can$ = US$0.76, then sterling must equal Can$2.63158. Since the market rate is sterling = Can$2.58, triangular arbitrage is possible. Starting with US dollars, sell them for Canadian dollars, getting Can$ 1.3158 for each US$. Buy sterling with the Can$ proceeds for $2.58, meaning that every Can$ becomes 0.51 pounds. Sell sterling for US$2.00, getting $1.02 for every 0.51 pounds. The original US dollar becomes US$1.02, producing a profit of US$0.02 for each dollar. If enough people do this, the Canadian dollar cost of sterling must rise to Can$2.63158, a level at which no arbitrage profits are available.

CHAPTER 14

INTERNATIONAL DERIVATIVES: FOREIGN EXCHANGE FORWARDS, FUTURES, AND OPTIONS

IMPORTANT POINTS

1. Foreign exchange forward contracts, futures, and options are examples of derivatives. These financial tools do not involve direct ownership of an asset and fluctuations in the value of the asset results in gains or losses for the owner of the derivative.

2. Through the forward exchange market, foreign currency can be purchased today for delivery and payment at a fixed date in the future. Contracts usually mature in 30, 60, or 90 days. Using the forward market is one way to reduce the risk associated with transactions requiring currency exchange. For example, a foreign investor in short-term U.S. dollar money market assets may sell forward dollars today, locking in a specific price in order to reduce a potential loss if the dollar depreciates over time. Trading in forward contracts occurs in the same environment as the spot market except settlement occurs in 30, 60, or 90 days rather than in 2 days. The spot and forward rates often differ in value due to expectations about the future. If a currency is worth more in the forward than in the spot market, a forward premium exists. If the spot rate exceeds the forward rate, a forward discount exists. The differences between spot and forward rates are usually quoted in annual percentages, making comparisons to interest rates easier.

    A futures market also exists for foreign exchange. This arrangement differs slightly from the forward market. All futures mature on the same day of the month while forward contracts close on a fixed number of days after they are signed. A secondary market also exists for futures contracts, while forward contracts usually have to be held until maturity.

3. Foreign exchange options are another international financial instrument. These contracts provide the opportunity to purchase or sell a fixed amount of currency at a specific price (the strike price) during a given period. The buyer of the option has the alternative of not exercising the purchase or sale. A put option gives the owner the

right to sell the currency. A call option gives the owner the right to purchase the currency. The owner of the option pays a fee for the contract. Purchasing puts or calls is a way to minimize the risk of any loss due to exchange rate volatility or to gamble on exchange rate changes with a limited downside risk.

4.   Three interrelated reasons exist for forward trading. First, the forward market is a means of hedging risk associated with credit terms on import/export business. If a department store imports products from abroad, payment may not be required for 30 days. If the dollar depreciated during this time, the imported goods became more expensive. The forward market allows the importer to lock in a specific price for the imported goods. Under a fixed rate system, the risk of volatile exchange rates was much less and the forward market was less frequently used for this purpose, but forward activity increased sharply with the early 1970s adoption of floating exchange rates by many industrialized countries.

    Another reason for the use of the forward market is to cover risks arising from interest rate arbitrage. When investors place money in foreign assets, they run the risk that the exchange rate may move in such a way to eliminate any investment profit. Using the forward market can eliminate this risk.

    Speculators also use forward markets. If people believe a currency will appreciate in the next 90 days to a level above the forward rate, the speculators will buy currency in the forward market. For example, if sterling is trading on the spot market at $2.00 and $2.02 in the 90-day forward market and the speculator believes the appreciation of the spot rate would be more than 2 cents, he or she could buy forward sterling and wait. In 90 days if the exchange rate were $2.04, he or she would take delivery of sterling at $2.02 and sell at the spot rate, for a net profit of 2 cents times the number of sterling in the contract. If the spot rate moved the opposite direction from the speculator's expectation, he or she would lose money.

5.   Two possible explanations exist for forward exchange rate determination, but they turn out to be closely related. Interest parity theory suggests that forward rates are determined through the interest rate arbitrage process. If the differential between foreign and local interest rates exceeded the premium on the local currency, investors would buy foreign assets and sell the foreign currency in the forward market. This process would cause the interest rate differential and the exchange rate gap to decline, thus eliminating the profitability of the transaction. For example, suppose the interest rate in Britain is 12% and the interest rate in the U.S. is 9%, when the forward price of sterling is at a 2% discount (Spot rate exceeds the forward rate.). The covered differential is 1%. Thus, the UK asset is the more attractive investment since the differential in the interest rates is not offset completely by the forward exchange rate discount. As investors demand UK assets, interest rates in the UK fall. As demand for US assets declines, US interest rates rise. As sterling is purchased on the spot market, the pound appreciates on that market while it depreciates in the forward market as forward sales occur. These pressures cause the covered interest differential to diminish. Thus, the arbitraging process produces the following outcome:

$$\text{Sterling forward discount} = r_{UK} - r_{US} \tag{14.1}$$

$$\text{Sterling forward premium} = r_{US} - r_{UK}. \tag{14.2}$$

Whenever sterling does not trade at a forward discount/premium that equals the interest differential, arbitrage opportunities exist. This analysis assumed that all assets are perfect substitutes and that transaction costs are insignificant. Differences in risk can generate interest differentials greater than the forward premium or discount.

Several reasons exist for the appearance of profits with covered interest-rate arbitrage: the assets are not of the same degree of risk, fear of exchange controls, or the possibility of double taxation.

6. Another approach to the determination of the forward rate focuses on expectations. If the spot rate is 2% higher than the forward rate, the market expects sterling to depreciate by 2%. If this were not the case, speculators would undertake transactions that move the forward rate to a level in line with the market consensus. This approach is related to the interest arbitrage theory in that both are dominated by differences in expected rates on inflation. If national currencies are claims on real goods and services, exchange rates should reflect differences in the relative purchasing power of these currencies. If the United States interest rate exceeds the British rate by 4%, expected inflation in the United States must be 4% higher than expected inflation in Britain to produce the same real interest rates. If people expect inflation to be higher in one currency than another, a higher nominal interest rate is needed to attract investment in that currency. Thus, while the nominal interest rates may differ, real interest rate would be arbitraged together. A forward discount on sterling implies that more inflation is expected in Britain than in the United States. The following equation summarizes this conclusion:

$$\text{exp. inflation}^{UK} - \text{exp. inflation}^{US} = r_{UK} - r_{US} = \text{forward sterling discount.} \tag{14.3}$$

The forward rate reflects both differences in the nominal interest rates and expected changes in the spot rate, where both are generated by differences in expected rates of inflation between countries. Figure 14-1 in the text highlights the relationship between the interest arbitrage and the expected-spot rate approaches to forward rate determination.

7. In addition to options, futures, and forward contracts, other international derivatives exist. With interest rate swaps, exchange interest payments denominated in one currency are exchanged for those payable in another currency. The maturity of these derivatives may differ. With foreign exchange swaps, simultaneous transactions in the spot and future markets occur.

CHAPTER OBJECTIVES

After studying the concepts in Chapter 14, you should be able to answer the following questions:

1.   Describe the spot market for foreign exchange. How does this market differ from the forward and futures markets for currency? What types of customers use each of these markets?

2.   Explain in detail the two alternative theories for forward exchange rate determination and how they became one theory. What role do differences in expected inflation rates play in your answer?

GLOSSARY TERMS

- call
- Clearing House International Payments System (CHIPS)
- covered return
- depreciation
- devaluation
- floating exchange rate
- forward exchange market
- futures market for foreign exchange
- gold standard
- hedging
- interest rate parity
- London Interbank Offer Rate (LIBOR)
- long position
- managed or dirty floating exchange rate
- par value
- put
- real interest rate
- revaluation
- short position
- spot market
- swap

CHAPTER 14 STUDY GUIDE QUESTIONS

Multiple Choice Questions

1.   If the spot exchange rate is greater than the forward rate, this means that

    a.   the currency is expected to depreciate in the future.
    b.   the currency is expected to appreciate in the future.
    c.   the spot rate is overvalued.
    d.   the forward rate is undervalued.

2. If the spot exchange rate is less than the forward rate, this means that

a. the currency is expected to depreciate in the future.
b. the currency is expected to appreciate in the future.
c. the spot rate is overvalued.
d. the forward rate is undervalued

3. A call option contract gives the owner

a. the right to sell a fixed amount of currency during a fixed period of time at a guaranteed price.
b. the right to purchase a fixed amount of currency during a fixed period of time at a guaranteed price.
c. the right to sell a fixed amount of currency during a fixed period of time at the current market price.
d. the right to purchase a fixed amount of currency during a fixed period of time at the current market price.

4. A put option contract gives the owner

a. the right to sell a fixed amount of currency during a fixed period of time at a guaranteed price.
b. the right to purchase a fixed amount of currency during a fixed period of time at a guaranteed price.
c. the right to sell a fixed amount of currency during a fixed period of time at the current market price.
d. the right to purchase a fixed amount of currency during a fixed period of time at the current market price.

5. A forward contract

a. allows for the purchase or sale of a foreign exchange today for delivery at an unspecified date in the future.
b. allows for the purchase or sale of a foreign exchange today for delivery at a specific date in the future, which is usually less than 2 days.
c. allows for the purchase or sale of a foreign exchange today for delivery at a specified date in the future, which is greater than 2 days.
d. allows for the purchase but not the sale of a foreign exchange today for delivery at an unspecified date in the future.

Use the following information to answer questions 6 through 8:

The Canadian dollar trades at US$0.6715 in the spot market and US$0.6713 in the 30-day forward market.

6. Based on this information, the Canadian dollar is trading at

a. a forward premium
b. a forward discount
c. a future premium
d. a future discount

7.   If the interest rate on Canadian 30-day assets equals 10% and the interest rate on similar US assets equals 11%, interest rate arbitrage would result in

a.   an increase in the Canadian interest rate and a decrease in the US interest rate.

b.   a decrease in the Canadian interest rate and an increase in the US interest rate.

c.   an increase in the Canadian interest rate and an increase in the US interest rate.

d.   a decrease in the Canadian interest rate and a decrease in the US interest rate.

8.   If the interest rate on Canadian 30-day assets equals 10% and the interest rate on similar US assets equals 11%, interest rate arbitrage would result in

a.   an appreciation of the Canadian dollar in the spot market and a depreciation of the Canadian dollar in the forward market.

b.   an appreciation of the Canadian dollar in the spot market and an appreciation of the Canadian dollar in the forward market.

c.   a depreciation of the Canadian dollar in the spot market and an appreciation of the Canadian dollar in the forward market.

d.   a depreciation of the Canadian dollar in the spot market and a depreciation of the Canadian dollar in the forward market.

Use the information provided below to answer questions 9 and 10.

Interest rate on British assets: 5%
Interest rate on French assets: 8%
Spot exchange rate: 1£=Fr.3
Forward exchange rate: 1£=Fr.2.9

9.   If the assets are of similar risk, you would invest in
a.   British assets
b.   French assets
c.   both assets
d.   neither asset, since you need to know more about risk differences between assets.

10.   If the assets are of different risk, you would invest in
a.   British assets
b.   French assets
c.   both assets
d.   neither asset, since you need to know more about risk differences between assets.

TRUE, FALSE, UNCERTAIN, AND WHY QUESTIONS

When answering the following questions, be sure to support your assertion of true, false, or uncertain with two or three sentences.

1. If a U.S. firm was in the midst of negotiations to buy a French company and knew approximately what the franc price would be, a franc put option contract would allow the U.S. firm to hedge risks associated with exchange rate fluctuations.

2. If a currency is trading at a forward discount, the spot rate exceeds the forward rate.

3. The difference in real interest rates is related to differences in expected rates of inflation. If the real interest rate in the United States exceeds the interest rate in England by 2%, expected inflation in the U.S. exceeds expected inflation in England by 2%.

4. If the pound sterling is trading at a forward premium against the dollar, interest parity suggests that the interest rate on sterling assets must exceed the interest rate on dollar assets

5. If the pound sterling is trading at a forward discount against the dollar, the interest rate on sterling assets must be greater than the interest rate on dollar assets.

SHORT ANSWER QUESTIONS

1. Sterling is trading at $2.00 in the spot market and $1.99 in the 90-day forward market. British interest rates on 90-day paper are 12% while U.S. yields on the same maturities are 6%. Why is this situation unusual? If all four prices (2 exchange rates and 2 interest rates) move to produce the more normal situation, in which direction do each of the four move?

2. Sterling is trading at $2.00 in the spot market and $2.01 in the 90-day forward market. British interest rates on 90-day paper are 7% while U.S. yields on the same maturities are 10%. Why is this situation unusual? If all four prices (2 exchange rates and 2 interest rates) move to produce the more normal situation, in which direction do each of the four move?

3. The Canadian dollar is trading at $0.90 in the spot market and $0.91 in the 180-day forward market. U.S. yields on 180-day paper are 12%. What must the interest rate in Canada be? Why? What does this imply about the expected inflation rate differential?

4. Continuing from question 3, a new governor of the Bank of Canada promises to accelerate money supply growth by 4% when the Canadian economy is close to full employment. What happens to the earlier situation?

5.   Suppose the nominal interest rate in the US equals 10% and the nominal rate in Mexico equals 15% and the rates of inflation in the United States and Mexico are equal to 4 percent. What is the real interest rate in each country?

ANSWERS TO CHAPTER 14 STUDY GUIDE QUESTIONS

Multiple Choice Questions

1.   a
       When the value of the forward rate is lower than the spot rate, the currency's value is expected to fall (depreciate) in the future.

2.   b
       When the value of the forward rate is greater than the spot rate, the currency's value is expected to increase (appreciate) in the future.

3.   b
       A call option gives the owner the right (meaning he or she does not have to fulfill the contract) to purchase a fixed amount of currency during a specific period of time for a specific exchange rate (the strike price).

4.   a
       A put option gives the owner the right (meaning he or she does not have to fulfill the contract) to sell a fixed amount of currency during a specific period of time for a specific exchange rate (the strike price).

5.   c
       A futures contract allows for the purchase or sale of a currency for a specific price with settlement in (usually) 30, 60, or 90 days.

6.   b
       Since the forward rate is less than the spot rate, the currency is trading at a forward discount, implying the Canadian dollar is expected to depreciate against the US dollar.

7.   a
       Investors will choose the US investment, since risk-free profits are possible. (Invest in US dollars and sell dollars on the futures market allows for profit opportunity.) These flows increase the demand for US assets and decrease the demand for Canadian assets, causing the rate on US assets to fall and the rate on Canadian assets to rise.

8.   c
       As investors move funds into US assets, demand for US dollars increases and the US dollar appreciates and the Canadian dollar depreciates in the spot market. Demand for forward Canadian dollars increases, implying the Canadian dollar appreciates in the forward market.

9. b

Suppose you have £100. Investing in British assets yields £105. Investing in French assets yields £111.72. (To find this number: convert £100 into Fr. using spot rate (£100x (Fr.3/£)), invest in Fr. asset (Fr. 300x1.08), and convert into £ using forward rate). Since the French asset yields the higher return and the assets are of similar risk, you will invest in the French asset.

10. d

If the assets are of different risk, you cannot make an informed investment decision without additional information about the risk differential.

True, False, Uncertain and Why Questions

1. False. If the U.S. firm wanted to hedge its risk against exchange rate fluctuations, the firm should purchase a franc call option which locks in a specific price at which the firm can purchase foreign currency.

2. True. When the spot rate exceeds the forward rate, the currency is trading at a forward discount.

3. False. Differences in nominal exchange rates are related to differences in expected inflation rates. If the expected inflation rate in the U.S. exceeds the expected inflation rate in England, the nominal interest rate in the U.S. should exceed the nominal interest rate in England by the same amount.

4. False. When sterling trades at a forward premium, interest rate parity suggests that the interest rate on US assets must exceed the interest rate on UK assets. If the interest rate differential does not equal the forward premium, the opportunity for risk-free profits exist.

5. True. When sterling trades at a forward discount, interest rate parity suggests that the interest rate on UK assets must exceed the interest rate on US assets. If the interest rate differential does not equal the forward premium, the opportunity for risk-free profits exist

Short Answer Questions

1. Since the forward discount on sterling does not equal the interest differential, riskless profits can be made. An investor should buy sterling assets. As capital flows out of dollar denominated assets and into sterling denominated assets, the interest rate in the U.S. rises and the interest rate in England falls. Investors demand spot sterling, which appreciates the currency (depreciates the dollar). In the forward market, the dollar appreciates as investors sell sterling and buy dollars.

2. Since the forward premium on sterling does not equal the interest differential, riskless profits can be made. An investor should buy dollar assets. As capital flows out of sterling denominated assets and into dollar denominated assets the interest rate in the U.S. falls and the interest rate in England rises. Investors demand spot dollars which

appreciates the currency (depreciates sterling). In the forward market, sterling appreciates as investors sell dollars and buy sterling.

3. A 2.22% annual premium exists on Canadian dollars:

$$\frac{(0.91 - 0.90)}{0.90} \cdot \frac{360}{180} = 0.022 = 2.22\%$$

The first term on the left-hand side of the equation is the percent change between the forward and spot rates. Since the forward rate is not an annual rate and the interest rate is an annual rate, the percent change must be converted into annual terms (represented by the second term on the left-hand side of the equation).

According to interest rate parity, the differential between the US and Canadian interest rates must equal to annual premium on Canadian dollars. This implies that the Canadian interest rate must be lower than the interest rate in the United States. It equals 9.778% (US interest rate - Canadian dollar premium = 12.0% - 2.22%).

This implies inflation in the U.S. is expected to be higher than in Canada by 2.22% because real interest rates are arbitraged together.

4. Canadian expected inflation would increase by 4%. The Canadian nominal interest rate must rise by 4% to maintain equal real interest rates. Therefore, the Canadian forward premium of 2.22% becomes a forward discount of 1.778%. The interest rate differential must equal the exchange rate differential. Previously, the US interest rate exceeded the Canadian interest rate, implying a forward premium of 2.22%. Assuming the US interest rate remains constant at 12% and the Canadian interest rate increases from 9.778% to 13.778%, the forward premium becomes a forward discount.

5. The real interest rate equals the nominal rate less inflation. Therefore, the real interest rate in the United States equals 6% and the real interest rate in Canada equals 11%.

CHAPTER 15

ALTERNATIVE MODELS OF BALANCE OF PAYMENTS OR EXCHANGE RATE DETERMINATION

IMPORTANT POINTS

1. This chapter explores the source of changes in the autonomous items in the balance of payments, which cause either payment disequilibria or fluctuations in a floating exchange rate regime. Conditions that generate a balance of payments surplus in the fixed exchange rate world would cause a currency appreciation if the exchange rate was flexible. The chapter also examines why some countries frequently have a deficit (or depreciating currencies) while others seem to experience prolonged surpluses (or appreciating currencies).

2. Balance of payments disequilibria have several effects on an economy. Deficits are of special concern. In a fixed rate world, a continuing deficit implies that the country is losing foreign exchange reserve assets. Eventually, the country will exhaust the supply of reserves and the nation will be unable to pay for any additional imports. If the foreign produced goods are necessities such as oil or food, life within this country can become very difficult. Countries faced with dwindling reserves frequently have unattractive options available. One possibility is a loan from a multilateral organizations such as the International Monetary Fund (IMF). Such loans tend to have stringent conditions attached that may be politically difficult to implement.

3. In addition to the reserve constraint, a payments deficit has other implications. The loss of export sales has a recessionary impact on a Keynesian macroeconomy. The reduction in exports decreases aggregate demand, lowering total output and income through the multiplier effect. For example, if the multiplier is 2 and exports fall by $100 billion, output decreases by $200 billion. If the economy was already weak, the decrease in output may generate a nasty recession.

4.   Balance of payments disequilibria under fixed rates also affects the money supply. A balance of payments surplus requires the central bank to sell local currency (or buy foreign currency) in the exchange market. This increases member bank reserves of the commercial banks, increasing the money supply. If the economy is operating close to full employment, this expansionary monetary policy could be inflationary. If the central bank wanted to pursue a contractionary monetary policy, a balance of payments surplus hinders its effectiveness. Table 15-1 shows the effects of the surplus on the domestic money supply, assuming a reserve requirement of 10 percent and a payments surplus of $5 million dollars (MBR denotes member bank reserves, FXR denote foreign exchange reserves, and DD denotes demand deposits).

Table 15-1:   Effect of Balance of Payments Surplus on the Domestic Money Supply

Central Bank		One Commercial Bank		All Commercial Banks	
+$5m FXR	+$5m MBR	+$5m MBR	+$5m DD	+$5m MBR +45m loans	+$50m DD

Through the deposit multiplier effect, the initial increase in member bank reserves causes an increase in the money supply of $50 million. The money supply increases regardless of the wishes of the central bank. If the central bank wants to offset the change in the money supply, it can sterilize. In the case of a surplus, the central bank must sell domestic treasury bills (or other domestic assets), which decreases the money supply. If the open market sale is enough to offset the increase in the stock of base money generated by the payments surplus, the net change in the money supply is zero.

Impacts of a balance of trade surplus can also be illustrated using the national income accounting identities. Recall that domestic output is given by:

$$Y = C + I + G + (X - M) \qquad (15.1)$$

$$(X - M) = Y - (C + I + G). \qquad (15.2)$$

The $5 million surplus (X > M by $5 million) means that the country is producing $5 million more real output than domestic residents are using. If the government's objective is to maximize the welfare of its citizens, chronic current account surpluses which accumulate foreign assets, may not be an optimal situation because domestic residents are compelled to absorb less than they produce in exchange for financial assets which may decline in value due to inflation.

5.   The same analysis can be applied to a deficit situation. In this case, the central bank must sell foreign exchange that diminishes the domestic money supply via the money multiplier. If the country is below full employment, the reduction in the money supply could push the economy into a recession. The central bank can sterilize by purchasing domestic assets and increasing the money supply. While sterilization can offset the

deficit's effects on the money supply, managing an independent monetary policy in the face of large payments disequilibria is difficult.

6. Chapter 15 examines two alternative theories of payments disequilibria. The traditional or Keynesian approach to balance-of-payments equilibrium focuses on the current account. The capital account is analyzed separately, with capital flows driven by risk and rates of return differences. The monetarist model, associated with neo-classical macroeconomic theory, looks at the accounts as a whole and is less concerned with individual items within the accounts.

In the Keynesian model, the balance of trade (BOT) is defined as the world price of exports times the amount exported minus the total import bill. This definition can be expressed as follows:

$$BOT = P_X \cdot Q_X - P_M \cdot Q_M \qquad (15.3)$$

If the country does not possess any market power in trade, the prices of imports and exports are fixed. Imports are viewed as a function of income and the real exchange rate:

$$Q_M = f(\overset{+}{Y_D}, \overset{+}{XR_R}) \qquad (15.4)$$

Imports rise with the real exchange rate and domestic income. If the real exchange rate increases, imports become cheaper since domestic currency can buy more foreign goods. Imports tend to be cyclical, falling during recessions and increasing during periods of prosperity.

Exports depend on the level of foreign incomes and the real exchange rate:

$$Q_X = f(\overset{+}{Y_F}, \overset{-}{XR_R}) \qquad (15.5)$$

If income in foreign countries increases, foreigners consume more of all goods including exports from this country. This means that the volume of goods exported to the rest of the world rises. If the real exchange rate increases, meaning that the domestic currency has become stronger, exports decline due to a loss of price-competitiveness. For example, suppose one dollar exchanges for one pound and British citizens import $10 billion worth of United States' goods. If both countries have the same rate of inflation and the dollar appreciates against the pound, causing one dollar to exchange for more than one pound, British imports of U.S. goods decline since U.S. products are relatively more expensive.

Substituting (15.4) and (15.5) into equation (15.3) yields:

$$BOT = f(\overset{+}{P_X}, \overset{-}{P_M}, \overset{-}{Y_D}, \overset{+}{Y_F}, \overset{-}{XR_R}) \qquad (15.6)$$

The balance of trade is positively related to the world price of exports and the level of foreign income. The balance of trade is negatively related to the world price of imports, the level of domestic income, and the real exchange rate. The terms-of-trade (P_X/P_M) are determined in world markets. The stability of the price ratio depends, to a degree, on the structure of the export and import markets. If the markets are highly competitive, prices could fluctuate sharply. If the market is oligopolistic, prices tend to be more stable. If the terms-of-trade are volatile, which is frequently true for developing countries, the trade balance for the country will also be volatile.

7. The role of domestic income in the Keynesian model suggests the cyclical linkage between trading partners. When the country experiences a boom, the trade balance for the country worsens while the balance of trade for its trading partners improves. On the other hand, if the rest of the world experiences a boom, the trade balance for the domestic economy improves as exports to its trading partners increase.

8. The capital account can be viewed as the result of moving funds from one country to another in search of the highest possible return. Differences in risks also generate capital flows. For example, if an investor decides to place his or her money in either sterling or rupee denominated assets, the differences in risk as well as interest rates and forward premiums or discounts influence his or her final choice. If the rupee yields a 2% higher real rate of return, the investor may opt for the pound asset if the rupee asset is considered risky. The capital account can be expressed as:

$$KA = f(\overset{+}{r_D},\ \overset{-}{r_F},\ \overset{-}{risk_D},\ \overset{+}{risk_F}). \tag{15.7}$$

If the domestic rate of interest exceeds the foreign rate, capital will flow into the economy. If the domestic asset is believed to be more risky, capital will flow out of the country. Thus, the capital account is positively related to the domestic interest rate and foreign level of risk, and is negatively related to the foreign rate of interest and the domestic level of risk.

9. A different approach to the capital account, known as the portfolio balance approach, focuses on the behavior of an investment manager. This individual has a fixed stock of capital to invest at any given time. The investment manager knows the past yields and risks associated with alternative assets and uses this information to form expectations about future yields. Based on past information and expectations about the future, the investment manager develops an ideal portfolio, designed to maximize yield subject to a risk constraint. Diversification is an important way to reduce risk. Placing all capital in similar investments (such as 100 shares of IBM and 100 shares of Apple Computer) does little to reduce the portfolio's exposure to risk since most events which decrease the value of IBM stock will tend to lower the value of the Apple stock as well. Diversity in types of assets reduces overall risk in the portfolio. The investment manager may seek to diversify internationally in order to reduce risk since countries tend to experience different timing in their business cycles. Once the actual portfolio matches the desired portfolio, capital flows cease, despite the continued existence of interest differentials.

When expected yields change, the ideal or desired portfolio is affected. If foreign interest rates increase, capital will flow toward the area of increased yield until the adjusted portfolio matches the optimal one. Capital flows cease once adjustment to the recent changes in interest rates is completed. The capital account can be represented as

$$KA = f(\overset{+}{\Delta r_D}, \overset{-}{\Delta r_F}, \overset{-}{\Delta risk_D}, \overset{+}{\Delta risk_F}) \qquad (15.8)$$

where the Δ denotes change. Thus, the capital account is a positive function of the recent change in domestic interest rates and foreign risk perception. The account is negatively related to recent changes in the foreign interest rate and domestic risk perception.

10.   Combining the expression for the capital and current accounts yields the following expression:

$$BOP = f(\overset{+}{P_X}, \overset{-}{P_M}, \overset{-}{Y_D}, \overset{+}{Y_F}, \overset{-}{XR_R}, \overset{+}{\Delta r_D}, \overset{-}{\Delta r_F}, \overset{-}{\Delta risk_D}, \overset{+}{\Delta risk_F}). \qquad (15.9)$$

An increase in P_X, Y_F, Δr_D, or $\Delta risk_F$ will cause an improvement in the balance of payments, or an appreciation. An increase in P_M, Y_D, XR_R, Δr_F, or $\Delta risk_D$ will generate a worsening of the balance of payments, or a depreciation.

11.   As noted in chapter 13, the volume of capital account transactions has become greater than current account transactions as sources of demand for and supply of foreign exchange for industrialized countries. Thus, many economists view the exchange markets and the balance of payments as financial entities and ignore the impact of factors that influence the current account. The exchange market is viewed as reflecting the supply and demand for financial assets denominated in various currencies. If demand for foreign assets decreases, a payments surplus or appreciation occurs. The asset market approach uses these concepts to model the balance of payments. Two sub-categories of the asset market approach exist; the portfolio balance theory, described above, and the monetarist model. The difference between the two approaches centers on the degree of substitutability between foreign and domestic assets. The portfolio balance model assumes that these assets are viewed as imperfect substitutes due to problems of risk. The monetarist model assumes away any risk differentials, meaning that foreign and domestic assets are viewed as perfect substitutes.

12.   The monetarist model assumes that markets are perfectly competitive and automatically adjust toward equilibrium if a shock occurs. Money is neutral, meaning that changes in the money supply do not have any permanent effect on real output or employment. Investment managers view foreign and domestic assets as perfect substitutes. Walras' law also is basic to this approach. It states that, if an economy is modeled as an all-inclusive set of markets, when one market is in excess demand, another market must be in excess supply. Since the asset market approach emphasizes financial transactions, the relevant markets are the money market, and the bond (and goods) market. Thus, if incomes fall causing an excess supply of money (at the current level of the real money supply), Walras' law necessitated that an excess demand for bonds/goods exists.

The demand for money is assumed to be a stable function of GNP. If real income rises by 10%, money demand also rises by 10%. If the central bank, trying to expand output, increases the money supply by 12%, money demand still only increases by 10%. In a closed economy, this excessive monetary expansion generates a 2% increase in the price level, which lowers the rate of real money supply growth to 10%.

With an open economy under the assumptions of perfect competition, zero transportation costs or other barriers to entry, prices of the same good in two countries should be equal. The law of one price depicts this relationship:

$$P_D = \frac{P_{ROW}}{XR_n} \qquad (15.10)$$

The domestic price of tradable goods (P_D) must equal the foreign price (P_{ROW}) divided by the nominal exchange rate (XR_n). If this equality does not hold, profits can be made buying goods in one country, shipping them to the other country for resale, (assuming no tariffs or transportation costs) which will force the prices to equality. The existence of non-traded goods is ignored. If the law of one price holds in financial markets and assets are perfect substitutes, the domestic and foreign interest rates should be identical. Any increase in the domestic interest rate will generate capital inflows, causing a reduction in the differential. Thus, any disequilibrium in either the goods market or the bond market causes large balance of payments flows.

13. In the monetarist model, the balance of payments is the mechanism through which domestic market imbalances are corrected when exchange rates are fixed. Suppose all markets are in equilibrium and the money supply is increased by 10%. An excess supply of money exists. Walras' law states that this excess supply of money is matched by an excess demand for goods and bonds. The shortage of goods and assets generates an increase in imports of goods and financial assets as domestic residents seek to lower the amount of cash they hold. The trade and capital accounts move toward deficit, which reduces the money supply until the money market equilibrium is restored. Thus balance of payments disequilibria are both the result of monetary policy errors and the source of their reversal. The balance of payments will automatically adjust the markets for money, goods, and bonds to equilibrium if the central bank does not interfere with the process through sterilization.

14. A simple mathematical model of the monetary approach is developed. Money demand is a positive function of income and a negative function of the interest rate under the assumption that money itself does not pay interest:

$$\overset{+ \ -}{M^D = f(Y, r)} \qquad (15.11)$$

The money supply is a function of the reserve requirement (rr) and the stock of base money (which is the sum of domestic assets (DA) of the central bank and foreign exchange reserves (FXR) held by the central bank):

$$M^S = 1/rr \cdot (stock \ of \ base \ money) \qquad (15.12)$$
$$base \ money = DA + FXR$$
$$(due \ to \ the \ balance \ sheet \ identity \ for \ the \ central \ bank) \qquad (15.13)$$

$$M^S = 1/rr \cdot (DA + FXR) \qquad (15.14)$$

In equilibrium, $M^D = M^S$. Setting (11) and (14) equal to each other implies:

$$f(Y, r) = 1/rr \cdot (DA + FXR) \qquad (15.15)$$

Since interest rates cannot change (law of one price in the bond market) and the reserve ratio is assumed fixed, the change in money demand can be written:

$$f(\Delta Y) = \Delta DA + \Delta FXR \qquad (15.16)$$

The balance of payments equals changes in foreign exchange reserves. Rewriting (16) in terms of ΔFXR:

$$\Delta FXR = BOP = f(\overset{+}{\Delta Y}, \overset{-}{\Delta DA}) \qquad (15.17)$$

The balance of payments is a positive function of a change in income and a negative function of a change in domestic assets of the central bank.

15. The monetarist model is not without criticisms. In this analysis, the central bank was assumed to be an autonomous agency. In many countries, monetary policy is not independently carried out by the central bank but instead is dominated by the finance minister and/or the president or prime minister. If the country is running a budget deficit, the central bank may be forced to monetize that deficit. This pattern is particularly common in developing countries. Thus, placing blame on the central bank for excessive monetary policies may not be warranted because the ultimate cause of the payments deficit is a large budget deficit that the central bank is compelled to monetize.

16. Another problem with the monetarist approach centers on the stability of the demand for money. A stable relationship between GNP and the demand for money (measured by the velocity of money) is an important component of the theory. Empirical studies in recent years indicate that the velocity of money has become more volatile. One possible reason for the change is currency substitution. The monetary model assumes that within the borders of a country, the domestic currency has a monopoly as the local money. This means that in England, all transactions are carried out in sterling. While exchange in goods occurs primarily in sterling, financial accounts may be denominated in several currencies. Thus, individuals or firms can substitute among currencies as the expected yield or value of the exchange rate changes. This weakens the linkage between output and the demand for local money.

17. Empirical evidence suggests that these models of the balance of payments perform reasonably well for countries with fixed exchange rates. With flexible exchange rates, these models are not as successful in explaining changes in the exchange rate. One

possible reason for this difficulty is speculative capital flows that are particularly important in a flexible exchange rate market.

CHAPTER OBJECTIVES

After studying the concepts presented in Chapter 15, you should be able to answer the following questions:

1. Why are balance of payments deficits of special concern to a country? Why can a country not maintain a payments deficit indefinitely?

2. What impact does a large deficit have on the effectiveness of monetary policy? What is the role of sterilization?

3. How is the capital account modeled under the portfolio balance approach?

4. What role do balance of payments imbalances play in the monetary model? What is the relationship between payments deficits or surpluses and the money market? Explain.

GLOSSARY TERMS

- asset market model of the balance of payments
- base money
- law of one price
- monetarist model of the balance of payments
- portfolio balance model
- purchasing power parity
- Walras law

CHAPTER 15 STUDY GUIDE QUESTIONS

Multiple Choice Questions

1. In the portfolio balance model, international capital flows

    a. respond to differences in yield levels.
    b. respond to differences in yield and risk levels.
    c. respond to changes in yields.
    d. respond to changes in yields and risks.

2.   A balance of payments deficit requires that the central bank

   a.   sell domestic currency, which increases the domestic money supply.
   b.   sell foreign exchange reserves, which increases the domestic money supply.
   c.   sell foreign exchange reserves, which decreases the domestic money supply.
   d.   purchase foreign exchange reserves, which decreases the domestic money supply.

3.   According to the Keynesian model, the volume of goods exported is

   a.   positively related to foreign incomes and negatively related to the real exchange rate.
   b.   negatively related to foreign incomes and negatively related to the real exchange rate.
   c.   negatively related to foreign incomes and positively related to the real exchange rate.
   d.   positively related to foreign incomes and positively related to the real exchange rate.

4.   According to the portfolio balance approach, risk is reduced through

   a.   investing in only highly rated bonds.
   b.   avoiding risky growth funds.
   c.   diversification.
   d.   investing in similar types of equities.

5.   According to the monetarist model,

   a.   money is neutral, meaning that purely monetary factors have permanent effects on real variables.
   b.   money is neutral, meaning that purely monetary factors cannot have permanent effects on real variables.
   c.   money is not neutral, meaning that purely monetary factors have permanent effects on real variables.
   d.   money is not neutral, meaning that purely monetary factors cannot have permanent effects on real variables.

6.   Walras' Law states that if excess demand exists in one market,

   a.   the price of that good must increase.
   b.   all other markets must have an excess supply.
   c.   another market must have an excess supply.
   d.   the price of that good must decrease.

7. According to the monetarist model, excessive expansion in the money supply in a closed economy causes

    a. output to expand at a proportional rate.
    b. money demand to fall.
    c. an decrease in the unemployment rate.
    d. price inflation.

8. If the exchange rate is two pounds to the dollar and the British price of golf clubs is £1200 pounds, the U.S. price must be $600. This is known as

    a. the law of equal cost.
    b. purchasing power parity.
    c. the law of one price.
    d. exchange rate parity.

9. One problem with the monetarist approach is the fact that

    a. the law of one price is frequently violated.
    b. the velocity of money may not be stable.
    c. both a and b.
    d. neither a nor b.

10. According to the monetarist model of the balance of payments, an increase in domestic income will

    a. increase the interest rate
    b. increase exports
    c. decrease the interest rate
    d. increase foreign exchange reserves

True, False, Uncertain and Why Questions

When answering the following questions, be sure to support your assertion of true, false or uncertain with two or three sentences.

1. According to the portfolio balance model, a decrease in the risk associated with a particular asset will generate permanent capital flows.

2. According to the Keynesian model, a country's trade balance is positively correlated with domestic and foreign income levels.

3. By investing half of your portfolio in 30-year Goodyear bonds and half in 30-year IBM bonds, the risk associated with your portfolio is significantly reduced.

4.   According to the monetarist model, an increase in income cannot permanently affect the balance of payments.

5.   According to the monetarist model, an increase in the money supply will create a balance of payments surplus.

Short Answer Questions

1.   Assume a balance of payments deficit decreases the stock of base money by $10 million dollars. Show the effects of the deficit on the money supply of the country. Assume the reserve requirement equals 10 percent.

Central Bank	One Commercial Bank	All Commercial Banks

2.   Continuing from question 1, show the effects on the domestic money supply if the central bank decides to sterilize.

Central Bank	One Commercial Bank	All Commercial Banks

For questions 3 through 5 use the monetarist model of the balance of payments to explain in Walrasian terms what happens in Country A in each of the given situations.

3.   Country A imposes a 10 percent tariff on all imports and uses the resulting funds to provide a 10 percent subsidy for all export sales. All goods are either exported or imported.

4.   A significant revaluation of the local currency. What impact does the size of the tradable goods sector have on the process?

5.   A decrease in the share of people's wealth that they desire to hold in the form of money, and an offsetting increase in the share they desire to hold as bonds.

ANSWERS TO CHAPTER 15 STUDY GUIDE QUESTIONS

Multiple Choice Questions

1.   d
The portfolio balance approach is a stock adjustment view of the capital account. Capital flows are generated by changes in yields or risks. Because assets are not perfect substitutes, yield differentials between assets can exist without generating continuing capital flows.

2.   c
A balance of payments deficit implies an excess demand for foreign exchange and an excess supply of domestic currency. The central bank must sell foreign exchange reserves and purchase domestic currency, which decreases the domestic money supply.

3.   a
If foreign incomes increase, country A's exports rise (through the foreign marginal propensity to import). If the real exchange rate increases, exports become more expensive and the volume of goods exported declines.

4.   c
To reduce risk, a portfolio manager should invest in different types of assets. If the portfolio consists solely of equities or solely of bonds, risk is not greatly reduced. If, however the portfolio consists of equities, bonds, and short-term assets, risk is reduced.

5.   b
According to the monetarist model, changes in monetary variables do not permanently affect income or employment. Thus, money is considered to be neutral.

6.   c
According to Walras Law and assuming an all-inclusive set of markets, if one market is not in equilibrium, an offsetting or opposite equilibrium must exist elsewhere in the economy.

7.   d
Since money is neutral, expansion of the money supply causes inflation, meaning the real money supply remains unchanged.

8.   c
The law of one-price states that the same good, under certain assumptions, will have the same price in different countries and currencies, once the exchange rate is considered.

9.   c
       Money demand (velocity of money) is not stable and the law of one price is frequently violated.

10.   d
       The higher income level increases money demand that creates an excess demand for money at the current interest rate. According to Walras' Law, an excess demand for money must be offset by an excess supply of goods/bond, creating a balance of payments surplus. As a result of the surplus, foreign exchange reserves increase to restore equilibrium.

True, False, Uncertain and Why Questions

1.   False. A change in risk associated with a particular asset generates only temporary capital flows.

2.   False. A country's trade balance is positively associated with foreign income levels since an increase in foreign income increases the country's exports, improving the trade balance. The balance of trade is negatively related to the country's own level of income since an increase in this value will increase imports (through the marginal propensity to import) which worsens the trade account.

3.   False. To reduce risk, the portfolio should include different types of assets. IBM and Goodyear 30-year bonds are close substitutes, when the value of IBM bonds falls, the value of Goodyear bonds probably falls as well. Only default risk is reduced.

4.   True. An increase in income increases the demand for money that generates a temporary balance of payments surplus. The money supply adjusts to restore money market equilibrium and eliminate the payments surplus.

5.   False. An increase in the money supply creates an excess supply of money and an excess demand for goods and bonds, resulting in a balance of payments deficit. The subsequent decrease in foreign exchange reserves decreases the money supply until equilibrium is restored.

Short Answer Questions

1.

Central Bank		One Commercial Bank		All Commercial Banks	
-$10m FXR	-$10m MBR	-$10m MBR	-$10m DD	-$10m MBR -$90m loans	-$100m DD

where

FXR = foreign exchange reserves
MBR = member bank reserves
DD = demand deposits

2.

Central Bank		One Commercial Bank		All Commercial Banks	
+$10m TB	+$10m MBR	+$10m MBR	+$10m DD.	+$10m MBR +$90m loans	+$100m DD.

where TB = domestic treasury bills

3.   As a result of the tariff and subsidy, prices of all goods in country A rise by 10%. The real money supply (M/P) falls by 10%. An excess demand for money exists so, according to Walras Law, an excess supply of goods and bonds must also exist. This results in a balance of payments surplus that increases the nominal money supply, as the central bank buys foreign exchange. This process of adjustment continues until the nominal money supply increases by 10% and the country is back in equilibrium with the real money supply unchanged.

4.   The dominant impact of a revaluation is to reduce the price of tradable goods. Eventually this extends to the prices of non-tradables, so that the overall price level falls by the percentage of the revaluation. The more open the economy, the smaller the role of non-tradables prices, and the more rapid the process. As the price level falls, the real money supply rises. The real money supply now exceeds money demand, so there is excess demand for goods and bonds. The balance of payments goes into deficit, which drains the excess money out of the system. This should continue until the real money supply has fallen to its original level.

5.   This is another reason for a decline in money demand, but the offset is now only an excess demand for bonds, not for goods. Only the capital account goes into deficit, not the current account. The balance of payments deficit lowers the money supply as

bonds flow in from abroad. This continues until domestic residents have the increased holdings of bonds and reduced holdings of money that they desire.

CHAPTER 16

PAYMENTS ADJUSTMENT WITH FIXED EXCHANGE RATES

IMPORTANT POINTS

1. This chapter examines the balance-of-payments adjustment process under the assumption of fixed exchange rates. One mechanism for the elimination of payments surpluses or deficits is the specie flow mechanism. This system, associated with David Hume, is automatic. In other words, the restoration of equilibrium does not depend on the decisions of a central bank or another government official. Under specie flow, national currencies are backed completely by gold, which is the only foreign exchange reserve asset. This means that the money supply of a country is solely determined by the stock of gold held by the central bank or government. A balance-of-payments surplus means that gold flows into the country's central bank, which increases the money supply. The higher money stock lowers domestic interest rates, generating capital outflows, and reducing any surplus in the capital account. The price level also increases causing imports to rise and exports to fall (which affects the current account). The level of economic activity and income also rises, which raises imports. If, however, the economy is operating close to full employment, real output and incomes cannot rise, so inflation increases. This adjustment process continues until equilibrium is restored in the balance-of-payments.

When a country experiences a payments deficit, specie flow generates the same sort of adjustment process. The money supply falls as a result of the loss of gold caused by the deficit. The decrease in the stock of money causes interest rates to rise, prices to fall, and output to decline, all of which reduce the deficit. This automatic adjustment process is recessionary. If prices are downward sticky and the economy is significantly below full employment output, the process of adjustment is extremely painful.

Some small countries use the currency of another country rather than having their own currency. The specie-flow mechanism describes the process by which balance of payments adjustment occurs.

Currency boards are similar to central banks in the sense that that they hold foreign exchange reserves. These institutions cannot, however, purchase domestic assets. This implies that the currency board cannot sterilize the effects of a balance of payments disequilibrium. A payments deficit will lower the money supply as foreign exchange reserves decrease.

The specie flow payments model operates as the adjustment process between regions within a country. When North Carolina residents receive more payments from non-residents than they send outside the state, a payments surplus exists. The stock of dollars held by North Carolinians increases by the amount of the surplus. Member bank reserves for North Carolina banks also rise as checks clear (assuming that payments are made in the form of a check), which increases the amount of money the banks have to lend to residents. Higher incomes and inflation in North Carolina cause the surplus to decline. Thus, the adjustment process is similar to the one previously described for a country.

2.   A useful tool for analyzing the balance-of-payments adjustment process is the IS/LM/BB approach, which is an extension of the Keynesian model. The domestic economy is divided into a real sector (representing the goods market) and a money market. Equilibrium in the real sector is represented by the IS line and occurs whenever intended investment (I_i) equals savings (S). Intended investment, which does not include unintended inventory accumulation, is a negative function of the interest rate (r). If the interest rate increases, investment becomes more expensive, and businesses are less willing to borrow money for expansion or other investment purposes. Savings depends upon the level of domestic income (Y). Through the marginal propensity to save, an increase in income generates a rise in savings. The IS line represents all values of the interest rate and income which correspond to the $S = I_i$ identity.

Figure 16-1: The IS Curve

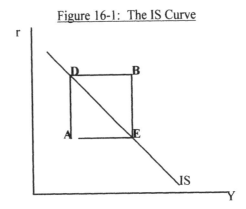

At point A, I_i exceeds S. In order to reestablish the equality between savings and investment, either interest rates must increase (moving to point D with lower I_i) or income must rise (moving to point E with increased savings), or some combination of both. At point B, savings exceeds I_i. If income falls (moving to point D with reduced savings) or interest rates decrease (moving to point E with higher I_i), savings will equal intended investment. Thus, along the IS curve, GNP is at its equilibrium level.

The slope of the IS curve measures the sensitivity of the economy to changes in the interest rate and the marginal propensity to save. A relatively steep IS curve implies either that investment is insensitive to changes in the interest rate or a high marginal propensity to save. Thus, any fluctuation in interest rates or income generates a movement along the curve. A change in the marginal propensity to save or the degree of investment sensitivity to the interest rate will change the slope of the IS line.

Due to the limitations of two-dimensional graphs, only the effects of two variables that influence the savings/investment relationship can be shown. Obviously, factors such as fiscal policy or a change in exports affect income, which, in turn, affects the savings and investment identity. Any change in these exogenous variables will shift the IS curve. For example, an increase in foreign income (increasing exports) or government spending (G) will shift the IS curve outward. Equation (6.1) illustrates the relationship between the exogenous factors and savings and investment (I is actual investment. Only in equilibrium will intended investment equal actual investment):

$$I = S_P + (T - G) + (M - X). \tag{16.1}$$

3. Equilibrium in the money market, which is represented by the LM curve, occurs when money demand (M^D) equals money supply (M^S). The demand for money is a positive function of the level of income and a negative function of the interest rate. As GNP rises, more transactions occur, and money is demanded to complete those transactions. A rise in the interest rate increases the opportunity cost of holding money. Residents hold income in either money or bonds. As interest rates rise, residents want to hold more bonds and less money. The money supply is determined outside the model (by the central bank, represented by equation (16.3)). The relationship between money demand and money supply can be shown:

$$M^D = f(\overset{+}{Y}, \overset{-}{r}) \tag{16.2}$$

$$M^S = M^S_0 \tag{16.3}$$

$$M^D = M^S. \tag{16.4}$$

The LM curve represents all combinations of interest rates and income levels that satisfy equation (16.4). Along the LM line, the money supply is constant at MS_0. If the central bank increases the money supply, the LM curve shifts outward (to LM'). If the central bank decreases the money supply, the LM curve shifts to the left (to LM"), as shown in Figure 16-2.

Figure 16-2: The LM Curve

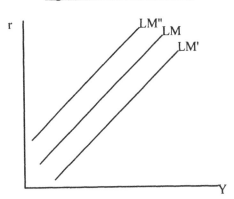

4. Domestic macroeconomic equilibrium can be shown using the IS/LM framework. Figure 16-3 illustrates the equilibrium values of r and Y that maintain both goods market and money market equilibrium. When the interest rate is r1 and income is Y1, savings equals intended investment and money demand equals money supply. Expansionary fiscal policy (an increase in G or decrease in T) causes the IS curve to shift to the right. Income rises through the multiplier effect. As income increases (to Y2), the demand for money rises, placing upward pressure on the interest rate (to r2) in order to choke off the excess money demand. Figure 16-3 shows the impact of expansionary fiscal policy.

Figure 16-3: The Effects of Expansionary Fiscal Policy:

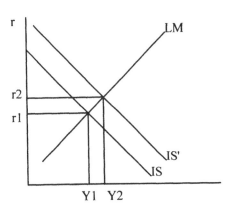

If the LM line was vertical, the expansionary effect of fiscal policy would be completely crowded out by the increase in the interest rate.

5. To represent equilibrium in the balance-of-payments, the BB line is added to the IS/LM analysis. Payments equilibrium occurs whenever the sum of the capital (KA) and current (CA) accounts equals zero. The current account depends upon the level of income. If income rises, residents increase consumption of all goods, imports included, which worsens the trade account. When the domestic interest rate fluctuates, the balance on the capital account changes as capital flows to the area of highest

return. The slope of the BB line indicates the impact of the interest rate on the capital account relative to the effect of domestic income on imports. If capital markets are highly integrated and capital flows are highly responsive to interest rate changes, the BB line is relatively flat. If the marginal propensity to import is low, an increase in income generates a small increase in the quantity of imports, which would also make the BB line relatively flat. Figure 16-4 shows the BB line.

Figure 16-4: The BB Curve

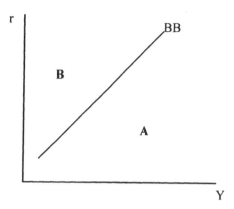

All points (such as point A) to the right of the BB line represent a balance-of-payments deficit. All points (such as point B) to the left of the BB line represent a balance-of-payments surplus. A change in foreign income, foreign interest rates, or the exchange rate causes a shift in the BB line. For example, an increase in foreign income increases foreign demand for local goods, increasing the level of exports and shifting the BB curve to the right.

6. Introducing the BB curve to the IS/LM framework shows balance-of-payments equilibrium as well as equilibrium in the goods and money markets. Figure 16-5 shows an economy experiencing a balance-of-payments deficit.

Figure 16-5: IS/LM/BB Graph with a Payments Deficit

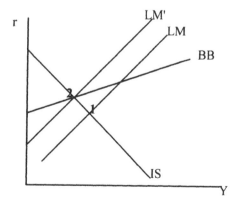

At point 1, only the goods and the money markets are in equilibrium. A balance-of-payments deficit exists. Under the specie-flow system, the balance-of-payments deficit reduces the money supply, shifting LM to the left (to LM'). Both external and internal equilibrium are restored at point 2.

7. The international financial system developed at Bretton Woods tried to avoid the total lack of monetary policy independence inherent in the specie flow model. For minor and temporary disequilibria, the system was to operate without macro policy changes. Deficits were to be financed with reserve losses, with the monetary effects of the losses offset by sterilization. If payments problems were more serious, both fiscal and monetary policies were to be used. Deficit countries should implement restrictive monetary and fiscal policies while the surplus nations were supposed to use expansionary policies. If the payments problem appeared to be chronic, a change in the exchange rate should be used. If the country was experiencing a deficit, its currency would be devalued, increasing exports and reducing imports.

The effects of tight monetary policy are similar to those described in Figure 16-5. Figure 16-6 shows the effects of tight fiscal policy under a payments deficit.

Figure 16-6: Tight Fiscal Policy with Payments Deficit

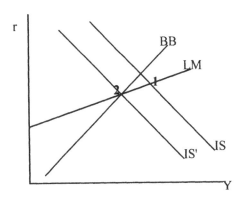

As the government reduces spending or increases taxes, income falls, shifting the IS curve to the left (to IS'). While the tightening of fiscal policy eliminates the deficit, the reduction in GNP is smaller with monetary policy, as can be seen by noting how much LM would have to shift to the left in Figure 16-6 to restore equilibrium.

Figure 16-6 assumed that the LM line was flatter than the BB line. This may not be the case. When capital is extremely mobile between countries, the BB line can be flatter than the LM line. This change in the slope of the curves changes the type of fiscal policy needed to eliminate the deficit. Figure 16-7 illustrates this example.

Figure 16-7: Expansionary Fiscal Policy with Payments Deficit

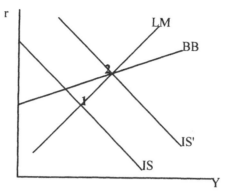

When BB is flatter than LM, the appropriate fiscal policy is an increase in government spending or a decrease in taxes. This shifts the IS curve to the right (to IS'), and restores balance-of-payments equilibrium at a higher level of income (pt. 1 to pt. 2). The expansionary fiscal policy increases the domestic interest rate, generating large capital inflows.

8.   The use of monetary and fiscal policy to correct payments disequilibria under the Bretton Woods system was not too successful. Surplus countries were often unwilling to implement expansionary policies. Without help from these nations, deficit countries had to tighten policies by even more. Such recessionary measures are very painful and deficit countries often used other means such as protectionism and capital controls to reduce the payments imbalance.

9.   The Meade conflict cases describe four situations in which a country may find itself:

1.   Balance-of-payments surplus and a domestic recession.
2.   Balance-of-payments deficit and domestic inflation.
3.   Balance-of-payments surplus and domestic inflation.
4.   Balance-of-payments deficit and domestic recession.

        Both problems in cases one and two can be solved using domestic macro policies. Case one calls for expansionary fiscal and monetary policies that will reduce the surplus and spur recovery from the recession, while case two calls for the opposite policies. Cases three and four present problems, and are known as the Meade conflict cases. If a country tries to restore payments equilibrium, case three suggests expansionary policies are needed. However, these measures worsen inflation. Tight fiscal and monetary policies that reduce inflation worsen the payments surplus. Case four also presents a similar conflict. The deficit implies that tight monetary and fiscal policies should be used, which worsens the country's recession, while the expansionary policies that will end the recession would worsen the payments deficit.

10.   The policy-assignment model is an attempt to find a way out of the problems suggested by the Meade conflict cases. The idea is that if the government has at least

as many policy tools as it has goals, the government should be able to develop a set of policies that will reach all of the goals simultaneously. Each policy tool is targeted at the goal on which it has the greatest relative impact. According to proponents of this theory, monetary policy has the greatest effect on the balance-of-payments and should be used to correct any payments distortions. Fiscal policy should be used to influence the level of domestic output.

Figure 16-14 (in the text) illustrates how this model works. The DD line represents all combinations of fiscal and monetary policies that produce a desired level of output. The slope of the line indicates the relative effectiveness of the two policies on the domestic economy. When DD is flat, fiscal policy is more effective in influencing domestic output than monetary policy. The FF line represents all combinations of fiscal and monetary policy that produce a balance-of-payments equilibrium. When FF is steep, monetary policy is more powerful in correcting payments problems than fiscal policy. When attempting to move from a disequilibrium situation to the crossing point of the two lines, it is important that fiscal policy be used to deal with the domestic economy and that monetary policy be assigned to payments equilibrium. Incorrect assignment of the policies worsens the conditions the country is experiencing. If, for example, the country has a deficit and inflation, and implements expansionary fiscal policy to reach payments equilibrium and monetary policy to reach full employment, equilibrium does not occur (see Figure 16-15 in the text).

11. The policy assignment model can also be shown using the IS/LM/BB framework. In Figure 16-8, case four is presented.

Figure 16-8: IS/LM/BB with Payments Deficit and Recession

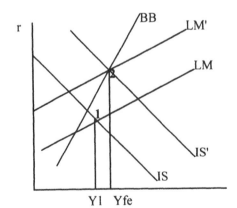

The economy is operating at less than full employment (Y1<Y_{FE}) and has a payments deficit (pt. 1). Using the policy assignment model, the money supply should be reduced, shifting the LM curve to the left (to LM'). Expansionary fiscal policy should be used to shift the IS curve to the right (to IS'). Equilibrium occurs at point 2, where output equals the full employment level and the payments disequilibrium disappears.

12. The policy assignment model is not without flaws. The capital account operate in a portfolio balance framework. If this is considered, the model will not work since high interest rates would only generate temporary flows of capital. The model also assumes that only two goals exist that the government cares about: the balance-of-payments and output at full employment. If the government is concerned with other things such as long-term economic growth, monetary and fiscal policies cannot be used solely to pursue the two goals of the policy assignment model. Additional policy tools are needed, which leads to a discussion of the exchange rate as the dominant route to balance-of-payments adjustment.

13. The previous discussion analyzed the effects of a single country's attempts to manage its balance of payments. A sizable literature focusing on the possibilities of coordinated macroeconomic policies has developed in recent decades, although neither the literature nor the experience of industrialized countries suggests that coordinated policy efforts can do much to restore equilibrium.

CHAPTER OBJECTIVES

After studying the concepts presented in Chapter 16, you should be able to answer the following questions:

1. Why are balance-of-payments surpluses or deficits temporary in the specie flow model?

2. How are the IS and LM curves derived? What information do the slopes of these lines tell you? What causes the slopes to change? What factors generate shifts in the curves?

3. What is the relevance of the BB line? When is the BB line flatter than the LM line? What factors shift the BB line?

4. Using the specie flow model and the IS/LM/BB diagram, show how equilibrium is restored if the country has a payments surplus (or deficit).

5. What are the Meade conflict cases? List each case and explain the appropriate fiscal and monetary policies to correct each problem.

6. What are the flaws in the policy assignment model?

GLOSSARY TERMS

- BB line
- policy assignment model
- LM line
- IS line

CHAPTER 16 STUDY GUIDE QUESTIONS

Multiple Choice Questions

1. According to the specie flow model, a balance-of-payments surplus

    a. raises domestic interest rates.
    b. puts upward pressure on the price level.
    c. puts downward pressure on real incomes.
    d. both a and b.

2. The IS line represents

    a. equilibrium in the domestic goods market.
    b. equilibrium in the investment savings relationship.
    c. equilibrium in the money market.
    d. equilibrium in the balance-of-payments.

3. The LM line represents

    a. equilibrium in the goods market.
    b. equilibrium in the investment market.
    c. equilibrium in the money market.
    d. equilibrium in the balance-of-payments.

4. The BB line represents

    a. equilibrium in the goods market.
    b. equilibrium in the investment market.
    c. equilibrium in the money market.
    d. equilibrium in the balance-of-payments.

5. The slope of the IS curve reflects

    a. the relative sensitivity of the demand for money to changes in incomes and interest rates.
    b. the relationship between the size of the marginal propensity to save and the impact of changes of the interest rate on intended investment levels.
    c. the relationship between the impact of the interest rate on the capital account and the impact of domestic incomes on imports.
    d. the relationship between the size of the marginal propensity to consume and the impact of changes of the interest rate on actual investment levels.

6.   The slope of the LM curve reflects

    a.   the relative sensitivity of the demand for money to changes in incomes and interest rates.
    b.   the relationship between the size of the marginal propensity to save and the impact of changes of the interest rate on intended investment levels.
    c.   the relationship between the impact of the interest rate on the capital account and the impact of domestic incomes on imports.
    d.   the relative sensitivity of the capital account to changes in incomes and interest rates.

7.   The slope of the BB line reflects

    a.   the relative sensitivity of the demand for money to changes in incomes and interest rates.
    b.   the relationship between the size of the marginal propensity to save and the impact of changes of the interest rate on intended investment levels.
    c.   the relationship between the impact of the interest rate on the capital account and the impact of domestic incomes on imports.
    d.   the relative sensitivity of the capital account to changes in incomes and interest rates.

8.   Under Bretton Woods, a country experiencing minor and temporary payments imbalances should

    a.   use exchange rate policy to correct the distortion.
    b.   use monetary and fiscal policy to correct the distortion.
    c.   use foreign currency controls to correct the distortion.
    d.   not actively attempt to correct the disequilibrium, but merely finance it.

9.   Under Bretton Woods, a country experiencing more serious payments imbalances should

    a.   use exchange rate policy to correct the distortion.
    b.   use monetary and fiscal policy to correct the distortion.
    c.   use foreign currency controls to correct the distortion.
    d.   not actively attempt to correct the distortion.

10.   Under Bretton Woods, a country experiencing chronic payments imbalances should

    a.   use exchange rate policy to correct the distortion.
    b.   use monetary and fiscal policy to correct the distortion.
    c.   use foreign currency controls to correct the distortion.
    d.   not actively attempt to correct the distortion.

True, False, Uncertain and Why Questions

When answering the following questions, be sure to support your assertion of true, false, or uncertain with two or three sentences.

1. Expansionary monetary policy shifts the LM curve to the left and is an effective way to increase the level of income within the economy.

2. Expansionary fiscal policy shifts the IS curve to the right and is an effective way to increase the level of income within the economy.

3. A country experiencing a balance-of-payments deficit and domestic inflation should use contractionary monetary and fiscal policies.

4. A country experiencing a balance-of-payments deficit and a domestic recession should use expansionary fiscal and monetary policies.

5. Under the Mundell-Fleming policy assignment approach, expansionary monetary policy and tight fiscal policy should be used if a country experiences a payments surplus and a domestic inflationary boom.

Short Answer Questions

1. A country faces a domestic recession and a balance-of-payments deficit. What set of policies would the Mundell policy assignment approach recommend?

2. Using the IS/LM/BB graph, illustrate the effects of the policy assignment model from question 1.

3. Starting from internal and external equilibrium, use the IS/LM/BB graph to show the effects of expansionary fiscal policy on the domestic economy. How does the degree of capital mobility affect your answer?

4. Starting from internal and external equilibrium, use the IS/LM/BB graph to show the effects of expansionary monetary policy on the domestic economy. How does the degree of capital mobility affect your answer?

5. A country is currently experiencing a balance-of-payments surplus and a domestic recession. Using the IS/LM/BB graph, show the correct policy assignments needed to restore equilibrium.

ANSWERS TO CHAPTER 16 STUDY GUIDE QUESTIONS

Multiple Choice Questions

1. b

    A balance-of-payments surplus increases the money supply that places upward pressure on the price level and worsens price competitiveness.

2. b

    The IS curve represents all combinations of income and the interest rate that equate intended investment and savings.

3. c

    The LM curve represents all combinations of income and the interest rate that equate money demand with a given money supply.

4. d

    The BB line represents all combinations of income and the interest rate that result in balance-of-payments equilibrium.

5. b

    If the marginal propensity to save is high or if intended investment is insensitive to the interest rate, the IS curve will be steep because large changes in the interest rate are required to offset a small change in income.

6. a

    A monetarist believes the role of income is far stronger than the role of interest rates, causing the LM curve to be steep. A Keynesian believes the role of interest rates is stronger and therefore believes the LM line is flatter.

7. c

    If the marginal propensity to import is very high and international capital flows are insensitive to domestic interest rate changes, the BB line is steep, and vice versa.

8. d

    Under the Bretton Woods system, a country experiencing minor payments disequilibria should sterilize exchange reserve changes and merely wait for equilibrium to return.

9. b

    With more serious payments problem, a deficit country should use more restrictive policies while surplus countries should implement expansive measures.

10. a

    For chronic payments disequilibria, the country should change the value of its domestic currency in the exchange market. Deficit countries should devalue and surplus countries should revalue.

True, False, Uncertain and Why Questions

1. False. Expansionary monetary policy shifts the LM curve to the right. If the country uses expansionary monetary policy to increase the level of income, the policy will be ineffective if the country starts from a point of equilibrium, since intervention in the foreign exchange market offsets any monetary policy change.

2. Uncertain. Expansionary fiscal policy shifts the IS curve to the right. The effectiveness of fiscal policy is influenced by the degree of capital mobility.

3. True. A country experiencing a payments deficit and domestic inflation should use tight fiscal and monetary policies to restore equilibrium.

4. False. Using expansionary monetary and fiscal policies will help eliminate the recession but will worsen the payments deficit.

5. True. According to the Mundell-Fleming policy assignment model, monetary policy should target the external goal (payments equilibrium) and fiscal policy should target the internal goal (full employment).

Short Answer Questions

1. The Mundell policy assignment model suggests that tight monetary policy (to eliminate the deficit) and expansionary fiscal policy (to eliminate the recession) be used in this case.

2. Expansionary fiscal policy shifts the IS curve to IS'. Tight monetary policy shifts the LM curve to LM'. Equilibrium is restored at point 2.

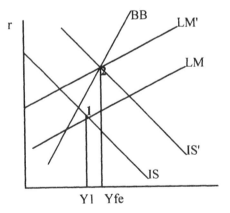

3. Expansionary fiscal policy shifts the IS curve to IS'. At point 2, a payments deficit now exists, meaning an excess supply of the domestic currency exists in the foreign exchange market. In order to maintain the fixed exchange rate, the central bank must intervene in the foreign exchange market and buy domestic currency or sell foreign

currency. This action reduces the domestic money supply, shifting the LM curve to LM'. Equilibrium is restored at point 3.

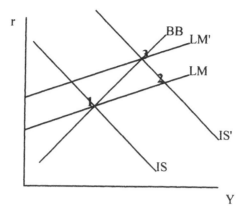

When BB is flatter than LM, expansionary fiscal policy generates an increase in the interest rate that causes huge capital inflows, creating a balance of payments surplus. The central bank must intervene and buy foreign exchange that increases the money supply.

4.   Expansionary monetary policy shifts the LM curve to LM' and created a payments deficit (pt. 1 to pt. 2). The central bank must intervene in the foreign exchange market to maintain the fixed exchange rate by selling foreign currency or buying dollars. This action decreases the domestic money supply which shifts the LM curve from LM' back to LM (pt. 2 to pt. 3).

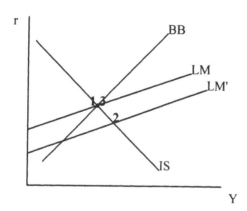

Expansionary monetary policy is also ineffective when BB is flatter than LM.

5.   The country should pursue expansionary fiscal and monetary policy. Expansionary fiscal shifts the IS curve to IS' while expansionary monetary policy shifts the LM curve to LM'. Equilibrium occurs at point 2, where the economy is operating at full employment output and the balance-of-payments is in equilibrium.

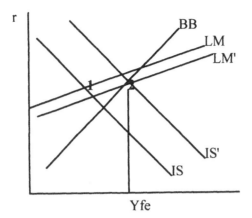

CHAPTER 17

BALANCE OF PAYMENTS ADJUSTMENT THROUGH EXCHANGE RATE CHANGES

IMPORTANT POINTS

1. This chapter examines the role of discrete changes in the exchange rate as the route to payments adjustment. In a most simple analogy, the exchange rate plays the same role in the foreign exchange market as the price of cars plays in the automobile market. If the demand for cars exceeds the supply, the price of automobiles rises. For example, if an excess supply for U.S. dollars exists in the exchange market because of a payments deficit, the price of dollars (the exchange rate) should decrease to eliminate the disequilibrium. A deficit in the United States' balance of payments corresponds to an excess demand for foreign currency (and an excess supply of dollars), causing the price of foreign currency to increase (and the price of U.S. dollars to decrease). When exchange rates are fixed, this adjustment process is not automatic. Instead, a government facing a payments deficit must devalue its currency (revalue in the event of a surplus).

2. Devaluations are not easily imposed and may not be successful. Certain conditions must be met in order for the devaluation to remedy the deficit problem. The Marshall-Lerner condition is one such requirement. The devaluation changes the relative price of exports and imports. Since the local currency is weaker after the devaluation, the local currency price of imported goods increases. Residents substitute away from the more expensive foreign goods toward cheaper domestic products. The size of the decline in imports depends upon the elasticity of demand. If this value is high, a small increase in the price of imports generates a large decrease in the quantity demanded, and the value of imports ($P_{imports}$ x quantity demanded) falls significantly. If demand is inelastic, the price rise causes a small reduction in the volume of imports, causing the total import bill to increase, when measured in the local currency.

The devaluation also affects the export market in two ways. First, the foreign currency price changes. If the local currency price of exports is constant, the foreign currency price falls by the amount of the devaluation (implying an infinitely elastic supply curve). For example, suppose that before the devaluation a U.S. good sells for $200 and the deutschmark is at $0.68, implying that the deutschmark price of the good is DM294.12. If the dollar is devalued by 10%, the U.S. cost of deutschmarks is $0.75. If the local price remains unchanged, the same $200 good costs foreigners only DM266.67, which should encourage foreign purchases of more U.S. goods. If the foreign currency price is fixed (implying an infinitely elastic foreign demand curve), the local price of exports increases by the amount of the devaluation. This should encourage domestic firms to increase the volume of goods sent to export markets.

If neither the demand nor supply curves for exports is infinitely elastic, the local price of exports will rise by less than the devaluation while the foreign price of exports will fall by less than the full percentage. Higher elasticity of demand for both imports and exports leads to a greater improvement in the balance of payments. If the demand elasticities are sufficiently low, the devaluation will worsen the trade balance. The Marshall-Lerner condition uses these conclusions to derive the critical values of the demand elasticities which ensure the success of a devaluation in restoring payments equilibrium under the simplifying assumption of infinitely elastic supply functions. Only when the sum of the demand elasticities (in absolute value terms) exceeds one, will the devaluation be successful.

When countries do not have any monopoly or monopsony power in trade, world prices are fixed. A devaluation of the local currency leaves the foreign currency price of exports unchanged. The supply curve for imports and the demand for exports are infinitely elastic at the world price (converted into the local currency price). In the export market, both price and quantity rise, increasing export revenues. On the import side, the amount of imports falls but the price increases. Expenditures on imports increase if the elasticity of demand is less than one. If either of the domestic elasticities exceeds zero, the trade account improves.

If a country has some market power in one or several export markets, the demand for exports is no longer completely horizontal, but is downward sloping. On the export side both price and quantity rise, increasing revenue (although export prices do not rise by the full amount of the devaluation). Import prices increase by the full amount of the devaluation, implying that the country's terms-of-trade deteriorates. The effect on import expenditures depends upon the elasticity of demand, discussed above.

3. The J-curve describes the existence of a time lag between the devaluation of a currency and the improvement in the country's payments situation. After devaluation, the trade balance follows a pattern resembling a "J", declining for a short period of time before rising steadily. This implies that countries may need assistance financing deficits occurring during this period.

4. How a devaluation affects a country's terms of trade depends on the size of the country in both export and import markets. When the following condition holds, a devaluation worsens the country's terms of trade:

$$e_s^{\,x} \cdot e_s^{\,m} > e_d^{\,x} \cdot e_d^{\,m} \qquad (17.1)$$

5.   More important factors influencing the effectiveness of a devaluation are macroeconomic in nature and include monetary and fiscal policies. Two alternative views to explain the effects exist: the Keynesian absorption model and the monetary approach. The absorption approach focuses on the impact of the devaluation on aggregate demand. As imports fall and exports increase, domestic incomes should increase via the multiplier effect. These expansionary forces may become excessive, especially if the country is close to full employment. This model can be illustrated using the following framework:

$$Y = C + I + G + (X - M) \tag{17.2}$$

$$(X - M) = Y - (C + I + G) \tag{17.3}$$

$$(X - M) = Y - A \tag{17.4}$$

$$\Delta(X - M) = \Delta Y - \Delta A \tag{17.5}$$

where

A = absorption, which is the total domestic use of goods and services and equals C+I+G

Δ = change.

The trade account improves only if output growth exceeds the growth of absorption. If the economy is producing $20,000 in output and absorbing $25,000, a $5,000 trade deficit exists. If the devaluation causes output to increase to $25,000 but absorption increases to $30,000, the devaluation did not reduce the trade deficit. Thus, the country must restrain the growth of absorption in order to allow an improvement in the trade account.

If the economy is at full employment, growth in output is restrained and any reduction in the trade deficit occurs at the expense of domestic absorption. This implies:

$$\Delta (X - M) = -\Delta A \ (since \ \Delta Y = 0). \tag{17.6}$$

Returning to the previous example, if a $5,000 trade deficit exists, policies targeting a reduction in absorption in the amount of $5,000 must be implemented.

6.   Using the savings/investment identity, the change in the trade balance can be expressed in terms of the change in S-I:

$$\Delta (X-M) = \Delta S_T - \Delta I. \tag{17.7}$$

If the devaluation is to succeed, either savings must increase, investment must decrease or some combination of the two. S_T includes (T-G), so this requirement implies tight fiscal policy.

7.   The IS/LM/BB framework can be used to show the effects of a devaluation. The devaluation shifts both the BB and IS lines to the right (to BB' and IS') as imports fall and exports rise. Figure 17-1 shows the devaluation's effects.

Figure 17-1: IS/LM/BB with a Devaluation

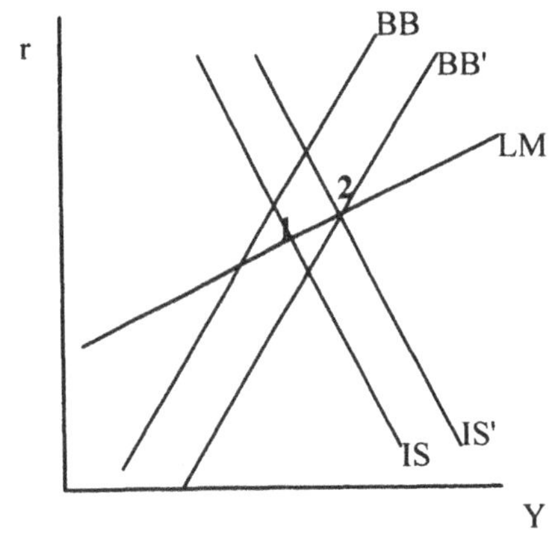

The devaluation moves the economy to equilibrium at point 2 with higher interest rates and income levels. If the IS curve shifts too far to the right, the payments deficit returns. A tighter fiscal policy is then needed to shift IS back to the left.

8.   The monetary model views payments disequilibria as a result of a problem in the money market. A deficit is caused by excessive monetary expansion, which causes a parallel increase in the demand for goods and bonds. Through the law of one price, a devaluation increases the price level that lowers the real money stock and eliminates the excess supply of money that created the payments deficit. According to the monetarist model, devaluations fail if the central bank allows a further increase in the nominal money supply, which creates another excess supply of money. In order for the devaluation to be successful, the central bank must maintain restrictive policies.

9.   Devaluations are unpopular for several reasons. The rise in the price level decreases the real incomes of residents, with particular impacts on those with fixed incomes. If the country has loans denominated in foreign currency, the cost of servicing the loans increases as the value of the local currency falls. The devaluation can also worsen the distribution of income within the country as individuals having assets abroad and speculators benefit from the devaluation. Also export and import-competing industries gain while the rest of the economy (the non-tradable goods sector) loses. The devaluation may also cause regional tension within the country when one area relies heavily on non-tradables (such as urban areas) and others depend on tradable goods (such as agricultural areas). The devaluation shifts income from the cities to the rural areas, which can result in political problems.

      For speculators, accurately anticipating a currency devaluation provides an opportunity for substantial capital gains once the currency loses some of its value. Such profit opportunities may be unpopular with those individuals and businesses adversely affected by the devaluation and make the policy politically unpopular.

10.   Revaluations have the same effects as the devaluation case, except in the opposite direction. The revaluation makes imports more affordable and exports less competitive. If the economy is near full employment, the recessionary impact of a revaluation is not too strong. On the other hand, if the country is simultaneously experiencing a recession and a payments surplus, the revaluation will worsen the recession unless accompanied by expansionary fiscal and monetary policies.

11.   The Meade cases discussed in Chapter 16 can be applied to exchange rate policy. Previously, monetary and fiscal policy conflicted when a country experienced either a payments surplus with inflation (case three) or a deficit with a recession (case four). The use of exchange rate policy can eliminate this problem. For case three, the appropriate policy is to revalue the local currency, while case four calls for a devaluation.

CHAPTER OBJECTIVES

After studying the concepts presented in Chapter 17, you should be able to answer the following questions:

1.   Why is the exchange rate often considered the most important price in an economy?

2.   What is the Marshall-Lerner condition? Why will a devaluation be successful if and only if this condition holds?

3.   Compare and contrast the Keynesian and Monetarist models of balance of payments adjustment. What role does the level of full employment income play in each theory?

4.   Why are devaluation and revaluations sometimes unpopular?

5.   How can the Meade conflict cases be resolved using exchange rate policy?

GLOSSARY TERMS

- absorption condition
- J-curve effect
- Marshall-Lerner condition
- specie flow mechanism

CHAPTER 17 STUDY GUIDE QUESTIONS

Multiple Choice Questions

1. The autonomous supply of foreign exchange represents

    a. domestic demand for foreign currency.
    b. foreign demand for domestic currency.
    c. domestic demand for domestic currency.
    d. none of the above.

2. An increase in British demand for foreign goods will

    a. shift the demand curve for pounds in the foreign exchange market.
    b. shift the supply curve for pounds in the foreign exchange market.
    c. cause British interest rates to change.
    d. cause foreign interest rates to change.

3. When a currency is devalued,

    a. the local price of foreign money increases, which raises the local price of imports.
    b. the local price of foreign money decreases, which raises the local price of imports.
    c. the local price of foreign money increases, which lowers the local price of imports.
    d. the local price of foreign money decreases, which lowers the local price of imports.

4. Suppose the dollar price of British sterling is $1.80 and the dollar is revalued by 20%. The new dollar price of British sterling is

    a. $2.16.
    b. $1.98.
    c. $1.62.
    d. $1.44.

5. Under the simple Marshall-Lerner condition, in order for a devaluation to be successful,

    a. the supply elasticities must sum to more than one in absolute value terms.
    b. the supply elasticities must sum to less than one in absolute value terms.
    c. the demand elasticities must sum to more than one in absolute value terms.
    d. the demand elasticities must sum to less than one in absolute value terms.

6.   A country with some monopoly power in one or more export markets but no
        monopsony power as an importer faces

        a.   an infinitely elastic import supply and export demand curves.
        b.   an infinitely elastic import supply curve and a sloping export demand curve.
        c.   an infinitely elastic export demand curve and a sloping import supply curve.
        d.   sloping import supply and export demand curves.

7.   A country with no monopoly or monopsony power in trade faces

        a.   an infinitely elastic import supply and export demand curves.
        b.   an infinitely elastic import supply curve and a sloping export demand curve.
        c.   an infinitely elastic export demand curve and a sloping import supply curve.
        d.   sloping import supply and export demand curves.

8.   A country with both monopoly and monopsony power in trade faces

        a.   an infinitely elastic import supply and export demand curves.
        b.   an infinitely elastic import supply curve and a sloping export demand curve.
        c.   an infinitely elastic export demand curve and a sloping import supply curve.
        d.   sloping import supply and export demand curves.

9.   According to monetarists, balance of payments deficits

        a.   can only be adjusted with contractionary fiscal policy.
        b.   can only be adjusted with expansionary monetary policy.
        c.   can only be adjusted if the excess supply of money is reduced.
        d.   can only be adjusted if the excess demand for money is reduced.

10.   A revaluation makes

        a.   imports and exports more expensive
        b.   imports and exports less expensive
        c.   imports more expensive and exports less expensive
        d.   imports less expensive and exports more expensive

True, False, Uncertain and Why Questions

When answering the following questions, be sure to support your assertion of true, false, or
uncertain with two or three sentences.

1.   Devaluations always succeed in adjusting a chronic balance of payments deficit.

2.   According to the monetarist school, a devaluation raises the price level and thereby
        increases the real money supply.

3. A country facing a balance of payments deficit and a domestic recession should devalue the local currency.

4. According to the absorption approach, a devaluation has effects that sharply decrease aggregate demand for domestic output.

5. An expected devaluation generates speculative capital outflows from the domestic country.

Short Answer Questions

1. What causes the J-curve effect? What implications does the J-curved effect have on the effectiveness of a devaluation in curing a chronic payments deficit?

2. A country with an ongoing payments surplus revalues its currency. What conditions are necessary for the revaluation to succeed in reducing or eliminating the surplus? Show the effects of the revaluation using the IS/LM/BB graph.

3. Of what relevance is the business cycle situation of the country at the time of the revaluation described in question 2? What fiscal or monetary policies would help the revaluation succeed?

4. What sectors of the economy gain from the revaluation? What sectors lose?

5. What are some of the impacts of a devaluation on an economy?

ANSWERS TO CHAPTER 17 STUDY GUIDE QUESTIONS

Multiple Choice Questions

1. b
    When foreigners demand domestic goods, services, and assets, they demand domestic currency to complete these transactions.

2. b
    An increase in British demand for foreign goods shifts the supply curve for pounds to the right since the amount of pounds they are willing to supply at every price increases.

3. a
    A devaluation reduces the purchasing power of the domestic currency, making imports more expensive relative to domestically produced goods.

4. d
    When the dollar is revalued, it takes fewer dollars to buy one pound. In this case, the revaluation decreases the dollar price of a pound by $0.36.

5.   c

According to the Marshall-Lerner condition, the sum of the demand elasticities must exceed one in order for a devaluation to be successful.

6.   b

If a country does not have monopsony power in its import markets, it faces an infinitely elastic import supply curve, reflecting the fact that it cannot influence the price of imports. If a country has some monopoly power in its export markets, it can influence price and faces a sloped export demand curve.

7.   a

A country without monopoly and monopsony power in trade faces infinitely elastic import supply and export demand curves since the country is unable to influence either the price it pays for imports or the price it receives for exports.

8.   d

A country with market power in both export and import markets can influence the price it pays for imports and the price it receives for exports. Thus, it faces sloping import supply and export demand curves.

9.   c

An excess supply of money means, according to Walras' law, an excess demand for goods and bonds which generates a balance of payments deficit. Eliminating the excess supply of money will eliminate the payments deficit.

10.   d

A revaluation means the purchasing power of local currency increases relative to foreign currency. Imports become cheaper as the domestic currency's value increases. Since foreign currency is worth less, exports become more expensive.

True, False, Uncertain and Why Questions

1.   False. The success of a devaluation depends upon whether the sum of the elasticities of demand exceeds is high (the Marshall-Lerner condition). When this condition does not hold, the devaluation will not help reduce the payments deficit. It also depends on a number of macroeconomic conditions including control of the money supply and a tight fiscal policy.

2.   False. A devaluation raises the price level that decreases the real money supply.

3.   True. The devaluation shifts the BB and IS lines to the right, which eliminates the payments deficit and the recession.

4.   False. Production of exports and import substitutes rises, which leads to higher incomes and greater consumption through the multiplier effect.

5.   True. If the devaluation was expected, it will generate speculative capital outflows.

Short Answer Questions

1. The effects of a devaluation are not instantaneous. Since some buyers may be locked into long-term contracts, individuals and firms may be unable to change spending patterns. This lag-time creates what is known as the "J-curve" effect. The trade account worsens over a period of time before improving and the country must have enough foreign exchange reserves to wait for this condition to pass.

2. Assuming infinitely elastic supply curves, the elasticities of demand for exports must sum to a value greater than one. In other words, the Marshall-Lerner condition must hold. The revaluation shifts the IS curve to IS' as imports increase and exports fall due to the change in the exchange rate. The BB line also shifts to the left (to BB') in response to the change in the exchange rate.

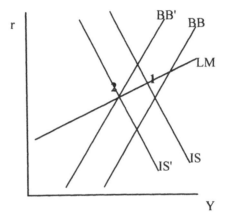

3. If an inflationary boom exists, the change in the exchange rate helps to stabilize prices. If a recession exists, the revaluation is painful. Therefore, expansionary fiscal policy would aid the revaluation efforts. This puts downward pressure on the price level that tends to increase the real money supply. The central bank may need to expand the nominal money supply so the real money supply increases even more if a recession exists.

4. The tradable sector loses since the price of tradables falls. Non-tradables gain from the revaluation. Foreign exchange net debtors win while net creditors lose from the revaluation.

5. A devaluation decreases the purchasing power of the domestic currency. Imports become more expensive and exports less expensive. Import competing and export sectors benefit.

CHAPTER 18

OPEN ECONOMY MACROECONOMICS WITH FIXED EXCHANGE RATES

IMPORTANT POINTS

1. This chapter introduces international trade to the traditional Keynesian macroeconomic model, under the assumption of a fixed exchange rate. Opening the economy to trade dampens the effects of economic shocks originating from domestic sources due to a smaller multiplier effect, but makes the country more vulnerable o business cycles originating abroad.

2. The simple Keynesian model is used in most introductory macroeconomic theory courses. Initially, the economy is assumed to have only business and household sectors. The existence of a government and the rest of the world is ignored. Prices are also assumed to be fixed. The output of the economy is measured by the money value of all final products (either consumption (C) or investment (I) goods) produced during the relevant time period. As goods are produced, an equal amount of income in the form of profits is created. The income (Y) is either saved (S) or consumed (C). These relationships can be expressed using identities:

$$Y = C + I \qquad (18.1)$$

$$Y = C + S. \qquad (18.2)$$

Investment includes both intended investment and accumulated inventories, and is determined outside the model. Consumption depends upon the level of income. The consumption function describes the relationship between these two variables:

$$C = C_a + bY. \qquad (18.3)$$

C_a is the level of consumption that is not dependent upon the level of income. The coefficient of Y is the slope of the consumption function and is called the marginal propensity to consume (b). More specifically, b is defined as the change in C divided by a change in Y (where $0 < b < 1$). This value measures by how much consumption increases when income changes. If income rises by \$100 and the individual spends

$75 of the $100 on goods, the marginal propensity to consume is 0.75. The remaining $25 is the amount of additional savings. Thus, the marginal propensity to save (s) is 0.25.

Plugging equation (18.3) into equation (18.1) yields the following equation:

$$Y = \frac{1}{1-b}(C_a + I) \qquad (18.4)$$

The $\frac{1}{1-b}$ coefficient is the Keynesian multiplier. Suppose the marginal propensity to consume is 0.80. If C_a is 100 and I equals 300, the level of income for the economy is 2000.

3.   The consumption function can also be represented graphically. Figure 18-1 illustrates the closed economy equilibrium.

Figure 18-1: The Consumption Function

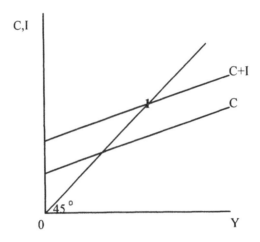

The 45-degree line represents all points where the amount of income equals the aggregated demand function (which is the C+I line). The equilibrium point for this economy is where savings equals investment and aggregate demand equals income (pt. 1). The level of savings is derived from the consumption function. For every level of income, the portion not consumed is the level of savings. If an individual consumes $0.75 of every dollar, the level of savings is $0.25. Thus, the sum of the marginal propensities to save and consume must equal one:

$$b + s = 1. \qquad (18.5)$$

4.   The multiplier can be used to determine the effects that an increase in investment has on the closed economy. Assuming that C_a remains unchanged, the following can be derived from equation (18.4):

$$\Delta Y = \Delta I(\frac{1}{1-b}) \tag{18.6}$$

The multiplier can be rewritten in terms of the marginal propensity to save:

$$k = (\frac{1}{1-b}) \tag{18.7}$$

$$k = \frac{1}{s} \tag{18.8}$$

Equation (18.8) gives the leakage from the circular flow of income. When income is spent on goods and services, the money remains in the income stream. When income is saved, the volume of money in the income flow is reduced, lowering the value of the multiplier. The larger the value of s, the smaller the value for k.

5.   The Keynesian model can be modified to include an additional sector representing international trade. Equations (18.1) and (18.2) become:

$$Y = C_d + I + X \tag{18.9}$$

$$Y = C_d + S + M \tag{18.10}$$

X and M represent exports and imports. The consumption function is modified in order to distinguish between consumption of domestically produced products and imports. Thus C_d refers to the consumption of domestic products. Using (18.9) and (18.10) yields the following relationship:

$$S - I = X - M. \tag{18.11}$$

In the absence of trade, savings had to be equal to investment. An open economy allows the country to invest more than it saves if imports exceed exports. From the balance of payments discussion in Chapter 12, the $(X-M)$ should be familiar. It is the balance of trade for the economy. Exports depend upon foreign incomes and tastes. For simplicity, the level of exports is exogenous and the exchange rate is fixed. Imports depend upon the level of domestic income. The marginal propensity to import (m) tells how much imports increase as income rises. The trade balance can be shown graphically. Figure 18-2 shows the $(X-M)$ curve. A trade surplus exists for values above the horizontal axis. The slope of the $(X-M)$ line is the marginal propensity to import with the opposite sign.

Figure 18-2: The X-M Curve

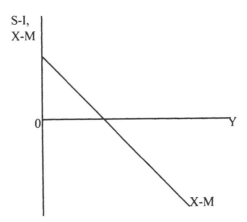

6.   By using a similar line to represent net savings in the domestic economy, the (S-I) =
        (X-M) identity can be illustrated. In Figure 18-3, equilibrium is at point A where
        savings equals investment and imports equal exports. (Note: The slopes of the S-I
        and X-M do not have to be equal, in absolute value terms.)

Figure 18-3: The X-M, S-I Equilibrium

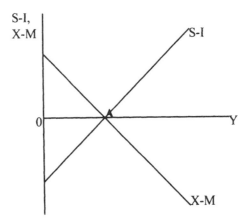

An increase in I (or decrease in S) causes the S-I curve to shift outward. An increase
in X (or decrease in M) generates a rightward shift of the X-M curve. If I increases,
shifting S-I to S-I', income increases (See Figure 18-4.) to the income level associated
with point A.

Figure 18-4: The Effect of an Increase in Investment

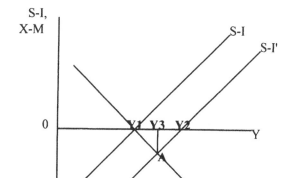

If the economy was closed (no X-M line), income would have increased to Y_2. The reason for the smaller income change is increased imports. As income rises, spending on all goods increases, imports included. If the economy does not trade, the total increase in spending is on domestic products. With trade, imports generate an additional leakage out of the circular multiplier process, generating a smaller rise in income.

If exports decrease, the X-M curve shifts down to X'-M, and Y falls. Obviously, if the economy was closed, this negative shock could not occur. The existence of exports and imports leaves the country susceptible to foreign economic shocks. Figure 18-5 illustrates the effects of the export decline. As exports fall, income declines causing a decrease in the quantity of imports consumed. Thus, the fall in exports is partially offset by a decrease in imports and the trade balance does not decrease by the full amount of the export change.

Figure 18-5: The Effects of a Decrease in Exports

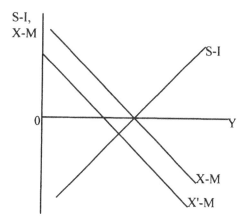

7.   The multiplier in the open economy differs from the one in equation (18.8). The multiplier is now defined as:

$$M = \frac{1}{s + m} \qquad (18.12)$$

When s or m is high, the multiplier is low.

8.   The previous discussion assumed an inactive government. The country was unable to insulate itself from any macroeconomic shocks. Using monetary and fiscal policy, governments are able to influence the level of savings and investment. These tools can be used to weaken the effects of any adverse shock. For example, if exports decline because of a recession in the rest of the world, a country can maintain its current level of income by using expansionary monetary and/or fiscal policy to shift the S-I curve. Figure 18-6 shows the effects of government intervention.

Figure 18-6: The Effects of a Decrease in Exports and Government Intervention

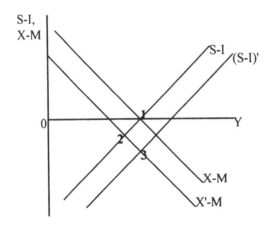

Exports decline as a result of a recession abroad (pt. 1 to pt. 2). To maintain a constant income level, the government increases I (or decreases S), shifting the S-I down, causing a larger trade deficit (pt. 2 to pt. 3).

9.   The analysis becomes more complicated if foreign repercussions are considered. When exports fall generating a decline in incomes and imports, the import decline reduces the foreign country's exports and therefore also affects the country in which the original export decrease began. The size and nature of the "bounce back" effect depends on the values for the marginal propensities to save and import in both countries.

10.   Using the IS/LM/BB model with international capital flows illustrates the effects of monetary and fiscal policies on GDP with fixed exchange rates. Equation (18.13) shows the effect of expansionary fiscal policy with fixed exchange rates.

(18.13)

$\downarrow \Delta MS_{MEX} \rightarrow \uparrow \Delta r_{MEX} \rightarrow \downarrow \Delta I_{MEX} \rightarrow \downarrow \Delta Y_{MEX}$

$\hookleftarrow \uparrow \Delta KA_{MEX} \rightarrow \uparrow \Delta BOP_{MEX} \rightarrow \uparrow \Delta FXR_{MEX} \rightarrow \uparrow \Delta MBR_{MEX} \rightarrow \downarrow \Delta r_{MEX} \rightarrow \uparrow \Delta I_{MEX}$

$\hookleftarrow$

$\uparrow \Delta Y_{MEX}.$

The decrease in the money supply generates an increase in the interest rate that decreases investment (and therefore income) and causes a capital account surplus as capital flows into the economy due to the higher interest rate. The balance-of-payments moves to surplus, increasing Mexico's foreign exchange reserves. This increase raised member bank reserves and the money supply, which lowers the interest rate, and eventually increases income. Thus, monetary policy is ineffective in contracting aggregate demand

The IS/LM/BB graph also illustrates the ineffectiveness of monetary policy with fixed exchange rates. If the Mexican central bank increases the money supply, the LM curve shifts to the right (See Figure 18-7.), generating capital outflows (pt. 1 to pt. 2). As the balance-of-payments moves to deficit, the central bank must sell foreign exchange reserves which decreases the money supply, shifting LM back to its initial level (pt. 2 to pt. 3)

Figure 18-7: IS/LM/BB with Fixed Exchange Rates and Expansionary Monetary Policy

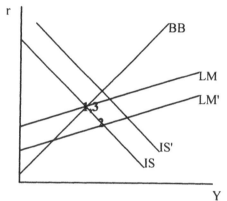

11.   If the government pursues fiscal policy, the effectiveness of the policy depends on the degree of capital mobility. Equation (18.14) illustrates the effect of restrictive fiscal policy with relatively mobile capital mobility:

(18.14)

$\downarrow \Delta (G-T) \rightarrow \downarrow \Delta Y \rightarrow \downarrow \Delta r \rightarrow \uparrow \Delta I \rightarrow \uparrow \Delta Y$

$\hookleftarrow \downarrow \Delta KA \rightarrow \downarrow \Delta BOP \rightarrow \downarrow \Delta FXR \rightarrow \downarrow \Delta MBR \rightarrow \downarrow \Delta MS \rightarrow \uparrow \Delta r \rightarrow \downarrow \Delta I$

$\hookleftarrow$

$\downarrow \Delta Y$

With fixed rates, a decrease in government spending causes a decrease in income through the multiplier effect. Money demand decreases, placing downward pressure on the interest rate that increases investment and income. The lower interest rate also generates capital outflows and a balance-of-payments deficit, which decreases foreign exchange reserves and the money supply. As the money supply falls causing an increase in interest rates, equilibrium in the money market is restored. With higher interest rates, investment falls, which lowers income. The net effect is a decrease in income.

With less capital mobility, the effects of fiscal policy are different. Equation (18.15) illustrates this case:

$$(18.15)$$

$$\downarrow \Delta(G-T) \rightarrow \downarrow \Delta Y \rightarrow \downarrow \Delta M \rightarrow \uparrow \Delta BOP \rightarrow \uparrow \Delta FXR \rightarrow \uparrow \Delta MS \rightarrow \downarrow \Delta r \rightarrow \uparrow \Delta I \rightarrow \uparrow \Delta Y$$

With fixed exchange rates, tight fiscal policy causes a decrease in income through the multiplier effect. As consumption falls for all goods, imports decrease, improving the trade account, and generating a balance of payment surplus. Foreign exchange reserves increase, increasing the money supply that decreases the interest rate. As investment rises, income also increases. Thus, if capital is relatively immobile, fiscal policy is ineffective with fixed exchange rates.

12. The IS/LM/BB graph can be used to illustrate the effect of fiscal policy. In Figure 18-8, capital is relative immobile (represented by a relatively steep BB curve) and contractionary fiscal policy shifts the IS curve to the left (to IS'). As income decreases (pt. 1 to pt. 2), demand for imports decreases and a balance of payments surplus exists. As a result of this imbalance, the central bank must buy foreign exchange. As a result of this transaction, the money supply increases, shifting the LM curve to LM' and income increases.

Figure 18-8: IS/LM/BB with a Fixed Exchange Rate and Fiscal Policy

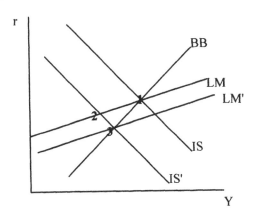

When capital is more mobile (represented by a relatively flat BB curve), contractionary monetary policy is more effective. Figure 18-9 illustrates this case. Tight fiscal policy shifts the IS curve inward (IS to IS'). As income falls, the demand for money decreases which decreases the interest rate and generates capital outflows. Since capital is relatively mobile, the capital account flows dominate current account and a balance of payments deficit exists. The central bank must sell foreign exchange, decreasing the money supply and shifting the LM curve inward (LM to LM').

Figure 18-9: IS/LM/BB with a Fixed Exchange Rate and Fiscal Policy

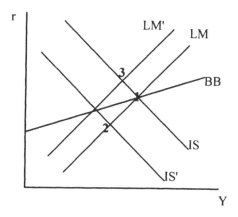

13. Under a fixed rate system, business cycles are transmitted through trade. Equation (18.16) illustrates how changes in US GDP affects its trading partner's economy, assuming little capital market integration.

$$(18.16)$$

$$\uparrow\Delta Y_{US}\rightarrow\uparrow\Delta M_{US}\rightarrow\uparrow\Delta X_{MEX}\rightarrow\uparrow\Delta Y_{MEX}$$
$$\hookrightarrow\uparrow BOP_{MEX}\rightarrow\uparrow\Delta FXR_{MEX}\rightarrow\uparrow\Delta MS_{MEX}\rightarrow\downarrow\Delta r_{MEX}$$
$$\hookleftarrow$$
$$\uparrow\Delta I_{MEX}\rightarrow\uparrow\Delta Y_{MEX}$$

When the United States experiences a boom, imports rise, increasing Mexico's exports and income. Higher exports create a current account surplus and the money supply increases. As the interest rate falls (to restore money supply and demand), investment increases which causes income to increase. Since capital integration is assumed low, capital account flows are ignored.

With more capital market integration, the increase in income generates an increase in US money demand which increases US interest rates. Capital inflows create a capital account surplus for the US and a capital account deficit for Mexico. Depending on the degree of capital integration, the capital account deficit may offset the current account surplus and a balance of payments deficit would exist. In this case, foreign exchange reserves decrease, generating a decrease in the money supply, increase in the interest rate. As the interest rate increases, investment falls and income decreases via the multiplier effect.

14. Fiscal and monetary policies enacted by one government may affect another country through the business cycle transmission process described in the previous section.

CHAPTER OBJECTIVES

After studying the concepts presented in Chapter 18, you should be able to answer the following questions:

1. What are the differences between the closed-economy Keynesian model and one including exports and imports? How does the multiplier change when the effects of international trade are considered?

2. What is the significance of the marginal propensity to consume? What is the relationship between this term and the marginal propensity to save?

3. Explain how the S-I and X-M curves are derived. What are the slopes of these lines? How can the closed economy equilibrium be represented?

4. What government policies shift the S-I curve? What causes the X-M curve to move? Explain how business cycles are transmitted. What steps can the government take to maintain the level of GNP if its trading partners enter a recession?

GLOSSARY TERMS

- foreign trade multiplier
- marginal propensity to import

CHAPTER 18 STUDY GUIDE QUESTIONS

Multiple Choice Questions

1. If the marginal propensity to import increases, the X-M curve

    a. shifts up.
    b. shifts down.
    c. becomes steeper.
    d. becomes flatter.

2. An increase in the GNP of the rest of the world will

    a. decrease country A's exports, shifting the X-M curve up.
    b. decrease country A's exports, shifting the X-M curve down.
    c. increase country A's exports, shifting the X-M curve up.
    d. increase country A's exports, shifting the X-M curve down.

3.   If the marginal propensity to consume is 0.75, C_a equals 0, and total income is $10,000, the amount of income spent on consumption equals

    a.   7500.
    b.   750.
    c.   2500.
    d.   250.

4.   If the marginal propensity to consume is 0.75, C_a equals 0, and total income is $10,000, the amount of income saved equals

    a.   7500.
    b.   750.
    c.   2500.
    d.   250.

5.   If a country faces a decline in the volume of its exports and decides to use domestic policy to offset the trade effects, this country should

    a.   increase domestic investment, shifting the S-I curve down.
    b.   increase domestic investment, shifting the S-I curve up.
    c.   decrease domestic investment, shifting the S-I curve down.
    d.   decrease domestic investment, shifting the S-I curve up.

6.   The open economy multiplier equals

    a. $\dfrac{1}{b-m}$

    b. $\dfrac{1}{b+m}$

    c. $\dfrac{1}{s-m}$

    d. $\dfrac{1}{s+m}$

7. In closed economy, the multiplier equals

   a. $\dfrac{1}{1-s}$

   b. $\dfrac{1}{c+s}$

   c. $\dfrac{1}{c-s}$

   d. $\dfrac{1}{s}$

8. The marginal propensity to import measures

   a. the amount of income spent on foreign goods.
   b. the fraction of additional income spent on imports.
   c. the fraction of consumption spent on imports.
   d. the amount of consumption that is in the form of imports.

9. The slope of the consumption function represents

   a. the amount of autonomous consumption.
   b. the amount of autonomous savings.
   c. the marginal propensity to consume.
   d. the average propensity to consume.

10. An increase in the interest rate will

   a. increase investment, shifting the S-I curve down.
   b. increase investment, shifting the S-I curve up.
   c. decrease investment, shifting the S-I curve down.
   d. decrease investment, shifting the S-I curve up.

True, False, Uncertain and Why Questions

When answering the following questions, be sure to support your assertion of true, false, or uncertain with two or three sentences.

1. When domestic income is zero, domestic consumption is also zero.

2. The amount of actual investment and intended investment are equal to each other.

3. With no government in the model, the sum of the marginal propensities to consume and save must equal zero.

4. A decrease in GNP in the rest of the world, according to the Keynesian model, will always result in a decrease in income in country A.

5. The size and nature of foreign repercussion depends upon the values of the marginal propensities to save and import in both countries only if both countries are large enough to affect the terms-of-trade.

Short Answer Questions

Use the S-I/X-M Keynesian model to show the effects of each of the following events. Start from the trade account being in balance, unless otherwise specified. Briefly explain why the line shifts occur.

1. Intended investment increases by $10 billion in the home country.

2. The home country adopts a tariff that reduces imports by $10 billion.

3. A foreign recession occurs.

4. People in the home country decide to save $10 billion more at every level of income.

5. This country devalues its currency in order to eliminate a trade deficit.

ANSWERS TO CHAPTER 18 STUDY GUIDE QUESTIONS

Multiple Choice Questions

1. c

    When the marginal propensity to import increases, the slope of line increases, and the line becomes steeper.

2. c

    An increase in the rest of the world's GNP increases country A's exports via the foreign marginal propensity to import. Higher exports shift the X-M curve up.

3. a

    The amount of income spent on consumption equals mpc · income = 0.75 · $10,000 = $7,500, assuming C_a equals 0.

4. c

    The amount of income saved equals total income - total consumption = $10,000 - $7,500 = $2,500, assuming C_a equals 0.

5. a

    A decline in the volume of exports shifts the X-M curve up, causing a trade deficit and a decline in income. To offset this decrease, the government can increase investment which shifts the S-I curve down. Income increases but the trade deficit worsens.

6. d

    The open economy multiplier is one over the sum of leakages in the economy.

7. d

    To find the multiplier, substitute the consumption function into the $Y = C + I$ equation and solve for Y. The coefficient of the exogenous variables is the multiplier.

8. b

    If income rises by $1,000 and m is 0.10, $100 is spent on imports (total consumption may increase more than $100).

9. c

    The marginal propensity to consume measures the change in consumption divided by the change in income.

10. d

    An increase in the interest rate decreases investment since the price of investment (the interest rate) is higher. If investment falls, the S-I curve shifts up.

True, False, Uncertain and Why Questions

1. Uncertain. If the consumption function contains a positive value for autonomous consumption, consumption will not equal zero when income is zero.

2. False. Actual investment includes unintended inventory changes while intended investment does not.

3. False. The sum of the marginal propensities to save and consume must equal one. Each dollar of income is either saved (in the form of personal or government savings) or consumed.

4. False. A decrease in GNP in the rest of the world will decrease country A's exports which, through the multiplier, will decrease income. However, the government can increase investment and, again through the multiplier, increase income.

5. False. The size and nature of foreign repercussions depends upon the values of the marginal propensities to save and imports in both countries regardless of the size of the countries.

Short Answer Questions

1.   The increase in investment shifts the S-I curve to the right, causing income to increase (pt. 1 to pt. 2).

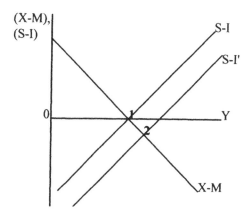

2.   The decrease in imports shifts the X-M curve to the right and increases incomes by more than $10 billion through the multiplier effect (pt. 1 to pt. 2).

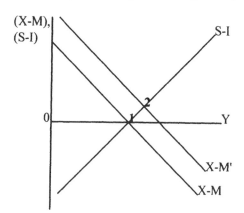

3.   A foreign recession decreases country A's exports which shifts the X-M curve to the
      left and decreases income through the multiplier effect (pt. 1 to pt. 2).

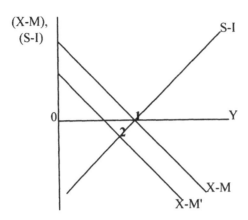

4.   An increase in savings in the amount of $10 billion will shift the S-I curve to the left,
      decreasing the level of income. The trade account moves into surplus (pt. 1 to pt. 2).

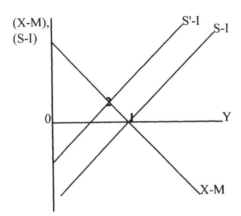

5.   Assuming the devaluation does not result in overshooting, this policy increases exports and decreases imports shifting the X-M curve to the right, eliminating the trade deficit and increasing income (pt. 1 to pt. 2).

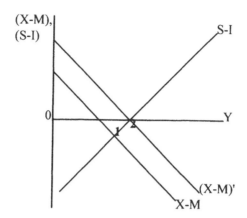

CHAPTER 19

THE THEORY OF FLEXIBLE EXCHANGE RATES

IMPORTANT POINTS

1. In 1973, a number of major industrialized countries adopted floating exchange rates, expecting to return to the fixed parity system in a short period of time. Certain macro shocks and financial conditions made such a return impossible. The chapter examines the floating exchange rate system, with emphasis on the transmission of business cycles and the impact of such an exchange rate regime on the effectiveness of fiscal and monetary policies.

2. A 'clean' or pure floating exchange rate is found primarily in economics textbooks. Countries instead maintain managed or "dirty" floats, meaning that the central bank intervenes in the foreign exchange market whenever the exchange rate moves too quickly or in a direction the government does not favor. This chapter assumes a pure float to clearly distinguish between the regimes of floating and fixed rates.

3. When balance-of-payments transactions are highly sensitive to changes in the exchange rate, the exchange rate tends to be more stable. For example, if a $20 billion capital outflow occurs, and trade flows are highly responsive to exchange rate changes, the exchange rate will have to fall only slightly to generate the offsetting transaction. If trade flows and other transactions respond weakly to the exchange rate, a larger depreciation will be needed to offset the capital outflow. Thus, when demand elasticities are low, the exchange rate is more volatile while a more elastic demand implies a more stable rate. In the short run, because of the J-curve effect, the exchange rate is likely to be more volatile, unless speculative capital flows are stabilizing..

4. The behavior of speculators plays a more important role in determining the degree of exchange rate volatility. If a currency is perceived to be stable (based on the credibility of central bank policy), speculators will believe any sizable rate fluctuation

to be temporary and their behavior will stabilize the exchange rate. For example, if the market views the deutschmark as being worth approximately $0.68, and has confidence that the policies of the Federal Reserve System and the Bundesbank are stable, any major deviation of the rate from this value will generate sales and purchases of the currencies, driving the rate toward the initial $0.68 value. In other words, if the deutschmark is worth $0.75, individuals will sell deutschmarks, driving the rate toward $0.68. As long as market participants have confidence in the future of the exchange rate, any the system will tend to absorb most macro shocks without excessive exchange rate movement.

When the market has little confidence in the central bank and fears that the rates may wildly change in the future, speculation is likely to be disruptive. For example, the rise in the deutschmark from $0.68 to $0.70 may signal the beginning of an upward trend in the value of the German currency (and a downward movement in the value of the dollar), generating an even larger appreciation, as speculators move funds into deutschmarks.

5.   In a managed-float system, the central bank can encourage stabilizing capital flows. If the currency begins to depreciate, the central bank may tighten monetary policy in order to support the weakened currency. If participants in the exchange market have confidence in the central bank's policies, they may be encouraged to buy that currency, thereby stopping its decline.

6.   The change from a fixed to flexible world affects international trade and financial interactions. When the exchange rate was fixed, companies faced little risk from currency appreciation or depreciation. With the flexible rate system, the degree of risk greatly increased. For example, suppose a wholesaler in the United States purchases a large amount of Orvieto wine for L4800 per bottle, with payment to be made in 90 days. Also suppose the current spot price of lira is $0.00083. If the price of lira doubles to $0.00166, the U.S. merchant pays a higher price for the wine since the dollar has depreciated against the lira. To avoid this risk, far more companies involved in international trade cover such risks in the forward market, than was the case under fixed exchange rates.

7.   A flexible exchange rate also influences the relative effectiveness of monetary and fiscal policy. Since the exchange rate moves to restore equilibrium, balance-of-payments surpluses or deficits cease to exist. The movement of the exchange rate affects both the domestic and foreign price of tradable goods, and eventually the price level. If a currency appreciates, the local price of tradable goods falls, while a depreciation generates an increase in the domestic price of tradables (assuming that markets are not monopolistic or oligopolistic, so that the law of one price holds).

8.   Under a fixed rate system, business cycles were transmitted through trade. Flexible exchange rates imply a different conclusion. Equations (19.1) and (19.2) show the differences between the fixed and flexible rate systems.

$$\uparrow \Delta Y_{US} \rightarrow \uparrow \Delta M_{US} \rightarrow \uparrow \Delta X_{MEX} \rightarrow \uparrow \Delta Y_{MEX} \tag{19.1}$$

$$\uparrow dY_{US} \rightarrow \uparrow dM_{US} \rightarrow \uparrow dX_{MEX} \rightarrow \uparrow dXR_{MEX} \rightarrow \downarrow dX_{MEX} \rightarrow \downarrow d(X-M)_{MEX} \tag{19.2}$$
$$\searrow \uparrow dM_{MEX} \nearrow$$

Equation (19.1) represents the fixed exchange rate system. When the United States experiences a boom, imports rise, increasing Mexico's exports and income. The flexible rate (equation (19.2)) weakens this chain of events. The boom in the U.S. increases Mexico's exports, causing the peso to appreciate which increases imports, decreases exports, and worsens the trade account. Thus, the flexible rate system weakens the transmission of business cycles, assuming central banks are willing to allow the exchange rate to fluctuate without interference.

9.   The effectiveness of monetary policy in a flexible system differs from the fixed parity case. As previously discussed, monetary policy is ineffective when rates are fixed. When rates are flexible, monetary policy is able to affect the economy. The differences between these two systems are highlighted in equations (19.3) and (19.4), which are respectively for fixed and flexible exchange rates:

$$\tag{19.3}$$
$$\downarrow \Delta MS_{MEX} \rightarrow \uparrow \Delta r_{MEX} \rightarrow \downarrow \Delta I_{MEX} \rightarrow \downarrow \Delta Y_{MEX}$$

$$\searrow \uparrow \Delta KA_{MEX} \rightarrow \uparrow \Delta BOP_{MEX} \rightarrow \uparrow \Delta FXR_{MEX} \rightarrow \uparrow \Delta MBR_{MEX}$$
$$\nearrow$$
$$\downarrow \Delta r_{MEX} \rightarrow \uparrow \Delta I_{MEX} \rightarrow \uparrow \Delta Y_{MEX}.$$

$$\tag{19.4}$$
$$\downarrow \Delta MS_{M} \rightarrow \uparrow \Delta r_{M} \rightarrow \downarrow \Delta I_{M} \rightarrow \downarrow \Delta Y_{M}$$

$$\searrow \uparrow \Delta KA_{M} \rightarrow \uparrow \Delta BOP_{M} \rightarrow \uparrow \Delta XR_{M} \rightarrow \downarrow \Delta X_{MEX} \rightarrow \downarrow \Delta (X-M)_{M} \searrow$$
$$\searrow \uparrow \Delta M_{M} \nearrow \qquad \downarrow \Delta Y_{M}$$

With fixed exchange rates (equation 19.3), the decrease in the money supply generates an increase in the interest rate which decreases investment (and therefore income) and causes a capital account surplus as capital flows into the economy due to the higher interest rate. The balance-of-payments moves to surplus, increasing Mexico's foreign exchange reserves. This increase raised member bank reserves and the money supply, which lowers the interest rate, and eventually increases income. Thus, monetary policy is ineffective in contracting aggregate demand.

If rates are flexible (equation 19.4), monetary policy can strongly influence the income level. The effects of a decrease in the money supply are similar to those in the fixed rate example except for one large difference, namely that the exchange rate is affected rather than the balance-of-payments. The capital inflows generate an appreciation in the value of the peso, increasing imports, decreasing exports and worsening the trade account which reduces income. Thus, under flexible exchange rates, monetary policy is far more effective.

10.   The IS/LM/BB framework also highlights the differences between fixed and flexible exchange rates.

        If the Mexican central bank increases the money supply, the LM curve shifts to the right (See Figure 19-1), generating capital outflows (pt. 1 to pt. 2) The peso depreciates, shifting the IS and BB curves to the right. Equilibrium occurs at point 3 at a higher level of income. If the exchange rate was fixed, the increase in the money supply generates the same shift in the LM curve. As the balance-of-payments moves to deficit, the central bank must sell foreign exchange reserves which decreases the money supply, shifting LM back to its initial level.

        The conclusion that flexible rates strengthen monetary policy depends upon whether the central bank is willing to allow the exchange rate to move without interference. If instead, the central bank wishes to avoid volatility, it may intervene in the foreign exchange market, which decreases the effectiveness of monetary policy and returns the system toward the fixed exchange rate conclusion.

Figure 19-1: IS/LM/BB with a Flexible Exchange Rate and Expansionary Monetary Policy

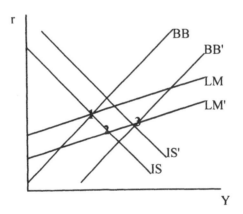

11.   Monetarists argue that the adoption of flexible exchange rates does not increase the effectiveness of monetary policy in the long run since the price level will change to move the real money supply back to its original level. Equation (19.5) shows this point:

(19.5)

$$\uparrow\Delta MS_{MEX}\rightarrow\uparrow ESM_{MEX}\rightarrow\uparrow EDGB_{MEX}\rightarrow\downarrow\Delta XR_{MEX}\rightarrow\uparrow\Delta Pt_{MEX}\rightarrow\uparrow\Delta P_{MEX}\rightarrow\downarrow RMS_{MEX}$$

        where   ESM = excess supply of money
                    EDGB = excess demand for goods and bonds
                    RMS = real money supply
                    Pt   = price of tradables

The increase in the nominal money supply creates an excess supply of money and, using Walras law, an excess demand for goods and bonds. The exchange rate depreciates which, according to the law of one price, leads to an increase in the price of tradables. Eventually, the overall price level rises, reducing the real money supply to its equilibrium value. Thus, any output effects are temporary.

12.   The effectiveness of fiscal policy with a flexible exchange rate depends upon the degree of capital mobility. When capital markets are highly integrated, the differences between the fiscal policy effectiveness with fixed and flexible exchange rates can be shown in equations (19.6) and (19.7):

$$\downarrow\Delta(G\text{-}T)\rightarrow\downarrow \Delta Y\rightarrow\downarrow\Delta r\rightarrow\uparrow\Delta I\rightarrow\uparrow\Delta Y \tag{19.6}$$

$$\downarrow\Delta KA\rightarrow\downarrow\Delta BOP\rightarrow\downarrow\Delta FXR\rightarrow\downarrow\Delta MBR\rightarrow\downarrow MS\rightarrow\uparrow\Delta r$$

$$\downarrow\Delta I\rightarrow \downarrow\Delta Y$$

$$\downarrow\Delta(G\text{-}T)\rightarrow\downarrow \Delta Y\rightarrow\downarrow\Delta r\rightarrow\uparrow\Delta I\rightarrow\uparrow\Delta Y \tag{19.7}$$

$$\downarrow\Delta KA\rightarrow\downarrow XR\rightarrow\uparrow\Delta X\rightarrow\uparrow\Delta(X\text{-}M)\rightarrow\uparrow \Delta Y$$

$$\downarrow\Delta M$$

With fixed rates (equation 19.6), a decrease in government spending causes a decrease in income through the multiplier effect. Money demand decreases, placing downward pressure on the interest rate which increases investment and income. The lower interest rate also generates capital outflows and a balance-of-payments deficit, which decreases foreign exchange reserves and the money supply. As the money supply falls causing an increase in interest rates, equilibrium in the money market is restored. With higher interest rates, investment falls, which lowers income. Thus, fiscal policy is able to decrease income.

    When the exchange rate is flexible (equation 19.7), fiscal policy is ineffective (assuming that capital is very mobile). The capital outflows cause a depreciation in the exchange rate, increasing exports, decreasing imports, improving the trade account, and increasing income through the multiplier effect.

13.   When capital is relatively immobile, the effectiveness of fiscal policy differs from the previous case. More specifically, fiscal policy is ineffective with fixed rates and powerful with a flexible system.

$$\downarrow\Delta(G\text{-}T)\rightarrow\downarrow \Delta Y\rightarrow\downarrow\Delta M\rightarrow\uparrow\Delta BOP\rightarrow\uparrow\Delta FXR\rightarrow\uparrow\Delta MS\rightarrow\downarrow\Delta r\rightarrow\uparrow\Delta I\rightarrow\uparrow\Delta Y$$
$$\tag{19.8}$$

$$\downarrow\Delta (G\text{-}T)\rightarrow\downarrow \Delta Y\rightarrow\downarrow\Delta M\rightarrow\uparrow\Delta XR\rightarrow\downarrow\Delta X\rightarrow\downarrow\Delta(X\text{-}M)\rightarrow\downarrow \Delta Y \tag{19.9}$$

$$\uparrow\Delta M$$

With fixed exchange rates (equation 19.8), tight fiscal policy causes a decrease in income through the multiplier effect. As consumption falls for all goods, imports decrease, improving the trade account, and generating a balance of payment surplus.

Foreign exchange reserves increase, increasing the money supply which decreases the interest rate. As investment rises, income also increases. Thus, if capital is relatively immobile, fiscal policy is ineffective with fixed exchange rates. When rates are flexible, the opposite conclusion holds. The decrease in imports generates an appreciation of the currency which worsens the trade account and decreases income.

14. The IS/LM/BB framework can also be used to highlight how the effectiveness of fiscal policy differs according to the exchange rate system and the degree of capital mobility. In Figure 19-2, the BB line is steeper than the LM line, meaning that capital market integration is weaker than the current account linkage to imports.

If the government increases spending, the IS curve shifts to the right (to IS'). As income rises (pt. 1 to pt. 2), demand for imports increases and the currency depreciates (pt. 2 to pt. 3). The IS and BB lines shift to the right (to IS" and BB') in response to the change in the exchange rate.

Figure 19-2: IS/LM/BB with a Flexible Exchange Rate and Fiscal Policy

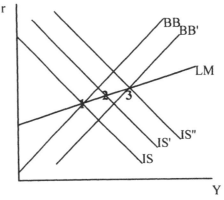

When capital market integration is stronger than the current account linkage to imports, BB is flatter than LM. This case is represented in Figure 19-3.

Expansionary fiscal policy generates higher income, increasing money demand and placing upward pressure on the interest rate (pt. 1 to pt. 2). As capital flows into the country, the currency appreciates, increasing imports, decreasing exports and lowering income (pt. 2 to pt. 3).

Figure 19-3: IS/LM/BB with a Flexible Exchange Rate and Fiscal Policy

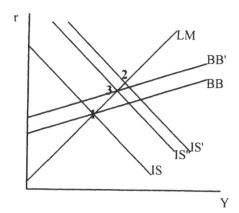

15.   Flexible exchange rates also have an impact on protectionist policies. A tariff, for example, reduces imports causing the local currency to appreciate, restoring payments equilibrium and leaving income and the trade balance largely unaffected.

CHAPTER OBJECTIVES

After studying the concepts presented in Chapter 19, you should be able to answer the following questions:

1.   Discuss the effects of a flexible rate on speculation in the foreign exchange market. What role does central bank credibility play in your answer?

2.   Compare and contrast the effectiveness of monetary policy with fixed and flexible exchange rate systems. Why do they differ?

3.   Compare and contrast the effectiveness of fiscal policy with fixed and flexible exchange rate systems. Why do they differ? What role does the degree of capital mobility play in your answer?

4.   Explain how the transmission of business cycles is weakened with a flexible exchange rate system. What happens if the central bank intervenes in the foreign exchange market to stabilize the exchange rate?

5.   Compare and contrast the monetarist model under fixed and flexible exchange rate systems. What role does the law of one price play in your discussion?

CHAPTER 19 STUDY GUIDE QUESTIONS

Multiple Choice Questions

1. An appreciation of the domestic currency

    a. increases the local currency price of tradable goods.
    b. decreases the local currency price of tradable goods.
    c. decreases the nominal money supply.
    d. decreases the real money supply.

2. With flexible exchange rates, a decrease in country A's exports will

    a. lead to a decrease in country A's income.
    b. cause a depreciation of the domestic currency which improves the trade balance and dampens the effects of the initial export decline.
    c. cause an appreciation of the domestic currency which improves the trade balance and dampens the effects of the initial export decline.
    d. lead to an increase in country A's income.

3. With fixed exchange rates, a decrease in country A's exports will

    a. lead to a decrease in country A's income.
    b. cause a depreciation of the domestic currency which improves the trade balance and dampens the effects of the initial export decline.
    c. cause an appreciation of the domestic currency which improves the trade balance and dampens the effects of the initial export decline.
    d. lead to an increase in country A's income.

4. In a flexible exchange rate system, the adoption of expansionary monetary policy

    a. decreases interest rates and encourages capital outflows, resulting in an increase of foreign exchange reserves.
    b. decreases interest rates and encourages capital outflows, resulting in a decrease of foreign exchange reserves.
    c. decreases interest rates and encourages capital outflows, resulting in an appreciation of the domestic currency.
    d. decreases interest rates and encourages capital outflows, resulting in a depreciation of the domestic currency.

5. In a fixed exchange rate system, the adoption of expansionary monetary policy

   a. decreases interest rates and encourages capital outflows, resulting in an increase of foreign exchange reserves.
   b. decreases interest rates and encourages capital outflows, resulting in a decrease of foreign exchange reserves.
   c. decreases interest rates and encourages capital outflows, resulting in an appreciation of the domestic currency.
   d. decreases interest rates and encourages capital outflows, resulting in a depreciation of the domestic currency.

6. According to the monetarist view, in a world of floating exchange rates, tight monetary policy

   a. creates an excess demand for money causing the domestic currency to appreciate, which decreases the price level and increases the real money supply.
   b. creates an excess demand for money causing the domestic currency to depreciate, which decreases the price level and lowers the real money supply.
   c. creates an excess demand for money causing the domestic currency to appreciate, which increases the price level and increases the real money supply.
   d. creates an excess demand for money causing the domestic currency to depreciate, which increases the price level and lowers the real money supply.

7. With flexible exchange rates, a tariff on imported goods

   a. improves the terms-of-trade for the country.
   b. decreases imports which causes the currency to appreciate, which worsens the trade account and decreases income.
   c. decreases imports which causes the currency to depreciate, which worsens the trade account and decreases income.
   d. decreases imports which causes the currency to depreciate, which improves the trade account and increases income.

8. When the BB line is flatter than the LM line, fiscal policy is

   a. powerful with both fixed and flexible rates.
   b. powerful with fixed rates and weak with flexible rates.
   c. powerful with flexible rates and weak with fixed rates.
   d. weak with both fixed and flexible rates.

9.   If fiscal policy generates a tendency toward a payments surplus and exchange rates are flexible,

a.   the value of the domestic currency will appreciate.
b.   the value of the domestic currency will depreciate.
c.   foreign exchange reserves will increase.
d.   foreign exchange reserves will decrease.

10.   If fiscal policy generates a tendency toward a payments surplus and exchange rates are fixed,

a.   the value of the domestic currency will appreciate.
b.   the value of the domestic currency will depreciate.
c.   foreign exchange reserves will increase.
d.   foreign exchange reserves will decrease.

True, False, Uncertain and Why Questions

When answering the following questions, be sure to support your assertion of true, false, or uncertain with two or three sentences.

1.   A floating exchange rate eliminates any central bank intervention in the exchange market.

2.   Fiscal policy is equally as effective with flexible exchange rates as it is with fixed ones.

3.   With flexible exchange rates, a decrease in exports causes a payments deficit that generates a depreciation in the domestic currency.

4.   With flexible exchange rates, an increase in foreign interest rates generates a payments deficit, causing a depreciation in the domestic currency.

5.   With flexible exchange rates, a policy generating capital inflows will not affect the value of the exchange rate.

Short Answer Questions

Contrast a regime of flexible exchange rates with a fixed parity system in terms of the following:

1.   The rest of the world adopts tight monetary policy. You are to explain what happens to this country, not the rest of the world (use the IS/LM/BB graph).

2.   With perfectly integrated capital markets, an expansionary fiscal policy is adopted by the domestic government (use the IS/LM/BB graph).

3. Starting from a point of equilibrium, fiscal policy is used to reduce inflationary pressures (use the IS/LM/BB graph).

4. The international transmission of business cycles.

5. The effect of changes in the value of the exchange rate.

ANSWERS TO CHAPTER 19 STUDY GUIDE QUESTIONS

Multiple Choice Questions

1. b
    An appreciation of the domestic currency increases the value of the currency in the foreign exchange market. This means, for example, that one dollar buys more pounds than previously if the dollar appreciates in value. This increases the domestic price of tradable goods.

2. b
    A decrease in country A's exports causes a depreciation of its currency. Country A's goods become cheaper as the currency depreciates which helps to reduce the effects of the drop in export sales.

3. a
    A decrease in country A's exports causes a payments deficit that reduces foreign exchange reserves, the money supply and income.

4. d
    An increase in the money supply decreases interest rates causing capital outflows. This causes the currency to depreciate, which strengthens the current account.

5. b
    An increase in the money supply decreases the interest rate causing capital outflows and a payments deficit. The central bank must sell foreign exchange reserves, which reduces the money supply, canceling the original monetary expansion.

6. a
    A decrease in the money supply causes an excess supply of goods and bonds (excess demand for money), causing the currency to appreciate and the price level to fall. This increases the real money supply.

7. b
    A tariff improves the trade account, causing the currency to appreciate. This appreciation decreases the price level and lowers income, making a mercantilist policy ineffective.

8. b
    With flexible rates, fiscal policy is offset by changes in the exchange rate. When rates are fixed, fiscal policy can effectively influence income.

9.   a

If the balance of payments moves toward a surplus and the exchange rate is flexible, the domestic currency will appreciate to restore equilibrium.

10.   c

If the balance of payments moves toward a surplus and the exchange rate is fixed, foreign exchange reserves will increase to restore equilibrium.

True, False, Uncertain and Why Questions

1.   False. Most countries having flexible exchange rates maintain a 'dirty' or managed float. If the value of a currency fluctuates greatly from the value most countries believe the currency should have, central banks may intervene in the exchange market to influence the currency's value.

2.   False. When BB is steeper than LM, fiscal policy is stronger under flexible rates. When BB is flatter than LM, fiscal policy is weaker under flexible rates.

3.   False. With flexible exchange rates, a balance-of-payments deficit cannot exist. In the case of an emerging payments deficit, the domestic currency depreciates causing an increase in exports and a decrease in imports which restores equilibrium.

4.   False. With flexible exchange rates, a balance-of-payments deficit cannot exist. In the case of an emerging payments deficit, the domestic currency depreciates causing an increase in exports and a decrease in imports which restores equilibrium.

5.   False. Assuming an initial payments equilibrium, a policy generating capital inflows creates an excess demand for domestic currency on the foreign exchange market. As a result, the value of the domestic currency appreciates.

Short Answer Questions

1.   FLEXIBLE RATES

The interest rate in the rest of the world increases, causing capital outflows out of country A. This shifts the BB line from BB to BB'. The currency depreciates which shifts IS to IS', and BB' to BB". Equilibrium occurs at point 2 where income has increased from Y1 to Y2.

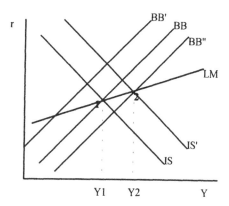

FIXED RATES:

The interest rate in the rest of the world increases which shifts the BB line to the left (to BB') as capital flows out of country A. A balance-of-payments deficit exists at point 1. The central bank must sell foreign exchange and buy dollars which decreases the domestic money supply and shifts the LM curve to LM'. Equilibrium is restored at point 2. Income falls from Y1 to Y2.

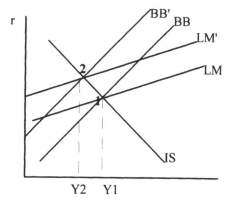

2.   Note: With perfectly integrated capital markets, the BB line is horizontal. If the BB line shifts, it moves horizontally, i.e., it slides along itself.

FLEXIBLE RATES:

The increase in government spending (or decrease in taxes) shifts the IS curve to IS'. The currency appreciates which shifts BB along itself and IS' back to IS. Income temporarily rises to Y2, until the appreciation occurs, which returns income to Y1.

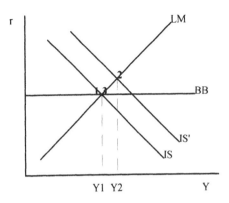

FIXED RATES:

The increase in government spending shifts IS to IS'. The balance-of-payments moves into surplus (pt. 2) and the central bank must sell dollars and buy foreign exchange which increases the domestic money supply and shifts LM to LM'. Income rises from Y1 to Y3.

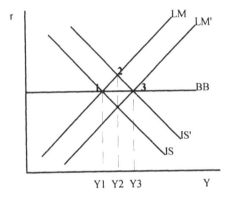

3.   Note: Let Yfe denote the full employment level of income.

FLEXIBLE RATES:

The decrease in government spending shifts the IS curve to IS' (pt. 1 to pt. 2). The currency appreciates, causing the BB line to shift to BB' and IS' to shift to IS". Income falls from Y1 to Yfe, reducing inflationary pressures (pt. 3).

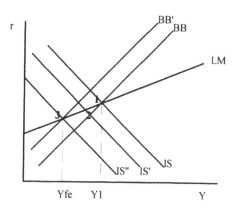

FIXED RATES:

The decrease in spending shifts IS to IS' and creates a payments surplus (pt. 2). (Income falls from Y1 to Y2.) This means the central bank must sell dollars and buy foreign exchange which increases the domestic money supply, and shifts LM to LM' (pt. 3).. Income rises from Y2 to Y3. With fixed rates, the intervention in the foreign exchange market dampens the contractionary effect of the decrease in spending.

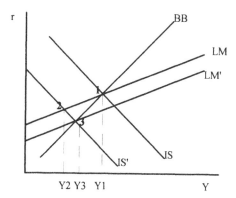

4.   With a fixed exchange rate, a decrease in the income of the U.S. decreases U.S. imports (Canada's exports). This decreases the income in Canada. The business cycle is transmitted.

With flexible rates (assume a clean float), the decline in U.S. imports causes the Canadian dollar to depreciate (the U.S. dollar to appreciate). This increases Canadian exports and reduces Canadian imports which increases Canadian income and causes the business cycle to be transmitted more weakly.

5.   With a flexible exchange rate system, any disequilibrium in the foreign exchange market results in a change in the value of the domestic currency. For example, if an event occurs which increases the demand for US dollars and the exchange rate is flexible, the dollar will appreciate against other currencies. If the exchange rate is fixed, the central bank must intervene to maintain the value of currency, selling dollars and buying foreign exchange.

CHAPTER 20

THE INTERNATIONAL MONETARY SYSTEM FROM 1880 TO 1973

IMPORTANT POINTS

1.   This chapter describes the international monetary experience under the pre-1914 gold standard until the end of the gold-exchange standard. The gold standard emerged in the latter part of the nineteenth century and was widely used until the outbreak of World War I. When a country went on the gold standard, its currency was defined in terms of gold and the central bank was required to buy and sell gold at a set price. As long as the public believed the central banks would adhere to the gold standard, the exchange rate was stable, its range of possible movement being determined by the transportation costs for gold.

        Any balance-of-payments disequilibria were adjusted through short-term capital flows. For example, if a currency's value fell below mint par, individuals and firms would buy the currency, driving the market rate toward the mint par value. Thus, payments disequilibria are corrected without large movements of gold. The crucial factor in the success of short-run capital flows in restoring payments and foreign exchange equilibrium is the public's confidence in the central bank and its ability to maintain the price of gold.

        Central banks were not passive under the gold standard. The "bank rate" is the rate of interest that a central bank charges when it makes loans to commercial banks. If a central bank faced a payments deficit, it would increase the bank rate, causing the interest rates in the country's financial sector to rise as well. This increase generates short-run capital flows from the rest of the world, increasing the demand for the country's currency and the value of the exchange rate.

2.   When balance-of-payments disequilibria were not temporary, adjustment involved changing prices, wages, and incomes. This process is similar to the one described in Chapter 16, in the section on species flow. If a country develops a balance-of-payments surplus and gold flows in, the resulting increase in the money supply and decrease in interest rates would generate upward pressure on all prices. Aggregate demand also tends to increase, generating an increase in the volume of imports, reducing the trade surplus, eventually ending the gold inflow.

        In the pre-1914 era, wages and prices were flexible enough to allow for this adjustment process. World trade rapidly expanded during this period, increasing the degree of integration of major nations' economies. Any single nation's ability to expand its money supply is limited by its balance-of-payments position. For the world as a whole, growth in the money supply was determined by the amount of new gold that was available to the central banks from the mining and smelting industry.

3.   During World War I, the gold standard ceased to function. After the war, countries resorted to inflationary reconstructive policies. Lingering political differences also influenced the pattern of trade between these countries. New countries emerged from old empires, changing the structure of the world economy. For numerous reasons, the pre-war exchange rate parities were no longer appropriate. During this time, exchange rates were allowed to float until international trade was sufficiently restored to allow a return to the gold standard. One problem centered on what the new equilibrium exchange rates should be. The theory of purchasing power parity was implemented to develop the appropriate exchange rates. The new set of exchange rates, it was believed, should reflect relative changes in purchasing power, indicated by relative rates of inflation. If a country experienced relatively more inflation than other nations, its currency should depreciate in value relative to the other currency. By the mid 1920s, many countries returned to the gold standard, but the new exchange rates differed from the pre-war parities. If the countries had returned to the foreign currency values that existed before the war, the exchange rates would have generated continual balance-of-payment deficits. Since all countries did not rejoin the gold standard simultaneously, a country often had to change its currency's parity as additional countries linked their currency to gold.

4.   During the inter-war period, pressures of nationalism also influenced the international monetary experience. Trade restrictions limited the flow of goods between trading partners. As the gold standard fell apart in the early 1930s, the world economy became more fragmented. Some countries attempted to limit exchange rate fluctuations through intervention in the foreign exchange market. Other nations pegged their currency to another currency, such as the dollar or the pound. These countries would intervene in the currency market to maintain its fixed rate vis-à-vis the dollar or the pound. When Britain went off the gold standard, many countries with significant ties to Britain pegged their currency to sterling. Some countries, fearing capital flight, imposed exchange controls, which limited the ability of individuals or firms to convert domestic money into other currencies.

5.   The Bretton Woods conference established the Articles and Agreements of the International Monetary Fund and also founded the World Bank. Most nations except the previous Communist bloc countries became members. One of the major sources of disruption during the inter-war period was volatile exchange rates, and countries wished to avoid the chaotic non-system of that period. Under Bretton Woods, each member agreed to set a par value for its currency in terms of the United States dollar (or its gold equivalent). Each member also agreed to take appropriate steps to ensure that its exchange rate did not deviate by more than one percent from that par value. For example, if the deutschmark has a parity of DM4.00 to $1.00 and the value of the deutschmark rises to DM3.96 to $1.00, the Bundesbank must intervene by purchasing dollars since the currency value has changed by the allowed 1 percent.

       If a country experienced fundamental balance-of-payment problems, its currency's par value could be changed to alleviate the problem. Thus, par values were to be stable but adjustable.

       Since all currencies were pegged to the dollar, the dollar was the numeraire of the system. The dominant role of the dollar had several implications for the United States. The U.S. did not have the power to set the exchange rate between the dollar and any other currency. In other words, the U.S. played a passive role in the determination of bilateral exchange rates. This is known as the nth currency problem. With n currencies, only n-1 dollar exchange rates exist. While the United States could change the level at which it set the dollar-gold price (set at $35 per ounce), it could not influence any exchange rate.

6.   On August 15, 1971, President Nixon announced that the United States would no longer buy and sell gold at $35 per ounce. In other words, the United States was no longer on the gold-exchange standard. Nixon also called for the devaluation of the dollar in hopes of improving the U.S. balance-of-payments position. In December 1971, the Smithsonian Agreement established a new system of exchange rates. The dollar was devalued by 8½ percent, which increased the price of gold to $38 per ounce and other currencies were revalued. However, the United States did not resume trading gold for dollars at this price, and the system collapsed within a year. In early 1973, speculation against the dollar caused several countries to let their currency float relatively freely in the foreign exchange market.

7.   During the 1960s, a major innovation in international banking occurred. Commercial banks in several countries began accepting deposits and loaning funds denominated in foreign currency. This market is known as the Eurocurrency market. Of particular interest to the United States is the Eurodollar component of the Eurocurrency market. Dollar deposits in foreign commercial banks are not subject to Federal Reserve restrictions (such as the reserve requirement). Until the mid-1980s, U.S. commercial banks were subject to Regulation Q, which specified the maximum interest rates U.S. banks could pay on time deposits. The Eurobanks were not subject to such regulations, making deposits in such banks more attractive since deposits could earn a higher rate of interest.

CHAPTER OBJECTIVES

After studying the concepts presented in Chapter 20, you should be able to answer the following questions:

1. Explain the process of adjustment under the pre-1914 gold standard. Why was this system successful?

2. Why did countries leave the gold standard during World War I? What problems did these nations encounter when they tried to re-establish the gold standard?

3. What were the major goals of the Bretton Woods Conference? Explain the process of balance-of-payments adjustment adopted at this conference.

4. What were some of the concerns of the negotiators at Bretton Woods? How did the experience of the inter-war years influence the Bretton Woods system?

5. Why did the Bretton Woods system collapse? Were the chronic U.S. balance-of-payment deficits of any relevance? Explain.

CHAPTER 20 STUDY GUIDE QUESTIONS

Multiple Choice Questions

1. When a nation went on the gold standard,

    a. it defined its currency in terms of gold and it allowed gold to be freely exported or imported.
    b. it defined its currency in terms of gold and did not allow gold to be freely exported or imported.
    c. it defined its currency in terms of the reserve asset (which was tied to gold) and it allowed gold to be freely exported or imported.
    d. it defined its currency in terms of the reserve asset (which was tied to gold) and it did not allow gold to be freely exported or imported.

2. The crucial factor that ensured the success of the gold standard was

   a. adherence to the rules of the system by most member countries.
   b. that the public had complete confidence that nations would abide by the rules of the system, by maintaining the fixed price of gold.
   c. the absence of speculation in the foreign exchange market.
   a. the existence of speculation in the foreign exchange market.

3. Under the gold standard, short-term capital tended to flow into sterling assets

   a. when the dollar fell in terms of pounds.
   b. when the pound rose in terms of dollars.
   c. when the pound fell in terms of dollars.
   d. when the pound stays constant in terms of dollars.

4. If a country develops a payments surplus, and gold flows into the country,

   a. interest rates and the money supply fall, putting downward pressure on wages and prices.
   b. interest rates and the money supply fall, putting upward pressure on wages and prices.
   c. interest rates fall and the money supply rises, putting upward pressure on wages and prices.
   d. interest rates rise and the money supply falls, putting downward pressure on wages and prices.

5. The theory of purchasing power parity states that

   a. a new system of exchange rates should reflect absolute changes in purchasing power, as indicated in relative changes in price levels.
   b. a new system of exchange rates should reflect absolute changes in purchasing power, as indicated in absolute changes in price levels.
   c. a new system of exchange rates should reflect relative changes in purchasing power, as indicated in absolute changes in price levels.
   d. a new system of exchange rates should reflect relative changes in purchasing power, as indicated in relative changes in price levels.

6. According to the Bretton Woods system, each member country agreed

   a. to specify a par value for its currency in terms of gold.
   b. to specify a par value for its currency in terms of British pounds.
   c. to specify a par value for its currency in terms of U.S. dollars.
   d. to specify a par value for its currency in terms of U.S. dollars or its equivalent in gold.

7.   The Eurocurrency market consists of

   a.   U.S. commercial banks with European subsidiaries.
   b.   commercial banks in several countries accepting deposits and extending loans in currencies other than their domestic one.
   c.   commercial banks in several countries accepting U.S. dollar deposits and extending loans in currencies other than their domestic one.
   d.   European commercial banks with U.S. subsidiaries.

8.   If the dollar price of pounds is $2 and the dollar price of deutschmarks is $4, the cross rate implies that the pound price of deutschmarks is

   a.   £0.50.
   b.   £2.00.
   c.   £4.00.
   d.   £0.25.

9.   According to the Bretton Woods system, each member agreed to keep its currency within one percent of its par value. If the pound par value is $2, this means that intervention is need whenever the dollar value of the pound

   a.   moves from $2.00.
   b.   moves to $1.98.
   c.   moves to $2.02.
   d.   moves to $1.98 or to $2.02.

10.   According to the Articles of Agreement, if a member found its payments to be in fundamental disequilibrium, it could

   a.   change its par value by a large amount without prior IMF approval.
   b.   change its par value by a large amount with prior IMF approval.
   c.   not change its par value unless it has the approval of the United States.
   d.   not change its par value unless other countries were willing to also change their par values.

True, False, Uncertain and Why Questions

When answering the following questions, be sure to support your assertion of true, false, or uncertain with two or three sentences.

1.   When countries operated on the gold standard, the payments adjustment process necessitated large transfers of gold between countries.

2.   The gold standard was equally as effective in the leading industrial nations as in developing countries.

3. Under the gold standard, long-term capital movements sometimes continued for a long time and enabled countries to maintain current account disequilibria.

4. Draws from the IMF are similar to short-term loans.

5. If a country tried to stimulate its economy by reducing interest rates, funds will tend to flow out of the country that tends to equalize interest rates in different financial markets.

Short Answer Questions

1. During the 1930s, an advisor to President Roosevelt suggested increasing the price of gold. What was the purpose of this proposal? What were the effects of this policy?

2. Why did some countries place direct controls on international transactions during the 1930s? What were the implications of this policy?

3. What is the scarce currency clause? How was this policy supposed to help balance-of-payments adjustment?

4. Why did the U.S. balance-of-payments deficit pose a problem for the United States and the rest of the world?

5. What implications did expansionary fiscal policy in the 1950s and 1960s have for the United States' balance-of-payments position?

ANSWERS TO CHAPTER 20 STUDY GUIDE QUESTIONS

Multiple Choice Questions

1. a
    A nation on the gold standard defined its currency in terms of gold, meaning the central bank was required by law to buy and sell gold without limit at the stated price.

2. b
    If the public did not have complete confidence in the ability of countries to adhere to the rules of the system, the market exchange rate between currencies would not be fixed within narrow limits.

3. c
    When the pound falls in terms of dollars, institutions with large holdings of short-term assets would see the low pound price as an opportunity to make profits as the pound rose within the band created by the gold points. Also, the Bank of England would be expected to raise interest rates as the pound declined.

4.   c

The gold inflow increases the money supply and decreases the interest rate. This causes an increase in aggregate demand and puts upward pressure on wages and prices.

5.   d

If Mexican prices double while US prices remain unchanged, one Mexican peso will buy half as much as it did before. Purchasing power parity suggests that the exchange rate should reflect this fact.

6.   d

Countries could set the value of the domestic currency in terms of dollars or in terms of the dollar price of gold.

7.   b

Eurocurrency deposits can be denominated in various currencies.

8.   b

For this example, £0.50 = $1.00 and DM0.25 = $1.00. This implies that £0.50 = DM0.25 or £2 =DM1.

9.   d

The exchange rate cannot fluctuate more than one percent of the par value. When the dollar price of pounds is $2.00, this implies that the value must not fall to $1.98 ($2.00 - [0.01]*$2.00 = $1.98) or rise to $2.02 ($2.00 + [0.01]*$2.00 = $2.02).

10.   b

A country submits a proposal to the IMF that decides whether to approve the change.

True, False, Uncertain and Why Questions

1.   False. The sensitive response of short-term capital to exchange rate changes is one reason why large movements of gold between countries in response to payments disequilibria did not occur.

2.   False. The gold standard was more effective in industrialized countries. Some individuals have argued that the cyclical fluctuations occurring under the gold standard fell heavily on suppliers of raw materials .

3.   True. The long-term capital flows meant that some nations did not have to balance their merchandise imports and exports, or even their capital account.

4.   True. Drawings from the IMF must be repaid once the payments position improves and are therefore similar to short-term loans.

5.   True. The existence of the international capital markets affects the autonomy of domestic monetary policy. Even with exchange controls, capital will find ways to get around the regulations.

Short Answer Questions

1. By increasing the price of gold, thereby devaluing the dollar, domestic prices of tradables may increase by the same proportion that the gold price was increased. A devaluation of the dollar (higher price for gold) will stimulate exports, lower imports, and cause an inflow of gold that increases the money supply and the price level. This period of adjustment may be very long, however.

2. Controls took the form of import quotas, foreign currency controls and other policies. The programs sought to insulate the domestic economy from direct influences of foreign economies. This system was inefficient, making most transactions a matter of political negotiation.

3. The scarce currency clause provides that if the IMF's holding of any national currency should be depleted, that currency could be declared scarce and member nations could impose discriminatory restrictions on imports from the scarce-currency country. This policy was designed to encourage countries running chronic surpluses to adjust, but was never used.

4. The deficits were welcomed in the early 1950s because they increased the world's supply of foreign exchange reserves, but when they continued into the 1960s, they undermined confidence in the system.

5. During this period, the U.S. balance-of-payments moved to a deficit. With stable exchange rates, the deficit country is expected to come under deflationary pressure. This did not occur. The U.S. sought to stabilize wages and prices but did not try to force them down.

CHAPTER 21

INTERNATIONAL MONETARY RELATIONS FROM 1973 TO THE PRESENT

IMPORTANT POINTS

1. This chapter focuses on the international monetary system since the Bretton Woods system collapsed in 1973. Since countries have maintained different systems since 1973, the world cannot be classified as being either on fixed or floating exchange rates. Some nations have freely floating currencies while others peg their money to a specific foreign currency such as the French franc or U.S. dollar. Table 21-1 (in the text) describes the various exchange rate structures that currently existed as of early 1994.

2. When many countries adopted floating rates in March of 1973, the move was expected to be temporary since fixed exchange rates were believed to be the best structure for the international monetary system. The oil embargo of 1973, however, discouraged a return to fixed rates. OPEC members experienced large trade surpluses, which introduced more uncertainty into the system. As described previously, short-term capital flows can be a source of volatility. No one could predict the possible investment strategies of the OPEC surplus nations. In light of this uncertainty and other effects of higher oil prices, returning to fixed rates was not feasible.

    By 1976, the floating rate system settled into a stable pattern. However, this soon changed. In 1977, the U.S. Secretary of the Treasury said that the dollar was too strong. This announcement, combined with uncertainty regarding the policies of the Federal Reserve system, led to speculative capital flows that caused the dollar to depreciate. Inflation during this period was also accelerating, which also influenced expectations about the future value of the dollar.

In late 1979, the Federal Reserve System, under the leadership of Paul Volcker, tightened monetary policy. Confidence in the policies of the central bank increased, and capital began flowing into the U.S., increasing the value of the dollar. The dollar's appreciation was the result of specific macroeconomic policies in the United States. The federal budget deficit grew as taxes were cut and government spending (particularly defense expenditures) increased. As the Treasury borrowed to finance the deficit, monetary policy continued to be tight and interest rates rose sharply. U.S. inflation was believed to be under control, which, combined with high nominal rates, implies that the real rate of interest also increased. The stronger dollar weakened the U.S. trade account as exports fell and imports increased.

The value of the dollar peaked in early 1985 and began to depreciate. The central banks of the industrialized countries also intervened in the foreign exchange market to facilitate the falling dollar. Major trading partners of the United States allowed their currencies to appreciate relative to the dollar in part because of fear of rising protectionist sentiment in the U.S.. Although a weaker dollar discourages imports and encourages exports, the U.S. trade account continued to deteriorate until 1987 before beginning a sizable improvement.

3.   In Chapter 18, the difference between real and nominal exchange rates was discussed. Previously accepted theory suggested that nominal rates should only move to roughly offset differences in inflation, leaving real rates relatively unchanged. Empirical evidence does not support this claim. Instead, real exchange rates have been very volatile. Changes in real rates have implications for income distribution within a country. For example, if a currency appreciates in real terms, the price of tradable goods falls relative to prices of non-tradables. Thus, the non-tradable sector gains and the tradable sector loses, as real income is redistributed within the economy. The instability of real rates has implications for the effectiveness of monetary policy. If the central bank wishes to slow the depreciation of its currency, it should implement contractionary monetary policy. If, however, the country is in a recession, the domestic effects of tight money will not be desirable. The Meade conflict cases return in a new form. The desire to stabilize the exchange rate can conflict with the monetary policy needs of the domestic macro economy.

The models of exchange rate determination presented in previous chapters have been tested empirically. These models have performed poorly. For example, Rudiger Dornbusch tested the monetarist model, which performed poorly; some of the coefficients had the wrong sign and others were not significant.

4.   Other possible international monetary systems have been proposed. Since speculative capital flows are often a source of currency market instability, a ban on such transactions has been suggested. Exchange market controls are one mechanism that could be used. However, this proposal has several problems. Since capital flows to the area of highest return, exchange controls or similar mechanisms will only distort the flows from the most efficient use to a less productive one. Regulations on capital flows can also be circumvented through a variety of means, such as transfer pricing or false invoicing.

Another proposed alternative to floating rates is a crawling peg following purchasing power parity. Fixed exchange rates are used, but they can be adjusted frequently to offset differences in rates of inflation. While this approach successfully incorporates an important cause of payments disequilibria, the crawling peg has one problem. If the payments problem has a cause other than difference in rates of inflation (such as shifts in the rates of return to capital or a country's terms-of-trade), the crawling peg does not prove a route to payments adjustment.

Thus, the flexible system of exchange rates remains intact, not because it is an ideal mechanism, but instead because a better alternative has not been found.

5.   In 1979 the European Monetary System (EMS) was created. Members agreed to maintain the exchange value of their currencies within 2¼ percent of each other (except for Italy that had a wider band).

In 1991, the members of the European Union signed the Maastricht Treaty, which provided for greater economic and political coordination between member countries. In the early 1990s, the viability of this treaty was tested. The German central bank adopted tight monetary policy. In order to maintain the currency bands, other countries had to follow the same policy. The United Kingdom suspended the exchange rate mechanism in 1992.

In order for a country to join the European Monetary Union (EMU), several criteria must be met. These regulations include restriction on the inflation rate, long term interest rates, budget deficit, government debt to GDP ratio, and exchange rate volatility. Eleven countries are founding members of the EMU.

The EMU created the European Central Bank. Each country's central bank will act in a manner similar to the twelve federal reserve banks in the United States. Each country's currency is pegged to the euro, which is the currency of the EMU.

6.   Robert Mundell argued that a currency bloc should be no larger than the area over which labor is mobile. This suggests that the United States might consist of more than one currency bloc, since labor is not fully mobile within the U.S.. This definition of the optimal currency bloc size focuses on policy response to macroeconomic shocks. If all regions within the bloc experience the same economic conditions, the appropriate monetary policy is easily determined. If, however, part of the bloc enters a recession, calling for expansionary policies, while other areas do not need such measures, a single monetary policy is difficult to implement.

Ronald McKinnon's view of an optimal currency area suggests that the pact must be large enough to stabilize internal price level changes regardless of changes in the external exchange rate. When the currency area is large, the price index, which is includes the price of both tradable and non-tradable goods, is not as responsive to changes in tradable goods' prices as when a currency area is a small.

7.   The Latin American debt crisis, which has several causes, has had a large impact on the international financial system. One source of the crisis was that OPEC members deposited oil revenues in commercial banks, vastly expanding the amount of loanable funds. These institutions, lent money to LDC governments. As long as the price of primary products remained high, these nations experienced little problem servicing

their international debt. In the late 1970s, the prices of such goods started to decline sharply. These loans also had adjustable or floating interest rates that were tied to interest rates in the United States and Europe. When the U.S. tightened monetary policy in the early 1980s, the interest rates on these loans skyrocketed, and the debtors faced much higher interest payments.

Developing solutions to this problem is not as easy as finding what caused the crisis. Commercial banks have written off substantial amounts of outstanding debt. Some debtor nations' economies have improved, allowing for these countries to reduce their level of indebtedness. Debt-equity swaps have also made a small contribution to the solution.

8. The Basle Accord of July 1988 addresses several problems associated with banking system solvency. Four main issues were targeted during negotiations. These areas include capital adequacy, excessively risky loans, excessively concentrated loans, and exposure from off-balance-sheet items.

9. At the end of 1994, Mexico encountered problems rolling over short-term debts, causing a depreciation of the peso. In response to this problem, the Mexican government announced tight fiscal and monetary policies which, combined with the lower value of the peso, should generate a current account recovery.

10. In late 1997, several Asian countries began to have problems with international investor confidence. Beginning in Thailand, investors withdrew large quantities of financial capital, necessitating IMF loan packages to attempt to end the crises. The combination of capital outflows, IMF austerity measures, and a Japanese economy in recession greatly affected the economies of Thailand, South Korea, Malaysia, and Indonesia.

CHAPTER OBJECTIVES

After studying the concepts presented in Chapter 21, you should be able to answer the following questions:

1. Why was the movement to floating exchange rates in 1973 believed to be temporary? Why did many countries not return to fixed exchange rates?

2. Explain the effects of U.S. domestic monetary policy on the value of the dollar in the late 1970s and early 1980s. What role did public confidence in the policies of the central bank play in the changing dollar value?

3. What other international monetary systems have been proposed? What are some of the problems associated with these ideas?

4. Briefly explain the circumstances preceding the debt crisis. What possible solutions exist? Which proposal do you think would be the most successful? Why?

GLOSSARY TERMS

- European Currency Unit (ECU)
- Euro
- European Monetary System (EMS)
- Exchange Rate Mechanism (ERM)

CHAPTER 21 STUDY GUIDE QUESTIONS

Multiple Choice Questions

1. Many major industrialized countries shifted to a regime of flexible exchange rates because

    a. floating rates were proven to be more efficient than fixed rates.
    b. the academic arguments for floating rates had been accepted.
    c. the system of fixed parities collapsed twice within a period of two years.
    d. countries no longer wanted their currencies to be pegged.

2. The depreciation of the dollar in 1985 was a result of

    a. previously tight monetary policy and central bank intervention.
    b. previously loose monetary policy and central bank intervention.
    c. previously loose monetary policy and the lack of central bank intervention.
    d. previously tight monetary policy and the lack of central bank intervention.

3. Since 1972, nominal and real exchange rate movements

    a. have been relatively stable.
    b. have differed. Nominal rates have remained relatively stable while real rates have been volatile.
    c. have differed. Real rates have remained relatively stable while nominal rates have been volatile.
    d. have been relatively volatile.

4. The European Currency Unit (ECU) is

    a. a composite currency consisting of fixed amounts of the currencies of participating countries.
    b. a composite currency consisting of variable amounts of the currencies of participating countries.
    c. a composite currency consisting of fixed amounts of the currencies of the 10 largest exporting countries.
    d. a composite currency consisting of variable amounts of the currencies of the 10 largest exporting countries.

5.   One of the causes of the Latin American debt crisis is

    a.   high levels of inflation in Latin America.
    b.   myopic commercial bank lending officers in the United States.
    c.   tight monetary policy in the U.S. at the beginning of the 1980s.
    d.   all of the above.

6.   Between 1981 and 1985, the U.S. dollar appreciated by about 40 percent in real terms. This meant that

    a.   the cost competitiveness of U.S. firms operating in international markets improved significantly.
    b.   the cost competitiveness of U.S. firms operating in international markets worsened significantly.
    c.   the cost competitiveness of U.S. firms operating in international markets was minimally hurt.
    d.   the cost competitiveness of U.S. firms operating in international markets was minimally helped.

7.   The U.S. current account deficit reflects the

    a.   gap between U.S. investment needs and low savings rates.
    b.   gap between U.S. investment needs and high savings rates.
    c.   gap between U.S. consumption needs and low levels of income.
    d.   gap between U.S. consumption needs and high levels of income.

8.   The appreciation of the dollar in the early 1980s was particularly damaging to

    a.   the Northeast, because of the effect on the services industry.
    b.   the deep South, because of the effect on tobacco and similar crops.
    c.   the Midwest, because of the effect on agriculture and manufacturing.
    d.   the West, because of the effect on high-technology goods.

True, False, Uncertain and Why Questions

When answering the following questions, be sure to support your assertion of true, false, or uncertain with two or three sentences.

1.   Studies of the pattern of exchange rate movements suggest that the absorption approach to exchange markets is more relevant than the asset market approach.

2.   It is hoped that the European Currency Unit (ECU) may become a medium of exchange and store of value within Europe.

3. The desire to limit the depreciation of a currency implies the need for looser monetary policy.

4. Exchange market controls are an efficient way to reduce exchange rate volatility.

5. The creation of the EMU implies that member nations have complete monetary and fiscal policy autonomy.

Short Answer Questions

1. Why do some countries wish all countries would return to the fixed exchange rate system under Bretton Woods?

2. What impact did the OPEC oil embargo have on the exchange rate system? Why did countries believe it was not feasible to return to fixed parities?

3. Why did other industrialized countries support intervention in the exchange market that caused a depreciation in the dollar in the period of 1985-1987?

4. What are some of the ways that the LDC debt crisis has been eased, although not solved?

5. Suppose Greece and Spain favor expansionary monetary policy while France and Germany favor tighter monetary policy. What are the implications of jointly managed monetary policy under the EMU system for this situation?

ANSWERS TO CHAPTER 21 STUDY GUIDE QUESTIONS

Multiple Choice Questions

1. c
   Flexible rates were adopted because the fixed system collapsed in August 1971 and January/February 1973. The move to floating rates was thought to be only temporary.

2. b
   The easing of monetary policy to speed the recovery from the 1982 recession and the intervention of several central banks led to the depreciation of the dollar that started in 1985.

3. d
   Empirical evidence shows that both nominal and real exchange rates have fluctuated greatly since 1973.

4. a
   The ECU is a basket consisting of a combination of the currencies of member countries.

5. d
    Rapid inflation, tight U.S. monetary policy and unwise lending decisions by U.S. banks all contributed to the debt crisis.

6. b
    The appreciation of the dollar significantly hurt firms operating in international markets as exports fell and imports increased.

7. a
    The current account deficit is the excess of domestic investment over savings. Since the overall U.S. savings rate is quite low, foreign savings are needed to close the gap.

8. c
    An appreciation hurts the tradables sector and benefits the non-tradables. Since the Midwest has a heavy concentration of export and import-competing industries, this region was damaged by the appreciation.

True, False, Uncertain and Why Questions

When answering the following questions, be sure to support your assertion of true, false, or uncertain with two or three sentences

1. False. Evidence suggests that current account transactions are responsible for 10 percent of all foreign exchange trading in New York. This suggests that the asset market approach to the exchange market is better suited to explaining exchange rate changes.

2. True. Some banks accept deposits in ECU and ECU-denominated traveler's checks are available. Eventually, it is hoped, the ECU will become an actual circulating currency.

3. False. The desire to limit the depreciation of a currency implies the need for tight monetary policy that may differ from the domestic goals of the central bank.

4. False. Exchange controls are not efficient since they prohibit the movement of scarce capital from less to more productive locations. They are also very difficult or impossible to enforce.

5. False. The creation of the EMU means that member countries will have less autonomy setting monetary and fiscal policies.

Short Answer Questions

1.   Many developing countries that have not switched to floating rates fear that floating rates may mean excessive exchange rate volatility, and wish for the relative stability associated with the Bretton Woods years.

2.   The OPEC nations suddenly had large payments surpluses and needed to invest oil revenues. Not knowing where these funds would be invested, combined with instability generated by high oil prices, made the return to fixed rates difficult.

3.   Other countries supported the dollar's depreciation because of fears of the rising tide of protectionism in the United States. It was feared that if the trade deficit did not decrease, Congress would enact legislation, with veto-proof majorities, establishing higher trade barriers.

4.   Many commercial banks have written off some of loans, stronger economic performance in debtor countries, and IMF austerity programs are some of the ways in which the LDC debt problem has been eased.

5.   When countries have different preferences for the direction of monetary policy, a compromise must be reached.

For Product Safety Concerns and Information please contact our EU
representative GPSR@taylorandfrancis.com Taylor & Francis Verlag GmbH,
Kaufingerstraße 24, 80331 München, Germany

Printed and bound by CPI Group (UK) Ltd, Croydon, CR0 4YY

08/05/2025

01864546-0001